Gary Lovisi created *Paperback Parade* back in 1986, and has been entertaining book collectors with stories and information about the classic paperback era ever since. He also started the New York City Collectible Paperback Show and ran it for 25 years, hosting most of the famous paperback authors as guests. Lovisi is a well-known collector of genre fiction, and a seller on Ebay.

A Mystery, Crime & Noir Notebook collects nearly 50 articles by Lovisi from the pages of such publications as *The Armchair Detective, Crime Time, Mystery Scene, Blood & Thunder, Crime Factory, The Big Book of Noir* and, of course, *Paperback Parade*. He writes about collecting, about some the noteworthy paperback publishers, but mostly about the writers—from George Arnaud to Harold Q. Masur to Ennis Willie. It's a literary journey filled with discovery. And be sure to view his book videos on *YouTube*.

A MYSTERY, CRIME & NOIR NOTEBOOK

By Gary Lovisi

Stark House Press • Eureka California

A MYSTERY CRIME & NOIR NOTEBOOK

Published by Stark House Press
1315 H Street
Eureka, CA 95501, USA
griffinskye3@sbcglobal.net
www.starkhousepress.com

A MYSTERY CRIME & NOIR NOTEBOOK
copyright © 2023 by Gary Lovisi.

All the articles in this book are copyright in the respective years of their original publication. They have all been edited, rewritten and expanded for this special Stark House Edition and all are copyright 2023 by Gary Lovisi.

All rights reserved, including the right of reproduction in whole or in part in any form. Published by Stark House Press by arrangement with the author.

ISBN: 979-8-88601-054-1

Book and cover design by Mark Shepard, shepgraphics.com

PUBLISHER'S NOTE:
This is a work of fiction. Names, characters, places and incidents are either the products of the author's imagination or used fictionally, and any resemblance to actual persons, living or dead, events or locales, is entirely coincidental.
Without limiting the rights under copyright reserved above, no part of this publication may be reproduced, stored, or introduced into a retrieval system or transmitted in any form or by any means (electronic, mechanical, photocopying, recording or otherwise) without the prior written permission of both the copyright owner and the above publisher of the book.

First Stark House Press Edition: November 2023

CONTENTS

Introduction: 11

About Mystery, Crime & Noir
The Noir Trap: Money, Women, Love, Sex & Fame 13
The Hardboiled Way 17

Various Authors & Books:
Collecting Vintage Mystery Paperbacks 23
Avon Books: Centerpieces of Vintage Mystery & Crime 32
Dell Mapback Mysteries 37
Three Daring Divas of Paperback Pulp Fiction 44
Lion Books: Noir Paperback Icons 54
A Trio of Lion Books: Book Three 60
Hardboiled Paradise: Books to Remember 65
Crime and Mystery One-Shot Wonders 73
Mob Hits: True Crime Mafia & Gangster Paperbacks 83
Crime To Die For 93
A Closer Look At Falcon Books 98
Sex & Savagery in Pulp Paperback Crime Cover art 104

Specific Authors & Books:
Georges Arnaud:
Rediscovering *The Wages of Fear* 111
Michael Avallone:
A Giant Passed Our Way 116
Stephen Becker: (aka Steve Dodge)
Shanghai Incident & Others 118
Charles Beckman, Jr.:
Charles Beckman, *Honky-Tonk Girl* and I 122
Jazz Meets Murder on Honky-Tonk Street 124
Lou Cameron:
Angels' Flight: Cool Jazz & Hot Murder 128
James Hadley Chase:
Fiction Too Tough: James Hadley Chase 135
William L. Coons: (aka Dell Holland)
Sin Town — Sleaze Noir at It's Best! 145
N.R. DeMexico:
A Look At *Marijuana Girl* 150
Norman Firth:
Borrowed Love: Romance as Dark Noir 155

Bruno Fischer:
Bruno Fischer: A Writer We Should Remember 163
Rediscovering Bruno Fischer 166
Al Fray:
Hardboiled Paradise: Al Fray 170
Gardner F. Fox: (aka Rod Gray)
That Lady From L.U.S.T. 178
Charles Fritch:
Negative of A Nude Wth Murder 183
Otis Hemingway Gaylord, Jr.: (aka G.H. Otis)
The Search For Otis 185
C.J. Henderson:
C.J. Henderson, Jack Hagee and Me 190
E. Howard Hunt: (aka Robert Dietrich)
The Steve Bentley Thrillers 196
Kermit Jaediker:
Hero's Lust, A Top Crime Noir Sleeper 211
Richard Jessup:
A Cop Called Wolf 215
Barry Lake: (aka Joe Barry)
The Elusive Joe Barry 217
I Read "Homicide Hotel" 224
Lyndon Mallet:
The Taffin Series 227
Nick Marino:
A Ride Down *One Way Street* 233
Marijane Meaker: (aka Vin Packer)
Vin Packer: The Return 237
Harold Q. Masur: (aka Hal Masur)
Scott Jordan: The Hard-boiled Lawyer 243
Paul S. Meskil:
Falling Into The *Sin Pit* 240
Fan Nichols:
A Noir Unknown: *One By One* 248
James Ross:
One-Shot Wonder: *They Don't Dance Much* 257
Don Tracy:
Don Tracy and *Deadly To Bed* 258
Blackout is a Knockout! 260
Lionel White:
Seven Hungry Killers on The Run 264
Ennis Willie:
Fortune: Tough Guy Hero as Noir Poetry 268
Too Late To Pray 272

Bibliography 273
Biography 275

ACKNOWLEDGEMENTS

"Introduction" is original to this edition and is copyright 2023 by Gary Lovisi. "The Noir Trap: Money, Women, Love, Sex & Fame" originally appeared in *Noir Riot* copyright 2014 by Gary Lovisi. "The Hardboiled Way" appeared on the Gryphon Books website, copyright 2001 by Gary Lovisi. "Collecting Vintage Mystery Paperbacks" originally appeared in *The Armchair Detective* V28, #1, copyright 1995 by Gary Lovisi. "Avon Books: Centerpieces of Vintage Mystery & Crime", originally appeared in *Crime Time* (UK) copyright 2003 by Gary Lovisi. "Dell Mapback Mysteries" originaly appeared in *Mystery Scene*, copyright 2003 by Gary Lovisi. "Three Daring Divas of Paperback Pulp Fiction" originally appeared in *Mystery Scene*, copyright 2008 by Gary Lovisi. "Lion Books: Noir Paperback Icons" originally appeared in *The Big Book of Noir*, copyright 1998 by Gary Lovisi. "A Trio of Lion Books" originally appeared as an introduction to the Stark House book *A Trio Of Lion Books: Book Three*, copyright 2022 by Gary Lovisi. "Hardboiled Paradise: Books To Remember" originally appeared in the Australian magazine *Crime Factory*, copyright 2002 by Gary Lovisi. "Crime and Mystery One-Shot Wonders" originally appeared in *Mystery Scene* #55, copyright 1996 by Gary Lovisi. "Mob Hits: True Crime & Gangster Paperbacks" originally appeared in *Paperback Parade* #99, copyright 2017 by Gary Lovisi. "Crime To Die For" originally appeared in *Crime Time* (UK), copyright 2006 by Gary Lovisi. "A Closer Look At Falcon Books" appeared in *The Digest Enthusiast* #13, copyright 2022 by Gary Lovisi. "Sex & Savagery in Pulp Paperback Crime Cover Art" originally appeared in *Crime Time* #25 (UK), copyright 2001 by Gary Lovisi. "Rediscovering *The Wages of Fear*" appeared in *Big Sky* #2, copyright 2014 by Gary Lovisi. "A Giant Passed Our Way" originaly appeared in *Mystery Scene* #63, copyright 1999 by Gary Lovisi. "*Shanghai Incident* & Others" appeared on Steve Lewis' blog, copyright 2011 by Gary Lovisi. "Charles Beckman, *Honky-Tonk Girl* and I" appeared on Ed Gorman's blog, copyright 2011 by Gary Lovisi. "Jazz Meets Murder on Honhy-Tonk Street" appeared as the intro to *Honky-Tonk Girl*, copyright 2011 by Gary Lovisi. "*Angel's Flight*: Cool Jazz & Hot Murder" introduction to Black Gat Book, copyright 2016 by Gary Lovisi. "Fiction Too Tough: James Hadley Chase" originally appeared in *Paperback Parade* #77, copyright 2009 by Gary Lovisi. "*Sin Town* — Sleaze Noir At It's Best" originally appeared in *Paperback Parade*, copyright 2015 by Gary Lovisi. "A Look At *Marijuana Girl*" appeared in *The Digest Enthusiast*, copyright 2021 by Gary Lovisi. "*Borrowed Love*: Romance as Dark Noir" originally appeared in *Paperback Parade* #81, copyright 2012 by Gary Lovisi. "Bruno Fischer: A Writer We Should Remember" originally appeared in *De Papieren Cirkel* (Dutch), copyright 1999 by Gary Lovisi. "Rediscovering Bruno Fischer" Stark House book introduction to *The Bleeding Scissors & The Evil Days*, copyright 2015 by Gary Lovisi. "Hardboiled Paradise: Al Fray" originally appeared in *Crime Factory* #9

(Australia), copyright 2003 by Gary Lovisi. "That Lady From L.U.S.T." originally appeared in *Paperback Parade* #86, copyright 2014 by Gary Lovisi. "*Negative of A Nude* with Murder" originaly appeared in *Paperback Parade* #87, copyright 2011 by Gary Lovisi. "The Search For Otis" appeared as an introduction to Stark House book, 2020 copyright by Gary Lovisi. "C.J. Henderson, Jack Hagee and Me" originally appeared in *No Torrent Like Greed*, Bold Venture Press, 2014 copyright by Gary Lovisi. "The Steve Bentley Thrillers" originally appeard in *Paperback Parade* #101, copyright 2014 by Gary Lovisi. "*Hero's Lust*, A Top Crime Noir Sleeper" Stark House book inrtoduction to *A Trio of Lions: Book One*, copyright 2016 by Gary Lovisi. "A Cop Called Wolf" originally appeared in *Paperback Parade* #99, copyright 2017 by Gary Lovisi. "The Elusive Joe Barry" originally appeared in *Paperback Parade* #53, copyright 2019 by Gary Lovisi. "I Read "Homicide Hotel" appeared in *Paperback Parade* #53, copyright 2019 by Gary Lovisi. "The Taffin Series" originally apeared in *Paperback Parade* #100, copyright 2018 by Gary Lovisi. "A Ride Down *One Way Street*" originally appeared in *Paperback Parade* #83, copyright 2013 by Gary Lovisi. "Vin Packer: The Return" originally appeared in *Mystery Scene* #100, copyright 2007 by Gary Lovisi. "Scott Jordan: The Hard-boiled Lawyer" originally appeared in *Paperback Parade* #30, copyright 1992 by Gary Lovisi. "Falling Into The *Sin Pit*" appeared in *Paperback Parade*, copyright 2013 by Gary Lovisi. "A Noir Unknown: *One By One*" originally appeared in *Paperback Parade* #74, copyright 2010 by Gary Lovisi. "One-Shot Wonder: *They Don't Dance Much*" appeared in Crime Time (UK), copyright 2001 by Gary Lovisi. "Don Tracy and *Deadly To Bed*" originally appeared in *Paperback Parade* #92, copyright 2016 by Gary Lovisi. "*Blackout* is a Knockout!" originally appeared in *Paperback Parade* #88, copyright 2012 by Gary Lovisi. "Seven Hungry Killers on The Run" appeared in *Blood & Thunder*, copyright 2012 by Gary Lovisi. "Fortune: Tough Guy Hero as Noir Poetry" unpublished, copyright 2023 by Gary Lovisi. "Too Late To Pray" book introduction, copyright 2012 by Gary Lovisi. All Rights Reserved.

A MYSTERY, CRIME & NOIR NOTEBOOK

By Gary Lovisi

INTRODUCTION:

You are about to embark upon a wonderful journey into the wild world of mystery, crime and noir vintage era paperback books. Some of these books and authors you may know of, but I am sure there are many you have never heard of — or certainly not read — and that is one key purpose of this book, to introduce you to these fine books and make you aware of them.

This book is a compilation of almost 50 articles I have written over a period of almost 40 years. They include topics about some of my favorite books in the mystery, crime and noir genres. Many of these books are found only in scarce paperback editions — however some are being reprinted by modern savy publishers who are doing a great service to fans, readers and collectors offering new, beautiful and inexpensive editions of these timeless classics. Classics that have stood the test of time. All of the articles in this book have been published previously in a variety of venues. Each article has been substantially rewritten, expanded, and most notably updated, from their original appearance for this special Stark House Press edition. This *Mystery, Crime & Noir Notebook* is a celebration of these wonderful books and their talented authors.

In some ways, this book is a loving memoir — my love letter of sorts — to all the authors and books that I have enjoyed reading in this genre over so many years. It was a big job collecting all these articles from their various, and sometimes, obscure original appearances, along with the 140+ rare book covers that grace this edition, but I think all the time and hard work was worth it. I hope that you agree.

Many of the authors I have written about here, I know — *or knew*— personally. Sadly, too many of them have now passed away, but while their physical voices have been silenced forever — their written voices will live on forever in their work! Some of the articles in this book were written as introductions to their own books — for recent reprints. You will find a couple of the articles included here may overlap each other a bit, where a book may be mentioned in two different articles — but that is attributed to my unapologetic enthusiasm for a really fine crime novel!

Accompanying most of these articles are a representative sampling of some of the classic vintage era book covers. I hope you enjoy this visual aspect of the book — those classic covers are like postcards to us from the past — done by many master artists of the vintage era. That incredible cover art grabbed the attention of the book browser and reader — to turn them into a book buyer. Who could resist some of these amazing cover images? They have a certain charm, and show the kind of rough and tumble hard-boiled attitude readers and fans have always enjoyed in these works. While some of the cover art may not be politically correct by today's standards — which was the point back then — all I can say about it now, in a true hard-boiled attitude is — *I really don't give a damn!*

Thank you for taking this journey with me. I hope it will prove entertaining, eye-opening, inspiring and loads of fun. I am sure you will make some new and pleasant discoveries with authors and books you will want to read and look for. If so, then I have done my job. *Enjoy the search!*

Gary Lovisi
Brooklyn, New York
June 21, 2023

The Noir Trap:
Money, Women, Love, Sex, Fame

There's been a lot written about noir, and a lot of great noir stories. Both in fiction and non-fiction, crime aficionados are fascinated by all things noir. But what is it about noir that makes it so fascinating? What I think it is, is that noir is a sadistic little trap just waiting for anyone to get caught in its diabolical web. The noir trap knows no bounds and can spring up and evolve from nothing into anything at the drop of a hat. Like life itself, occurrences can be entirely random, or meticulously planned out — but of course in noir, nothing *ever* goes according to plan.

All that said, I believe there are five major components of noir that exemplify the classic noir trap. They are money, woman, love, sex and fame. There are other topics that also fit, to be sure, but I think these five topics, by far, exemplify classic noir.

Money: We all know about money and noir. Crooks out to make the big score. The little guy who finally makes it rich. The person who finds a sack of money dropped from the back of an armored truck, or who is sent a package by mistake, full of cash (or drugs, which translate into money), or anything else that can get you piles of cash — like naughty photos of a politician or movie star. You can even make the money legally, like winning the lottery. It doesn't matter how you get the cash — having it never turns out well. In noir, money is a curse and will become your doom — it will get you killed — or something worse. Usually worse, because there are things worse than mere death when it comes to noir. But that doesn't stop the noir protagonist (or sucker) from seeking bushels of money that are not his — the mythical 'big score'. The thing with noir is, that once you make the big score, that's when your problems really begin. In noir, for every step you take forward — you take three steps back. Into the dark. Into doom. In noir, money never helps you out, or makes things better. Money only buys trouble!

Women: We all know about women in noir, especially the femme fatale. Women in noir hold a special place, they are just as deadly, deceitful, betraying and low-down as the men — and often even worse. The women of noir — weather femme fatales or not — get the guys into all kinds of trouble and into situations which will make him wish he never met her by the time she is through with him. Think of James M. Cain's *Double Indemnity* (based on an actual 1927 murder, by the way). Here alluring Phyllis Dietrichson gets horn-dog, heel, too-smart-for-his-own-good sucker Walter Neff to kill her husband. Then the two of them are stuck with each other and their crime — hate each other — kill each other — *all the way down the line* — to the end. Both the book and film are brilliant examples of noir and the femme fatale. But what about so-called 'nice girls'? Noir women can be 'nice' as apple pie. They can be decent women and not dirty rotten tramps — but a nice girl can turn into one of them evil vixens even against her will. A good girl can be just as attracted to a bad boy as a femme fatale can be. A

good girl who has everything going for her will eventually meet a bad boy (a 'male fatale'?), that will use her, hurt her, turn her bad — or force her to do really bad things — like murder. Like murdering her bad guy's wife to get her out of the way. Or maybe even murdering her bad guy — defending herself from her abuser with murder, but she'll go down hard for it. I think the good woman has just as much to fear from noir as guys who make a bad pick-up of some femme fatale cutie in a dark smoky biker bar. Things can only get worse from that point on. One way or the other — women in noir always get their man!

Love: Of course love is a wonderful thing when it enters your life — but not in noir. In noir, love is a corrupt evil turd in disguise. It is often intermingled with the femme fatale but I'd like to look at love as a separate noir trap here. I call it the love trap. Usually that means a man falling hard for a hot dame and willing to do anything to do right by her. It can be, and often begins as honest, well-meaning love, but it doesn't stay that way for long. These days the noir love trap can be comprised of any combination of two people (or more), but the results will always be the same. Love and noir do not mix. In the love trap, people's feelings just don't get upset or hurt — they get squashed, trampled, utterly destroyed.

Lives get ruined. Betrayal and revenge will surely follow. Suicide is seen as one way out. Some people take that option. Even that doesn't help. Not really. In the noir love trap, something that beings so seemingly sweet and nice — will inevitably end in terrible tragedy. *Romeo and Juliet* could have been a noir love story and Shakespeare the first noir writer! Love in noir, is a cruel bedfellow!

Sex: Sex in noir is almost always associated with the femme fatale — but what sex really is in noir — is not so much the explicit sexual act — but a representation of unrestrained lust. And all that goes with it. That means lusting after a woman (or another person) — who is someone you have no right to be lusting after. A married woman, or a mob chief's wife, girlfriend, or daughter. That can land you in a world of hurt. Sometimes, the person who is betrayed will just kill the amorous luster quickly in a blind fit of rage. In noir, that could be considered taking the easy way out. In noir, if you lust after (and consummate that lust with the sex act), say with the wife-girlfriend-daughter of a mob boss, and you are caught — you might wish you were dead but it may take days or weeks before that event actually happens. It will almost certainly involve a blow torch. Which brings us to torture. Torture is another aspect of noir, but torture in noir is often of the mental, emotional, or spiritual variety — but it can also appear as extremely painful physical torture as well. Sex equals torture in noir.

Fame: This is one noir trap not often considered, but it seems to happen to too many young stars and celebrities today. Some are people who are famous for…just being famous. Whether it's a Lindsay Lohan or Justin Bieber, or Alec Baldwin and Charlie Sheen, these people seem to be leading lives that have fallen deeply into the noir trap. A person may spend an entire lifetime reaching for the brass ring, grasping for success or fame, and when they achieve it — they are still miserable. In noir, you are even more miserable when you achieve your desire than you were before you got what you wanted. Too many find fame a hollow victory, and in noir, it most certainly is. You lose all sense of self, self-worth, and what makes you an individual. In the old days, in films like *The Roaring Twenties* with James Cagney, all his character wanted to do was be 'somebody', to be a 'big shot'. Fredo in *The Godfather*, just wanted what he saw was his by right, by being the eldest son. He was passed over! He wanted to be somebody too, make a name for himself. He wanted respect! When that doesn't happen the person suffers and it rips him or her apart — it also causes them grievous harm. So the world keeps turning and the noir trap of fame keeps eating its young. Fame is an insidious noir trap.

Noir is a subject that encompasses many different, and often contradictory aspects, but to me these five topics exemplify the key aspects of classic noir. The noir trap is out there — in all its manifestations — watching and waiting for each one of us to enter it's deadly web. You can run but you can not hide. So watch your step!

The Hard-boiled Way

What is hard-boiled?

Hard-boiled is attitude. Attitude to the core. It's also a lot more. Some may think it's only fiction about violence, often very brutal violence, but that's not a necessary ingredient. Violence is there because we're talking about realistic crime fiction when we talk hard-boiled, and that means you lay it out truthfully to the reader. Don't sugarcoat the truth, don't play it cute. The attitude comes from realizing *that* truth. No matter how truly rotten or violent it may be. Knowledge of that truth can not help but effect the writer, or his characters, and if done well, the reader as well.

There's a lot of tough-guy talk and action in some hard-boiled fiction, but that's not all there is to it either. Others think all that's important is style, all that wonderful Chandleresque chit-chat which a lot of readers and critics like perhaps a bit too much, but too often these days has entered the area of nostalgia, pastiche, or even cliché. However, the real hard-boiler, Dashiell Hammett is, to those in the know still on top. Carroll John Daly had *real* heart. Mickey Spillane *made* you read him. Jim Thompson, David Goodis, Cornell Woolrich (in his William Irish noir days), Chester Himes, Donald Goines and Charles Willeford lived lives no writer could ever make up and their work soared because of it. Or, in spite of it. And modern hard-boiled fiction is all that and more.

Part of what hard-boiled is about is the adherence to a moral code in a world without any moral code or any moral values at all. Hammett and Chandler wrote about it in the old days. However these days, it can be a moral code as minimalist as that of Andrew Vachss' Burke, or as twisted as one of James Ellroy's cop heroes.

Today, more than ever, hard-boiled fiction is relevant fiction that has meaning and stands for something, unlike the broader spectrum of literature, and most other mass-market entertainment. Modern authentic hard-boiled material (not Chandler clones or blood and guts retro-pulp), seriously examines crime or social issues, often taking us to places and depths we'd rather not be taken into at all. The world is a cruel place, but for the hard-boiled hero (and the reader and writer by extension), it's far crueler than anyone can ever imagine. And that's part of the real story most people who do not read hard-boiled fiction do not want to face. Escape is, after all, so much more pleasant. And comforting. And easy. It can be so…cozy. And all the answers are laid out for you at the end.

What could be nicer? Well, folks, that ain't the way it is with authentic hard-boiled material. Oh, you might get a tidy answer at the end of the story, but if you do, there'll be little comfort in it I can assure you.

Hard-boiled fiction is not just about private eyes either. Even in the past, some of the best hard-boiled writers; W.R. Burnett (*The Asphalt Jungle*), and James M. Cain (*Double Indemnity* and *The Postman Always Rings Twice*), were certainly *not* writing private eye fiction. They were writing hard, cold truth. The way it was back then, the way they saw it every day of their lives. Dashiell Hammett did the same thing as a Pinkerton, he took that life he'd lived and molded it into his Continental Op stories, later on into Sam Spade and the stuff that dreams are made of. But the core truth and attitude is always there in Hammett's work. And it is no less true today than when his work was first published around 100 years ago.

Today the hard-boiled tradition comes on strong, in some ways even bolder than ever. Today there are serious issues and debates in hard-boiled work that you don't see any place else. And certainly not at this level of detail and intensity.

Hard-boiled deals with crime, naturally. But it goes deep down into the black heart of crime. The corruption crime can bring into a person's life, or into our society. The pain and decay it spawns on so many levels. The effect on the criminal *and* the victim. The reasons for it all.

Authentic hard-boiled fiction is also about real people trying to live their lives, to make it in the day-to-day and getting smashed down inch by inch, lower and lower. But they still hang in there. They refuse to go down for the count. They're not giving up one damn thing, because they've had to fight like hell every day of their life for what they've got – and they'll fight like hell every day of their life *to keep it*. And I'm *not* talking materialism here, folks. Not at all. I'm talking pride, honor, dignity, self-respect, the truth, going out of your way to help a friend, or going out of your way to fuck the enemy, days of blood and rage, a gut full of hurt, stand-up people in a sit-down shut-up world. That's hard-boiled! It's more true today than ever!

It's about attitude. And that still lives. It still has meaning. These writers are rebels all right, but they've *got* causes. *Real* causes and plenty of them. It's a new world now, and all that 1960s pseudo-angst crap just won't wash anymore. We're talking war. We're talking survival now.

So who are some of the people writing the good stuff that I admire and like to read? Too many to mention here so I'll just talk a bit about some of the best and some of my own favorites. On the top of any list is Andrew Vachss. His Burke novels, (such as *Dead And Gone*, Knopf, 2000), is fiction with a microscopic attention to detail and reality, showing the harsh truth about the world today. It can be a brutal truth, an ugly truth, but never to exploit, never to be gratuitous in any way. Vachss' fiction serves to illuminate and enlighten his readers and the public to the importance of child protection. Vachss put himself on the battle line every single day in this fight. He was a working attorney whose practice was solely devoted to child protection.

Eugene Izzi took it all a step further, the abused child as adult criminal, cop, con, ex-con, citizen trying to make it. His work was raw and sparse with the impact of a sledgehammer to the brain. It can knock you out. Or knock some sense into you. Izzi also wrote a trilogy as "Nick Giatano." He committed suicide a few years ago under strange circumstances.

Gerald Petievich did the same for Los Angeles, exposing us to crooked cops, counterfeiters (*One-Shot Deal*), government treasury agents on the hunt, L.A. gangs and cops out of control. His *Earth Angeles*, out years before the Rampart scandal in the LAPD was a warning that went unheeded. There's even a foray into a suicide/murder in the White House years before Vincent Foster's suicide (*Paramour*). Petievich stopped writing a few years back, he was so real good. I wish he would have picked up his pen and written more books, but he did give us some real winners.

Stephen Solomita writes tough crime novels. His Stanley Moodrow books, about a broke-down cop who knows all the ropes but still gets his

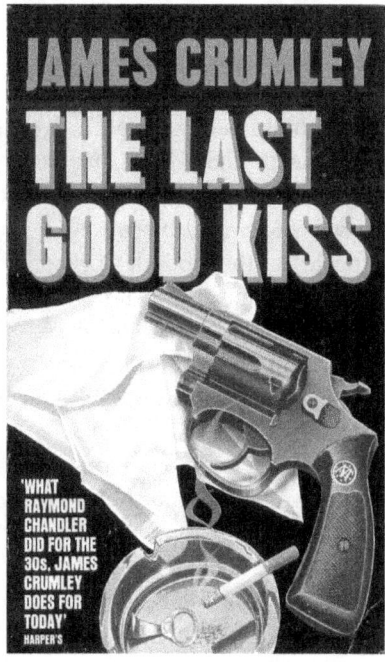

ass in trouble with the top brass, even as he solves their most complex cases (*A Twist of the Knife, Force of Nature*, etc), is just great stuff. *Keeplock*, written as by David Cray (Otto Penzler Books, 1995) is an intense crime caper that spells doom for all involved. In it an ex-con who wants to go straight takes a ride on the hellbound train. Along for the ride are crooked cops, crazy cons, killers, druggies, punks and Mafia bad guys. It's a must book to search for.

James Lee Burke (with his Dave Robicheaux series of novels) and James Crumely (Milo Milodragovitch and C.W. Sughrue are his detectives, and both appear together in *Bordersnakes*, Mysterious Press, 1996), have done some of the best work around. But not often enough, they were not prolific at all. But they were hard-boiled and often brutal, starkly real and full of heart. These guys expanded the bounds of the hard-boiled crime novel, expanded the bounds of crime itself, showing us the intermix with everyday life, and with everyday America. Social consciousness that shows the dark heart of America, as nasty and brutal as it has ever been. Burke even has Robicheaux enter the netherworld between his detective and the ghost of a dead Confederate general – and he pulls it off! Crumley's *The Last Good Kiss* is a kick-ass classic as good as anything Hammett and Chandler ever wrote — it is a must read.

James Ellroy (*The Big Nowhere, L.A. Confidential*, are what I consider his two classics, *White Jazz* and *American Tabloid* – may be hard to read but worth the effort) is another writer up there with the greats. He lifts the covers off pretense and hypocrisy and shows us all the wet slimy things that wriggle underneath. Ugly, brutal, but like a highway accident, you can not look away. Whether it's 1950s Los Angeles, or the modern world of cops and crims, Ellroy is right on target. And he pulls no punches.

Some other writers have also chalked up excellent work. Michael Connelly was a relatively new writer when I first wrote this article years ago. At that time he'd checked in with his first novel, *The Black Echo*. Since then has become a legitimate super star with many fine novels to his credit, *Black Ice, The*

Concrete Blonde, Void Moon, and many more. Connelly's detective, Harry (Hieronymus) Bosch is at odds with his own department, the F.B.I., and even himself, in an exciting series of books that twists and turns like a Hieronymus Bosch painting itself. His first book even won an Edgar Award, and many of his fine books have since been filmed into some terrific TV series and movies.

Truth is, most awards in the mystery field are bullshit, seemingly given out to stroke friends. And most of these award winners and their books will be forgotten – but authentic hard-boiled work transcends time, fad, *damnit*, it even transcends bullshit. Hard-boiled is real and true, it lives and breathes right there in that book as you read it. You can feel the cold breath of death, taste the anger and rage like bile, feel your bowels tighten as you see the outrage coming. The evil is on its way into your world – *and there's no one able to stop it!*

Russell James (*Payback, Daylight, Oh No, Not My baby!* etc.) is another guy who can write a hell of a good story, and who says Brits can't write true hard-boiled? This guy is good! James makes it all come starkly alive, dangerous and fascinating. Good characters and tight plotting make him someone to put on your reading list.

I.K. Watson, another British writer, tells a great story in his debut novel, *Manor* (Foul Play Press, 1996) about the Smith Family. They're the modern inheritors of the crime kingdom of the Krays and Richardsons who now find themselves under siege in this hard-boiled crime novel that I feel is destined to become a classic. As far as I know Watson has written one other book, *Wolves Aren't White*. Anyone got a copy?

Thomas Boyle has written three novels in his Brooklyn series *(Only The Dead Know Brooklyn, Post-Mortem Effects,* and *Brooklyn Three)*, all about a homicide cop named DeSales who's trapped between different worlds and different parts of himself. A hard-boiled Brooklyn cop trying to hold on to his decency and humanity while working at a job that every day tries its best to chip away whatever it can of his soul, his spirit and his honor. He does not give up. These are great, very underrated novels.

Wayne Dundee in his Joe Hannibal series (*Burning Season, The Skintight Shroud,* and *The Brutal Ballet*), writes a more humane type of private eye, hard-boiled but with a big heart. It's an interesting mix that works because the basic humanity of Hannibal (and Dundee) come through in his struggle to 'fight the good fight'. And sometimes he even wins!

Joe Lansdale, is another great. At the time I originally wrote this article, he was mainly known for fantasy and horror, but he's proved he can pen one hell of an incredible hard-boiled story when the feeling comes upon him. Urban horror or country horror – you don't need no supernatural nonsense in Lansdale's crime fiction to scarce the hell out of you. His Hap and Leonard books are classics, adventures of two pals in red-neck East Texas. *Mucho Mojo*, is a serial killer novel that grabs at your guts, twists hard, and just won't let you go. Pretty it ain't, but good it sure be. There are more books in this series, such as *Two Bear Mambo* is a sequel, more recent books keep the series going strong. Lansdale, with Vachss, even collaborated on a book, *Veil's Visit*, a collection of great short stories. Of course Lansdale's Hap and Leonard series has been made into a recent TV series attesting to the book's popularity and quality.

I'm sure that some of the authors who have written for my own crime magazine, *Hardboiled*, will become stars in the future. People like Mike Black, David Scholl, Rose Dawn Bradford, Royce Allen, Joy Hewitt Mann, Cindy Rosmus, Rebecca Hardy Black, Robert Skinner, and many more are writers who have offered hard, realistic, cutting-edge work. And there's true meaning and value to their work and all the writers whose work has appeared in the pages of *Hardboiled* over the years. These writers take a stand and tell a story without boundaries. They write serious, they have guts; they're not doing the usual crap. The fact that today, out-of-print copies of *Hardboiled* have now become rare collector's items, attests to the quality of the magazine.

To stand for something in life, as well as in your fiction as a writer, to tell the truth and let the chips fall where they may, to have guts and attitude, and not be afraid to take chances — that's real attitude — and that's the hard-boiled way.

Collectable Vintage Mystery Paperbacks

Paperback collecting has been a growing hobby for many years, especially those books published during the early vintage years (1939-1969), which is the focus of this piece since these form the majority of paperbacks with high demand and value. There are many reasons for this. Most of the interest has to do with the often gorgeous (and sometimes exploitive or risque) cover art.

This cover art, especially during the vintage years was highly illustrative, highly visual, and often full of raw passion, wild action, and for mystery addicts there's always the threat (or promise) of murder, mayhem, a dangerous but gorgeous femme fatale, or a woman in peril and in need of being rescued. The covers often tell a story all by themselves, sometimes separate but just as compelling as the book they illustrate. Paperbacks from the 1940's to the 1960's in 'Fine' condition [a collector term for a paperback that appears unread or almost 'as new'], with good mystery or hard boiled cover art, are often highly prized by collectors today, irrespective of the quality of the book they illustrate.

For the collector of mystery paperbacks there's another equally important aspect to the book. Which brings us to the Paperback Original (or PBO), perhaps the most important factor in the demand and value of a collectable mystery paperback of any era. PBO's are true first editions, original publications that have never appeared in print before, and there are a surprisingly large amount of them, many by some of the biggest and most collected names in the mystery field.

Though most paperbacks generally have less value than their hardcover edition, when you talk

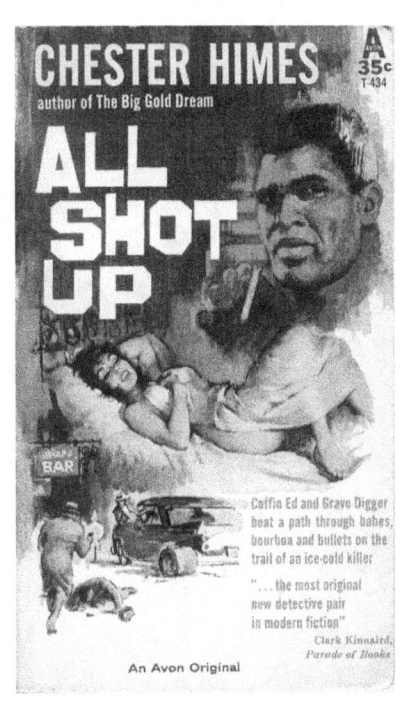

about paperback originals, you have *no* hardcover first edition at all. To make matters more involved, many times the PBO is the only edition of that book that was ever printed.

The paperback originally began as a medium for cheap reprint fiction, a place where hardcover publishers often dumped work to make a few extra bucks after their first edition had sold out. Today some hardcover collectors and dealers continue to hold to the arcane and elitist notion that paperbacks are only cheap reprints with little or no value. To their disadvantage. While there are many reprint editions with little value for collectors (though they may be collectable in their own right — and excellent books to read), while not every PBO is a collectable, there are many mystery paperback originals with high value and eagerly sought by collectors and dealers.

The paperback original phenomenon took off in 1950 with Gold Medal Books and later (their Crest line); Lion Books; Graphic Books; Dell First Editions, and others. However, it has its roots back in the early 1940's with Avon Books who published PBO's in their Murder Mystery Monthly digest-size series. Examples include: Raymond Chandler *(FIVE MURDERS*, MMM #19, PBO 1944; *FIVE SINISTER CHARACTERS*, MMM #28, PBO 1945; and *THE FINGERMAN*, MMM #43, PBO 1946); James M. Cain (*DOUBLE INDEMNITY*, MMM #16, PBO 1943; and *THE EMBEZZLER*, MMM #20, PBO 1944); and William Irish/Cornell Woolrich

(*IF I SHOULD DIE BEFORE I WAKE*, MMM #31, PBO 1945; *BORROWED CRIME*, MMM #42, PBO 1946). Many of these books in nice condition can be very pricey. Actually, some of those listed above strictly speaking are not PBO's, rather, they are new collections of previously published pulp magazine stories. However, they are true first editions and hence very collectable.

Other examples of crime and mystery paperbacks in the Avon series are the various incarnations of Robert Bloch's *THE SCARF OF PASSION* and later on, the various Avon original editions of the works of African-American author Chester Himes (#T-328, *THE REAL COOL KILLERS*, PBO 1959; #T-357, *THE CRAZY KILL*, PBO 1959; and #T-434, *ALL SHOT UP*, PBO 1960). These Himes titles can run you about $50-125 each in Fine shape. Chester Himes is still relatively undiscovered, but he may be the next writer whose PBO's will  become really hot in years to come. Donald Goines is another African-American writer whose crime novels all came out as PBOs and his work is rough — but terrific! His PBOs can fetch from $25 to $75!

There's a lot of collectable and valuable paperbacks in the mystery field. Some interesting for reasons besides being PBO's. First paperback printings can also be collectable, such as the reprint of Robert Bloch's (author of *Psycho*) hardcover edition of *SHOOTING STAR* (half of Ace Double #D-265) which is backed with the Block collection, *TERROR IN THE NIGHT*. On the other hand, there are also Bloch PBO's in the Ace series such as *SPIDERWEB* (Ace #D-59, PBO 1954) and *THE WILL TO KILL* (Ace #S-67, PBO 1954). These are excellent crime novels, scarce and highly collectable, dating from an era when Bloch was writing contemporary crime and mystery.

Another interesting item is the dust-jacket edition of *THE MALTESE FALCON* by Dashiell Hammett (Pocket Book #268). Dust-jackets were a publisher gimmick to re-package a book, usually with more provocative cover art, so they could put it on sale again. This edition of *FALCON* is not a PBO, it's not even a first paperback printing. My edition of the book is just a lowly 8th printing from 1945, but it does feature that rare and highly collectable dust jacket wrapped around it (the art later used for the cover on the Perma Book edition of this title). However, it is the dust jacket that makes all the difference. Dust jackets on any vintage era mass-market paperback are rare and much sought after by collectors. This one, because it is Dashiell Hammett, his most famous novel that features Sam Spade, usually sells at a premium. Condition is particularly important in dust jackets. A near Fine condition copy (near Fine dust jacket, that is, because it is the jacket that is key here) can easily sell for a hundred dollars or more. Other Dashiell Hammett collectable paperbacks were published by Mercury Mystery, Jonathan Mystery, and Bestseller Mystery in digest size.

Another example of an interesting and collectable mystery paperback is *PATTERN FOR MURDER* by David Knight (Graphic Book #48, PBO 1952) which is actually Richard Prather's first book under pseudonym, and the first Shell Scott novel (later reprinted as *THE SCARMBLED YEGGS*). We find a lot of this kind of thing with collectable mystery paperbacks, pseudonyms, retitles, new editions with new cover art, all guaranteed to make your collecting much more complicated — or more fun and interesting — depending on your interests.

In the 1950's Gold Medal Books and Lion Books led the pack publishing paperback originals and many of the books they published have become the blockbuster collectable titles so sought after today. Many of these books were also reprinted by currect publishers.

Tiny Lion Books, in a major coup, published eleven paperback originals by a fellow named Jim Thompson throughout the 1950's, including his first paperback book, *THE KILLER INSIDE ME* (Lion #99, PBO 1952). This is an incredible crime novel, a brutal story, and this first edition is valued in the $500-$1,000 range in near Fine condition, and is scarce.

Examples of other collectable Thompson titles in the Lion series are *A SWELL LOOKING BABE* (Lion #212, PBO 1954), *RECOIL* (Lion #120, PBO 1953), and *THE GOLDEN GIZMO* (Lion #192, PBO 1954). These Thompson Lion editions in Fine shape are all rare and expensive.

David Goodis also wrote for Lion Books; they published four of his paperback originals. These are great crime noir novels and highly collectable. They include: *THE BURGLAR* (Lion #124, PBO 1953); *THE DARK CHASE* (Lion #133, PBO 1953); *THE BLONDE ON THE STREET CORNER* (Lion #186, PBO 1954, with a gorgeous Robert Maguire cover); and *BLACK FRIDAY* (Lion #224, PBO 224). These can fetch from $100 to $300 in Fine shape.

Aside from Jim Thompson and David Goodis, there are many other collectable mystery PBO's in this Lion series, making it one of the toughest and most costly series to attain for the completest collector, or the crime fiction fan. Here's a few of the highlights:

THE LUSTFUL APE by Russell Gray (Lion #38, PBO 1950, was in fact written by mystery author Bruno Fischer under one of his horror pulp bylines).

SOMEONE IS BLEEDING (Lion #137, PBO 1953) and *FURY ON SUNDAY* (Lion #180, PBO 1953) are both by horror master Richard Matheson when he was writing crime fiction. There is also *THE KIDNAPPER* by Robert Bloch (Lion #185, PBO 1954). These are all much sought after titles. Of these four listed above, the first might be a $35 book; the last three, anywhere from $75 to $300 depending on condition.

Aside from the books already mentioned, there's much fine crime and mystery material in the Lion series. Books by David Karp, Stanley Ellin, Kenneth Millar, Day Keene, and Eleazar Lipsky are some of the best. There's also some hidden treasure. *BODIES ARE DUST* by P.J. Wolfson (Lion #83, 1952) is not a PBO, but it is a scarce and much sought-after incredible hard-boiled novel about a crooked cop on the way down. It's a great read, and was reprinted by Berkley Books in 1960 as *HELL COP* (Berkley #D2036). The Berkley reprint seems to be impossible to find.

G.H. Otis wrote two incredible hard-boiled thrillers for Lion in 1953, then seemingly disappeared from paperbacks. His first book was *BOURBON STREET* (Lion #131, PBO 1953), a few months later, *HOT CARGO* (Lion #171, PBO 1953) appeared, and that was it — but more on Otis elsewhere in this book. *BOURBON STREET* is about a loot-mad gunpunk on a rampage who takes apart New Orleans; *HOT CARGO* is a

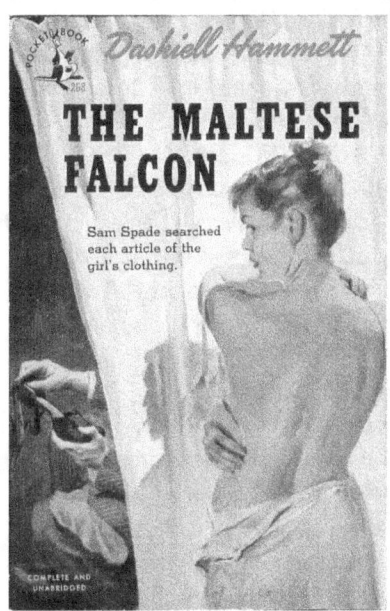

riveting tale of betrayal, spys, double-dealing, and more taking place on a tramp oil tanker on it's way to hell. Otis wrote only two books for Lion and for many years there was next to nothing known about him. Nevertheless, these scarce classics are very underrated and the PBOs are in demand.

Gold Medal Books was the leader in publishing original paperbacks in the 1950's, and was responsible for some of the finest work in the mystery field finding its way into print. Even today, most Gold Medals are still good reads, and with such fine authors as John D. MacDonald, David Goodis, Peter Rabe, Richard Prather, Day keene, Bruno Fischer, Gil Brewer, Lionel White, Vin Packer, Harry Whittington, Charles Williams and others — there's a lot here for the reader and collector. Gold Medal also offers some big money books, such as *THE BRASS CUPCAKE* by John D. MacDonald (#124, PBO 1950, his first novel); and these four by David Goodis, *CASSIDY'S GIRL* (#189, PBO 1951), *OF TENDER SIN* (#226, PBO 1952), *STREET OF THE LOST* (#256, PBO 1952), and *THE MOON IN THE GUTTER* (#348, PBO 1953). These can sell for about $100 each, and many paperbacks in this Gold Medal series of 1,000+ titles published up to 1960 are very collectable.

One of the hottest Gold Medal's is BLACK WINGS HAS MY ANGEL by Elliott Chaze (Gold Medal #296, PBO 1953) which is very scare and on just about every collectors want list — this time because it's a damn good hard-boiled mystery people *want* to read. Fans want a copy in any condition — just to read! Worn and torn copies easily go for $20, when you can find them, and Fine condition copies can go for big money. It was reprinted by Berkley Books as *ONE FOR THE MONEY* (#Y658, 1962) and that reprint is even tougher to find than the original Gold Medal edition. And collectable in it's own right. Go figure!

Crest Books, a Gold Medal imprint, also published an interesting mix, reprints with originals, much of it mystery fiction. Among these are five of the Joe Puma novels written by William Campbell Gault. All are PBO's. These are undervalued, underrated and excellent hard-boiled private eye novels that I would rate even higher than Gault's Brock Callahan books.

SWEET WILD WENCH (Crest #309) seems to be the toughest one to find of the five.

Of course, I've hardly mentioned some other series containing collectable mystery paperbacks, such as the William Irish titles in the Dell Ten-Cent series: *MARIHUANA* (#11, PBO 1951), and *YOU'LL NEVER SEE ME AGAIN* (#26, PBO 1951); nor the scarce Fred Brown edition of *THE CASE OF THE DANCING SANDWICHES* (#33, PBO 1951) all of which are incredibly collectable, valued in the $100-400 range. Fred Brown also had mystery titles published in the Bantam series, and though these were all reprints, they are still very collectable and fans search them out diligently. *WE ALL KILLED GRANDMA* (Bantam #1176) is a good example of a Fred Brown Bantam mystery from the late 1950's.

Speaking of Bantam, the LA Bantam series (no relation to Bantam Books) has many rare mystery editions. A few highlights: *THE SPANISH CAPE MYSTERY* by Ellery Queen (#1, 1939); *THE RED THREADS* by Rex Stout (#1A, 1939, in illustrated and non-illustrative cover versions); *THE SHADOW AND THE VOICE OF MURDER* by Maxwell Grant (#21, PBO 1940 also in two cover versions); and *THE BLUE GERANIUM AND OTHER TUESDAY CLUB MURDERS* by Agatha Christie (#26, 1941, in both cover versions). All LA Bantam's are rare, and with one exception, the mystery titles with illustrative cover art are the most desirable. These

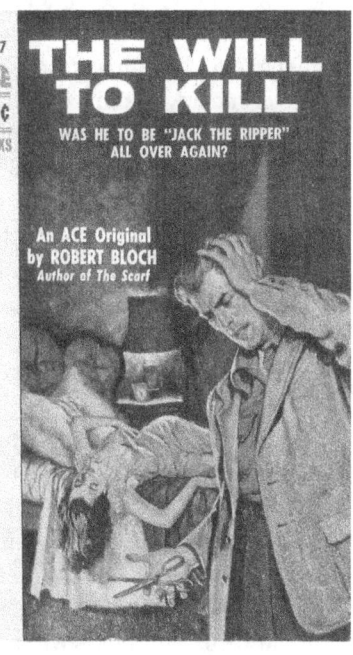

 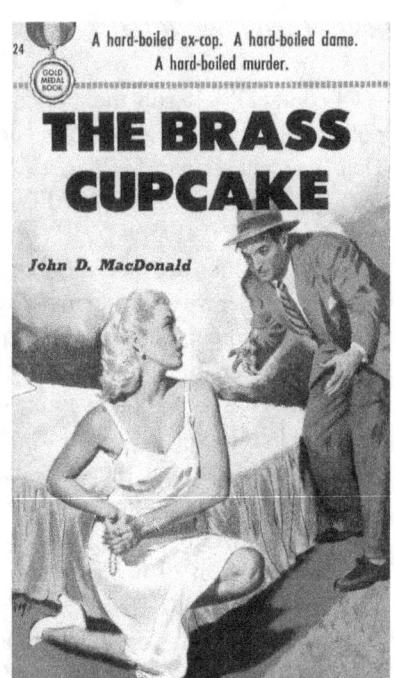

can range from $100 up to $500 or more in near Fine shape. Most go for $50-75 in almost any condition.

Charles Willeford is a writer who made his name in the mystery field with his fine Hoke Mosley novels, but Willeford had many earlier brutal sleaze crime novels published by low-end outfits like Beacon Books in the 1950's. *PICK-UP* (Beacon #B109, PBO 1955); *HIGH PRIEST OF CALIFORNIA* (Beacon #B-130, 1st separate edition, 1956); *LUST IS A WOMAN* (Beacon #B-175, PBO 1958) and *HONEY GAL* (Beacon #B-160, PBO 1958) are a few of his much sought after early titles that can run high in price. Willeford also wrote crime noir sleaze for Newstand Library another soft-core outfit. *THE WOMAN CHASER* (#U137, PBO 1960); *UNDERSTUDY FOR LOVE* (#U-170, PBO 1961); and *NO EXPERIENCE NECESSARY* (#U-182, PBO 1962) can easily fetch around $100 each.

Some later vintage books of note are the Richard Stark books published by Pocket Books. These are PBO's and the author is, of course, Donald Westlake. These are not often seen in nice condition. Then there are many of the early Ed McBain 86th Precinct police procedural novels that were PBO's, such as *THE MUGGER* (Perma #M3061, PBO 1956) and *KILLER'S PAYOFF* (Perma #M3113, PBO 1958); and others.

In the 1970's and 1980's we saw many more fine writers build up followings. They're big stars today. Lawrence Block had some of his books published as Gold Medal originals in the 1960's and 70's, as well as other titles under pseudonym such as his Chip Harrisons. All are collectable today. In fact, Block's first Evan Tanner novel, *THE THIEF WHO COULDN'T SLEEP* (#d1722) was first published by Gold Medal as a PBO in 1966. Meanwhile, *IN THE MIDST OF DEATH* (Dell #4037, 1976) featuring Matt Scudder was also published as a PBO. Many of Block's fine novels have been reprinted by Hard Case Crime in attractive new paperback editions.

Robert Campbell, who has seemingly fallen out of popularity these days, was a fine writer known for his hard-hitting crime fiction and has had at least one book, his first Jake Hatch novel, *PLUGGED NICKLE* (Pocket #64363, 1988) appear as a PBO which is well worth searching out.

Roger Crais, who began writing about his wacky contemporary P.I. hero Elvis Cole in the novel *THE MONKEY'S RAINCOAT* (Bantam #26336) had this first novel, appear as a PBO in 1987. It was a hot number years ago, but is still very collectable in that paperback original edition. Again, condition is key on all these books.

James Elroy — called the demon dog of American crime fiction — known for incredible and often brutal but serious crime fiction also had his first book, *BROWN'S REQUIEM* (Avon #78741) published as a PBO in 1981. It's his only PBO, and is difficult to find in nice shape.

New paperbacks are being published all the time, some becoming the mystery and crime collectables of the future. Mystery paperbacks are fun to collect. The older vintage era books (1939-1959) have a certain charm and ambiance to them that makes them special these days. You can still find some at flea markets an yard sales for as little as a quarter a piece. Even today it is still possible to make amazing finds! You just have to know where to look — and what to look for. So it's a hunt and it's a gamble, a game and a wonderful hobby for the rabid mystery fan and collector. *Good hunting!*

Avon Books:
Centerpieces Of Vintage Mystery & Crime

Some of the most collectable and valuable vintage mystery and crime paperbacks were published in the Avon Books series of the 1940s and 1950s. These included two major digest-size series (measuring 5.25 x 7.75") and early books in the regular Avon Books mass-market paperback rack-size series. And while many of these books were early paperback reprints of hard covers, some were first edition collections. For this reason, and because of their cover art, they command high collector prices today. While Avon published all kinds of books, in all genres, their mainstay was mystery and crime fiction and it is these books that offer fans and collectors a fascinating and fun group of books to collect. There are three basic Avon series of interest to mystery and crime fans and collectors.

The *Avon Murder Mystery Monthly* (AMMM) series began in 1942 and ran 49 issues. They are a gorgeous digest-size series with very nice cover art by William Forrest, Paul Stahr, Ann Cantor and others. The cover art shows various hard-boiled or criminal scenes or sexy bad-girl femme fatales. Examples include the cover for *The Green Ice Murders* by Raoul

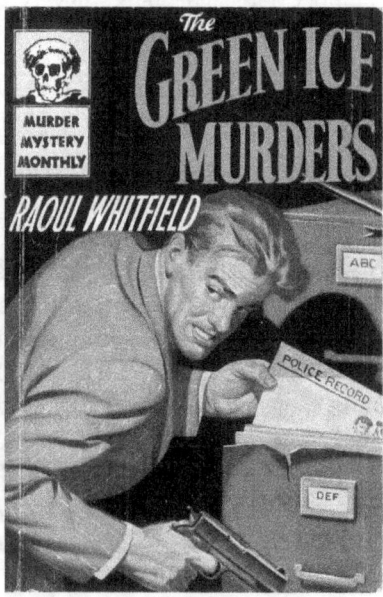

Whitfield (#46), an incredible hard-boiled novel showing a tough guy stealing police files. This scarce digest from 1947 could set you back a bundle, as with all these books, depending on condition.

Then there's the cover art on W.R. Burnett's hard-hitting noir novel *Nobody Lives Forever* (#33) showing tough mugs and their moll planning the crime caper in the novel. Gorgeous but deadly femme fatales are a staple of noir and they also appear on the AMMM covers: such as on James M. Cain's *Loves Lovely Counterfeit* (#44) showing a sexy dame in art by Don Milsop. There is also the more classy but deadly beauty drawn by Ann Cantor on the cover of *The Finger Man* by Raymond Chandler (#43, 1946). This is also a first edition in book form under this title. It, like many of the Avon digests and books in the early paperback series, were often reprinted later in the paperback series with a new number and new cover art. For instance, *The Finger Man* later appeared in the regular Avon paperback series as Avon Book #219 in 1951, and is itself collectable. Another example is *5 Murderers* by Raymond Chandler which originally appeared as AMMM #19 in 1944 and was later reprinted in the regular Avon series with new cover art as book #63. Avon published a number of new collections of Chandler stories under new titles and all are first editions and very collectable. The AMMM edition of Raymond Chandler's *The Big Sleep* (#7), was an early edition from 1942 and the first paperback edition of this classic Sam Spade novel.

Other classic AMMM digests include very collectable editions by A. Merritt, James M. Cain (*The Postman Always Rings Twice*, #6), Rex Stout, Agatha Christie, Frank Gruber, and William Irish/Cornell Woolrich, among others.

Avon Monthly Novels (AMN) were another key digest-size series that began in 1947 and ran for 21 issues. This series, similar to the previous AMMM's, included more sexy cover art or risqué books (for that era) which Avon would soon specialize in publishing – but it also included such books as the classic noir, *Sinful Woman* by James M. Cain (#1). Then there's *The Villain And The Virgin* by James Hadley Chase (#4, a sexy retitling of his hard-boiled gangster classic, *No Orchids For Miss Blandish*, also later reprinted in the regular Avon paperback series. There is also the incredibly insensitive and politically incorrect, *12 Chinks And A Woman*, also by Chase (#7, from 1948), which was reprinted in the regular Avon paperback series in 1952 with new and much more brutal cover art as Avon Book #485. There was also Robert Bloch's early, pre-*Psycho* serial killer novel, *The Scarf of Passion* (#9), also reprinted in 1949 as Avon #211.

However, there's another series that contains a glorious array of early key mystery and crime paperbacks, and that is the regular *Avon Books mass-market paperback rack-sized series* that began in 1941 and runs over a thousand titles. The Avon Books series delved into the mystery and crime genre early with their third book: *The Big Four* by Agatha Christie (#3, which can fetch $100 or more). From then on this series published hundreds of classic novels in the mystery and crime genre much sought after today by collectors.

All these Avon Books series are exciting and lovely to collect. Avon Books are just beautiful. The covers are blazing pulp explosions of color and action, with sexy girls, tough guys, guns, crime, terror, murder and mystery. Even the spines of the books, when lined up in a stack make an attractive display of bright color and design.

While there are hundreds of outstanding crime and mystery books in this Avon series, far too many to talk about here in this short article, I've chosen a dozen or so representative samples that illustrate various strengths and collectable points.

The earliest Avon Books did not have numbers on them until #42, and first printings of many of the early numbers contained 'globe end papers', in which the front and back inside covers had a globe map design. These appeared on the first four or five dozen titles but were soon discontinued on later numbers and on all reprints. Early books with globe end papers are scarce and in nice condition, these early mysteries especially, are quite collectable and expensive today.

For a brief period starting from about 1945 with books numbering from #80 on, and running to about #130, books in this series offered an attractive frame design on the cover. The use of this design was the result of a rivalry between Avon Books and Pocket Books, the two pioneer paperback publishers of the era. One stole this design from the other so that at the time the product of both companies looked very much alike — on purpose I imagine. Nevertheless, the design fit well with classic mysteries. Examples are the dead girl on the cover of Agatha's Christie's *Death In The Air* #89; the femme fatale on the cover of *The Dark Street Murders* by Peter Cheyney #93; the wild and gruesome cover showing a giant skull-headed fly menacing a woman on *A Taste For Honey* by H. F. Heard #108; and the tough gangster and gorgeous moll on the cover of *The Unconscious Witness* by R. Austin Freeman #122.

Some of the Avon Books also used, or reused, color photographs taken from the earlier Avon digests, or even from Avon comic books, as cover art for mystery titles in this series. These photos are raw, passionate, and colorful. They evoke nostalgia, but many also show sexy girls with quite significant cleavage – always a hit with the male collectors! Examples of these include the 'heated embrace' cover photos on *The Moving Finger* by Agatha Christie (#164, a traditional mystery); *The Scarf Of Passion* by Robert Bloch (#211, an early serial killer novel); or the sexy femme fatale photo on *No Orchids For Miss Blandish* (#355, a hard-boiled gangster novel).

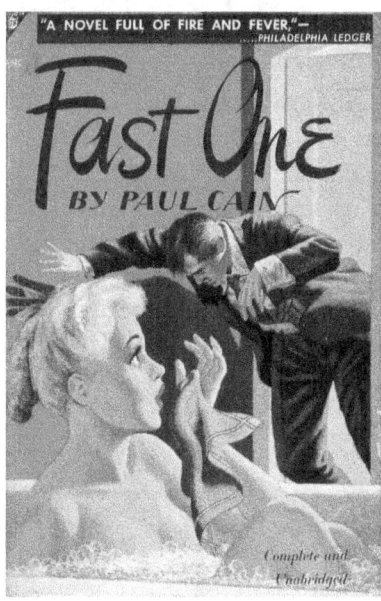

Besides such giants as Chandler and Christie, many classic novels and collections by collectable authors in the mystery and crime genre appear in the regular Avon Books series. These include, *Double Indemnity* by James M. Cain (#137, 1947, the book that was made into the classic noir film. This edition pre-dates the film. Others include *This Is Murder, Mr. Herbert* by Day Keene, (#159, 1948, an early first edition collection by this popular pulp crime author). Then there is *Fast One* by Paul Cain (#178, hard-boiled stories from *Black Mask*. The sexy girl in the bathtub cover art was replaced on a later 1952 printing on book #496).

Another perennially popular author in the Avon series was Rex Stout. His Nero Wolfe mysteries, such as *The Red Box* appeared as AMMM (#9, 1942); *The League of Frightened Men*, (Avon #20, 1942); *Over My Dead Body* (Avon #62, 1945); *The Red Box* (Avon #82, 1946, which reprints AMMM #9). There are many more Rex Stout reprints in the Avon series, most have new cover art, making even the reprints collectable. For instance, *The Case Of The Black Orchids* by Rex Stout (Avon #256 from 1950, reprints the earlier Avon Book #95, which was published under the shorter title, *Black Orchids*. Avon #95 from 1946.

Another very collectable author published by Avon was Cornell Woolrich (also his more hard-boiled work under his William Irish pseudonym). His early suspense and noir titles appeared in the AMMM series and all are scarce. These were also later reprinted with new cover art in the regular Avon paperback-size series. The earliest of these Avon Books reprints was *The Black Angel* (#96); others included: *If I Should Die Before I Wake* as by Irish (#104); *The Black Path Of Fear* (#106); and the haunting *I Married A Dead Man* by William Irish (#220). All are very collectable.

When you talk about classic books – hard-boiled crime or traditional mysteries – the various series published early on by Avon Books offer some of the best vintage paperbacks in the entire genre. With top authors, incredible pulp action stories, classic sexy girl cover art, bright colors, classic detectives like Philip Marlowe, Rex Stout, or Hercule Poirot, and prized and scarce first editions, they offer everything the rabid fan or collector could desire. They're exciting and fun books to collect and display. They are the vintage centerpieces of classic mystery and crime fiction.

Dell Map Back Mysteries:
They Just Don't Make 'em Like That Anymore!

The Dell Map Backs of the 1940s and 1950s were something really special. It wasn't only their elegant package, they were simply beautiful books and they hold their beauty over the years. They were sturdy, and had physical integrity as a quality package irrespective of their contents. The Early books had firm covers that were laminated, and they showcased often surreal or representational airbrushed covers by fine artists such as Gerald Gregg. Later books in the series featured more realistic cover illustrations by artists such as Bill George and Robert Stanley. A keyhole logo on the cover and a map on the back cover were the images most visible and remembered today from the early Dell Books. Inside, they also included various teaser pages; *"Things This Mystery is About"* or a *"Cast of Characters."* All relatively minor touches, but they made the books something special and the readers loved them. They just don't make 'em like that anymore.

A thin band on the cover proclaims to the reader *"with crime map on back cover."* That's what really made these books special and stand out, the incredible and beautifully rendered maps on the back cover of each

book. Beginning with Dell Book #5 in 1943, a mystery novel titled, *Four Frightened Women* by George Harmon Coxe, back cover maps would appear on an amazing 577 volumes until 1952.

These back cover maps were a truly lovely and original use for an often neglected part of the paperback book. No publisher had ever used the idea before, and no publisher put so much effort into producing quality and memorable paperback books than the Dell Books series. The maps were a scene-of-the-crime representation of what was going on in the story in that book. Dell issued a wide array of map backs in all genres, but mysteries formed 50% of all the books in the series and these are the books that are of special interest to us. They are a beautiful series of books and hold a special place in the hearts of mystery readers and fans, yesterday and today. They offer a treasure trove for the mystery fan and collector.

Map back books were 4-color cartographic fantasies and were the idea of Dell editor Lloyd Smith. Many of the maps were drawn by Chicago graphic artist Ruth Belew. She did at least 150 of the 577 maps. The maps themselves were often unique and imaginative. They showed anything from a nation or state with cities, streets, mountains, seas and lakes; to a Manhattan brownstone with diagrams of the various floors; or a country estate showing rooms, gardens and outbuildings.

While the cover art was important and often exceptional, some of the books did not have illustrations for the covers but used photos of stars

from the film made from the book. Examples of these early movie tie-in books include *Night And The City* by Gerald Kersh (#374) and *Death In A Doll's House* by Hannah Lees and Lawrence Bachman (#356) which had color photos of the stars who appeared in these films. The former shows stars Richard Widmark and Gene Tierney, and the later book – filmed under the title "Shadow on the Wall" – shows the stars of that film, Ann Southern and Zachary Scott.

Many authors had their books reprinted as gorgeous collectable Dell Map Backs to the thrill of fans. Rex Stout and his famous Nero Wolfe stories appeared beginning with Dell Book #9 in 1943. Stout's work was represented early in the series with *Double For Death*. There would be a dozen Rex Stout books published in this series with maps on the back, each offering a unique look at his classic stories and characters.

Dashiell Hammett had 7 books that spanned the era from #129 to #538 with airbrushed covers by Gerald Gregg on the lower numbers and later with action-oriented and sexy girl cover art by Robert Stanley. While the Hammett covers are very different in design and content, all are stunning and interesting. The maps on the back of these for the most part show the Continental Op's stomping ground in San Francisco. Various maps of 'Frisco appear on the back of at least 5 books: *The Continental Op* (#129) with a hanging man cover; *The Return of The Contenintal Op* (#154) with gun shooting shield cover; *Dead Yellow Women* (#308) with four dead Asian girls on a morgue slab; *Blood Money* (#486, reprints Dell #53) with man pulling dead woman from the water; and *The Creeping Siamese* (#538) with the cover showing a sexy girl holding a bloody dagger. Each shows various well-designed maps of the streets of the city where the stories take place. Hammett's *A Man Called Spade* (#411, reprints Dell #90) has a Robert Stanley cover showing his version of private dick Sam Spade; while on the back is a map of the apartment of Max Bliss, the scene of a murder in the title story in this crime collection. Some Dell Map Backs, were reprinted from an earlier Dell Map Back with new cover art. Then there's Dashiell Hammett's *Nightmare Town* (#379) with another fine Robert Stanley cover and another scene-of-the-crime map on the back cover.

Classic mystery author Agatha Christie had many books reprinted in the Dell series with maps on the back. Dame Agatha's first Dell Book, and her first map back, was an early one, *The Tuesday Club Murders*, (#8) from 1943. The series continued with many more of her fine books. Examples include: *Appointment with Death* (#105) a Hercule Poirot murder mystery with a stylish airbrush cover by Gerald Gregg of the Grim Reaper and a back cover map showing the Holy Land with an insert scene of Petra, the place of sacrifice that is a scene of a murder. *The*

Mysterious Mr. Quin (#570), shows colorful harlequins on the cover, while the back has a map of Canada, France, and scenes where the book takes place.

Some writers only had one book represent them in this series, but what a book! Popular suspense author Cornell Woolrich had *The Black Curtain* (#208) with a cover full of foreboding and dark atmosphere that matched his work. Popular noir icon David Goodis was represented by *Dark Passage* (#271), with a stark fleeing prisoner cover, on the back is a map of Irene Janney's apartment, the place the murderer uses as a hideout in the novel.

Other popular writers who had books in the series include David Dodge with *It Ain't Hay* (#27)) a crime and drug novel with an incredible cover showing death rowing a boat that carries a giant marijuana cigarette. On the back is a map of San Francisco *"where marijuana and murder make a thrilling story."* Clayton Rawson's Great Merlini books are also published in the Dell series. Merlini mixes magic with murder and were written by practicing magician, Rawson. One of the best of these was *The Headless Body* (#176) with a cover that shows a gruesome sideshow barker and a back cover map of the Mighty Hannun Show, the circus where the murder takes place. These are just a few of the Dell map back high points. There are many more.

Traditional mysteries held a center stage in the Dell Map Back series. For instance there's *The Cross-Eyed Bean Murders* by Dorothy B. Hughes (#48) with a map of Room 1000 at the Lorenzo Hotel; *The Window At the White Cat* by Mary Roberts Rinehart (#57); with a ghostly cat on the cover; *Ill Met By Moonlight* by Leslie Ford (#6), the 2nd Map Back with a map of April Harbor, the town that was the scene of the murder; *Hunt With The Hounds* by Mignon G. Eberhart (#546) with a map of the state of Virginia and Bedford County; and *The Accomplice* by Matthew Head (#346) with a haunting cover showing a dead beauty in a chaise lounge with the Eiffel Tower outside her window.

George Harmon Coxe was a popular pulp and hardcover author in the 1930s and 40s and his *Four Frightened Women* (#5) was the first Dell Map Back from 1943. He also had many more in the series. Examples include his Kent Murdock novel *Murder With Pictures* (#101) showing a bold blue map of the apartment where murder takes place in the book; or the Flash Casey novel, *Murder For Two* (#276) with a surreal cover of a giant pencil marking out two dead women. Then there's *Murder in Havana* (#423), a later novel with a women in bondage cover by Robert Stanley and a back cover map showing Cuba and scenes from the novel.

Brett Halliday was another author who did well for years with Dell Books chronicling the hard-boiled adventures of his tough Miami private eye, Mike Shayne. One such example is the dead girl in the water cover for *Blood on Biscayne Bay* (#268), with a map of Miami Beach and Biscayne Bay where the murder occurred.

Two popular mystery authors had books under pseudonyms in the Dell series. Erle Stanley Gardner, whose popular Perry Mason books were reprinted by rival paperback publisher Pocket Books also had a separate series reprinted by Dell chronicling the adventures of Bertha Cool and Donald Lamb written as by A.A. Fair. *Crows Can't Count* (#472) is one example of an A.A. Fair Dell title. John Dickson Carr not only had books published under his own name from Dell as Map Backs, but also under his popular pseudonym, Carter Dickson.

Mystery and crime novel covers in this series also spawn often surreal or intense images of death, skulls, or the Grim Reaper. The errie beckoning skeletal hand on *The Crooking Finger* by Cleve F. Adams (#104) is one good example. One better might be the skull and Grim Reaper image on the cover of *Midsummer Nightmare* by Christopher Hale (#150). The cover art on many Dells was imaginative and often riveting and with the colorful back cover maps it made a potent combination for sales success.

While there are some key mysteries in this series that can sell for $50, or even $100 if in Very Good condition or better, most will sell for about $15 to $25 in Very Good. Early titles go for more. They can still be found from time to time at flea markets or yard sales, but today the best place

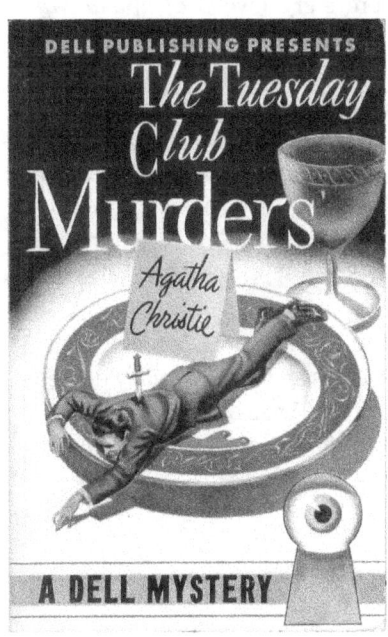

to find these gorgeous books is from a specialist collectable paperback dealer, at a paperback show, or on the Internet.

The design and style of the old Dell Map Backs has had a powerful impact upon editors, publishers and collectors over the years. Today these books are collected avidly. Dell collector and scholar William H. Lyles wrote an informative and groundbreaking examination of this publisher in his book, *Putting Dell on The Map: A History of the Dell Paperbacks* (Greenwood Press, 1983). Since then interest in the Dell series, and especially the Map Backs, has grown. Decades after the last Map Back was published in 1952, their influence still impacts the paperback market. For instance, in 1987, when IPL Books reissued *The Headless Lady* by Clayton Rawson, their edition showcased a back cover map drawn by Jennifer Place that was based upon the map on the back of Dell Book #176. Then there are the first two books published in 2000 by the small Hollywood outfit, Uglytown Productions. *By The Balls* and *Five Shots and A Funeral* both by Tom Fassbender and Jim Pascoe are Dashiell Loveless hard-boiled satires, but in their design and format they look and feel just like classic Dell Map Backs. These fun books have become collectable in their own right.

In 2003, I published a new trade paperback original crime novel in the classic Dell Map Back format and style. *A Trunkfull of Trouble* (Gryphon Books, 2003) is by veteran mystery author Julius Fast. Julius Fast, brother of famed author Howard Fast, was the winner of the first-ever MWA Edgar Award in 1947 for his first mystery novel, *Watchful at Night*. In *A Trunkfull of Trouble* he gives us an original traditional mystery set in Manhattan and a small Connecticut town where murder and two million dollars in cash is at stake. It's a thrilling crime novel with wonderful characters. The book harkens back to the classic Dell Map Backs in cover art, design, logo, "cast of characters" teaser pages and, of course, it has a beautiful, colorful map on the back cover that shows the main locations described in the text. The cover art and map design are by artist, Lucille Cali. This excellent mystery novel is a proud homage to this classic series of paperback books.

Dell Books published an impressive array of authors. Most of them were popular authors of the era in the 1940s and 50s, but many of them have gone on to become real legends today. These authors and these books are perennially popular. *They just don't make 'em like that anymore!*

A DOZEN TOP MAP BACK MYSTERIES

The following list contains 12 of the top mystery and crime Dell Map Backs. It does not include non-Map Back titles, key books in other genres, or puzzle books. The values include two ranges: from Very Good (VG) condition, books with moderate wear, to About Fine (AF) condition, books that are almost as new.

1: *Dark Passage* by David Goodis, Dell #221, $75-250.
2: *Blood Money* by Dashiell Hammett, Dell #53, $55-125.
3: *A Man Called Spade & Other Stories* by Dashiell Hammett, Dell #90, $50-125
4: *The Return of The Continental Op* by Dashiell Hammett, Dell #154, $50-120.
5: *Double For Death* by Rex Stout, Dell #9, $45-120.
6: *Dead Yellow Women* by Dashiell Hammett, Dell #90, $50-120.
7: *The Black Curtain* by Cornell Woolrich, Dell #208, $55-100.
8: *Scotland Yard: The Department of Queer Complaints* by Carter Dickson (John Dickson Carr), Dell #65, $45-100.
9: *The Continental Op* by Dashiell Hammett, Dell #129, $45-125.
10: *The Tuesday Club Murders* by Agatha Christie, Dell #8, $50-125.
11: *It Ain't Hay* by David Dodge, Dell #270, $40-90.
12: *Blue City* by Kenneth Millar, Dell #363, $40-125.

The Three Daring Divas of Paperback Pulp Fiction

In the pulp paperbacks of the 1950s three women dared what was almost impossible, writing about subjects that were never to be spoken of out loud, only veiled in whispers – especially for such nice young ladies. Crime, murder, matricide, juvenile delinquency, sex, including lesbianism. They wrote honestly about these topics and in doing so they helped usher in the era of the paperback original with stories that grabbed their readers as never before.

This article is a celebration of **Marijane Meaker**, **Ann Bannon** and **Julie Ellis** – three daring divas as I call them; pioneering woman writers who blazed a path for all women that would follow. I knew and liked each one of these talented ladies. They have been guests over the years at my annual book show in New York and I have interviewed each of them in my magazine, *Paperback Parade*. We have also been good friends and they are wonderful special people.

The 1950s and early 60s was a time of rigid morals and very traditional tastes. However, just below the surface, tension and change brewed. These three writers took chances and began to mine that fertile area of crime and sex often mixing the two together. They did so in the new paperback originals that were coming into vogue in the predominately male-dominated writing and publishing paperback world, and they began to produce work that broke all barriers, though each sometimes carefully masked their true identities behind pseudonyms. Decades later their work would attain cult status.

Each of these ladies presented strong female characters in their books, women much like themselves, full of life and passion who were not afraid to stake their ground in a world that was often hard and unforgiving. Their original paperbacks were big sellers and very popular. One reason was that these three women wrote for women about women's issues. They mined the fertile ground awash with love, passion, fear and especially sexual desires. Meaker, Bannon and Ellis gave vent to feelings not often found back then for women in paperback fiction.

While Marijane Meaker may not be that well known to many crime and mystery readers, the name Vin Packer is certainly well-known. It was a name associated with some of the best-written and most collectable paperback originals of the 1950s and 60s. Meaker's books as Vin Packer, give us outstanding mystery, crime, as well as realistic and truthful juvenile delinquent novels. Later, as Ann Aldrich, she would write lesbian-themed novels that were far ahead of their time. Still later, as M.E. Kerr, she would write many fine young adult novels.

Marijane Meaker was born in Auburn, New York in 1927 and began her long and successful writing career at 23 years of age when in 1952 she began writing original crime novels as Vin Packer for Gold Medal Books.

Originally, Meaker worked for Gold Medal as a secretary and when the new publishing line was introduced – paperback originals – she wrote a book for it. That was *Spring Fire* (GM #222) and it sold right away. It's "a story once told in whispers now frankly, honestly written" as the cover blurbs proclaim, a novel about Leda and Mitch that takes place at a women's college which also involves their lesbian romance. The cover by Bayre Phillips shows the two women in slips, sitting together upon a bed, but looking away from each other, as if highlighting the tension between them. It's an effective image and one that will often be used, in a variety of ways, on the covers of many books that deal with the subject.

Mystery critic Jon Breen has said of Meaker's Vin Packer books, "Her probing accounts of the roots of crime are richly detailed snapshots of their times, unconventional, intensely readable, and devoid of heroes, villains, or pat solutions."

When I asked her why so many of her characters seemed troubled, deluded or confused, Meaker told me, "I was following true crime cases and fictionalizing them. I was young and perhaps cynical but I was trying to create interesting characters and they usually, to my mind, are not happy-go-lucky, upbeat personalities, particularly in the crime field. I wasn't trying to *say* anything – just tell a good story."

Ed Gorman put it more simply, but to the point, "[Vin Packer] was one hell of a writer."

Some of her best Packer crime novels dealt with people living secret lives or trapped in complicated relationships that often led to murder. *Something in the Shadows* (GM#1146, 1961) is about Joseph Meaker (she sometimes used her own name as that of a character in her books), Maggie and Hart, who find themselves in a brutal story of horror and crime. In *Intimate Victims* (GM #1241, 1962), we have an amazing novel of people who have literally changed identities and the good and evil that results. Then in *5:45 To Suburbia* (GM #731, 1958) she shows the two sides of Charlie Gibsons' life. Charlie rode the 5:45 to Westport every day, he was an important publishing executive, well liked, but also addicted to a powerful woman who had made him the success he'd become, and he could not break away from her. Thus begins his downfall.

With *The Girl on the Best Seller List* (GM #976, 1960) and *The Damnation of Adam Blessing* (GM #1074, 1961) we have stories that seem torn from today's headlines, but they were written over 60 years ago! The former tells the story of a woman whose tempestuous book laid bare the secrets of the most influential people of a small town – and now they want revenge against her! The latter novel delves into the private and strange world created by a man, and the woman who entered it. Both covers for these classic Gold Medal paperback originals are by the super talented Robert McGinnis and capture the mood and style of these

Julie Ellis at the NYC Book Show, 2006

Meaker and Bannon with the author, 2006

novels perfectly.

Meaker's books also included three tough but truthful juvenile delinquent novels which back then were a popular sub-genre of crime fiction. *The Thrill Kids* (1955) give us kids on the prowl for kicks and murder. The cover art by James Meese captures the moment of lust and danger that runs through the book for one young woman. In *The Young and The Violent* (GM #581, 1956), the blurbs tell us, "expect to get hurt when you hit upper Park Avenue, where the asphalt battleground – and violence begin," it's a stunning crime novel of teenage armies and warrior gangs who rumble and murder each other to protect their concrete turf. A harrowing JD classic. Finally in *The Twisted Ones* (GM #861, 1959), we have another tense brutal novel of rape and murder among wild youth and gangs. These books were very popular and reprinted many times. And like all the books she wrote, as by Vin Packer, they were also based upon real cases that Meaker came upon in her research.

Perhaps her most intense and lauded crime novel is *The Evil Friendship* as by Vin Packer (GM #797). This brutal novel of murder and matricide is based on the famous 1954 Parker-Hulme murder case from New Zealand. Anthony Boucher characterized the story as "a lesbian Loeb-Leopold."

In fact, when I asked her about how she heard about the original case, Meaker said, "Boucher called the case to my attention. I sent for the trial transcripts. Juliet Hulme, it turned out, served only 5 ½ years and is writing best selling mysteries."

Marijane added in a recent email: "The name Juliet Hulme took after she got out of prison and wrote murder mysteries is a famous one: Anne Perry. She's now the very celebrated author of all those Victorian mysteries. I knew a long time ago she had taken that pseudonym but I never mentioned it until the New York *Times* did a big write up on it when the movie (based on the case), *Heavenly Creatures*, came out…"

Meaker's other Vin Packer novels concern race relations and crime in the deep South of the 1950s. In *3-Day Terror* (GM #689, 1957) a small town is torn apart by a vicious killer. In *Dark Don't Catch Me* (GM #624), one of the major premises is the sexual tension between blacks and whites that boils over into racial anger and inevitably murder. Meaker said she based the first book on the famous Emmett Till murder case, and the other novel was based on various news stories she heard during the period.

In 1955, Meaker broke in a new pseudonym, and broke new ground, as Ann Aldrich. Under that name she published her first overtly lesbian-themed novel, *We Walk Alone* (GM #509). While some of her Packer books touched upon this subject mixing it with crime (such as with

Spring Fire), the Aldrich books were expressly about lesbian lives and relationships and told their stories with an unapologetic honesty rarely seen in mainstream fiction dealing with this subject back then. The books were very popular with readers, male and female. Men bought and read books with lesbian subject matter for curiosity or titillation. However, women read them to discover a world they did not know existed, and for many women these books told them they were not alone, that the feelings they had for women, were felt by other women. It was a liberating feeling for many of these women.

"As a gay woman," Meaker said, "the themes were natural to me. I'm glad to see that after all these years, gay writing is viewed as a legitimate literature."

Marijane Meaker wrote 20 original paperback novels for Gold Medal Books from 1952 to 1965. She said, "I loved Dick Carroll!" – speaking of the legendary editor of the line and the originator of the paperback original – "I never knew the others [there]. Those were great days!"

Shortly after Dick Carroll died, Meaker stopped writing as Vin Packer.

Marijane Meaker later wrote books for teens and young adults as M.E. Kerr. She adds, "I think it's easier to see the adult in the child – and easier to reach the adult through the child."

Stark House has reprinted classic Vin Packer crime novels in attractive trade paperbacks that contain two Packer novels per book. These include *Something in the Shadows* & *Intimate Victims*, and two matricide novels, *The Evil Friendship* & *Whisper His Sin*. These books offer some of the best crime reading around and are real bargains in this new format.

Ann Bannon is a petite, outgoing woman who is a pleasure to be around and talk with, her smile just lights up any room she is in. Her work for the classic Gold Medal Books broke new ground in lesbian-theme paperback original fiction. Ann's writing began when she was just 21, as a young wife and mother, her writing explored lesbian lives and relationships. While her books have little or nothing to do with mystery and crime, what she wrote about could have been prosecuted as crimes itself back then. Such women could be arrested, lose custody of their children, lose their jobs if their "secret" got out.

"I discovered *The Well of Loneliness* by Radclyffe Hall. While the general gloom and weepiness of it frustrated me, I nonetheless found it fascinating, and followed up quickly with Vin Packer's (Marjane Meaker's) *Spring Fire*, a book set in a time and place that had more significance to me. Both books moved me. And I found them both on a drugstore kiosk in Philadelphia. They inspired me to try my own hand at story-telling."

Ann's first novel, *Odd Girl Out* (GM #653), was published by Gold Medal Books in 1957 and it turned out to be the second best selling original paperback of that year.

The book came about when Ann sent a letter to Vin Packer about a book she had written and Packer (Meaker) wrote back inviting Ann to New York to meet her own editor, Dick Carroll, at Gold Medal Books.

Bannon said, "(Marijane) worked for Gold Medal, witnessed the stunning success of Tereska Torres's 1950 lesbian story, *Woman's Barracks*, and believed she could write novels herself. When the editor-in-chief, Dick

Carroll, took a chance on *Spring Fire*, she got lucky. And so did Carroll, because the book was a huge success. It was dawning on him, and the other management types at Gold Medal, that tales of love between women were a potential gold mine. So when I showed up with a five-inch thick manuscript, I was more welcomed than I realized. Dick sent me home to whittle the big manuscript down, and to focus on the romance between the two sorority sisters. 'There's your story,' he said. I did it, and he published it as *Odd Girl Out* (his title) without changing one word."

However, for Ann, exploring what was then looked at by most as a literary back alley was difficult for a then married woman with children. So she used the pseudonym A. Bannon, soon to become Ann Bannon.

"Given the disreputable nature of the subject matter at the time, I always had spooky feelings that my every move was being charted by some shadowy government snoop. But I've never been able to find out for sure. I did take the precaution of switching to using only the Gold Medal address on notes to readers. And my children's welfare and my own parental rights weighed heavily upon my mind. God forbid I should jeopardize either by owning up to my writer's identity."

In 1957 when *Odd Girl Out* was published, and for many years afterwards, women who wrote such material – or worse in the terms of the period – actually lived those lives – could lose custody of their children in the courts. So Ann's concerns were well founded in those early days before tolerance and gay rights were ever even imagined.

Ann says her family for the most part, was relieved that she had not used her real name on the books. She said her mother "took it all fairly well. She never scolded me. Her major commentary was 'just don't ever show this to your grandmother, dear.' I never did."

Ann adds, "At the time I was writing, I remember feeling resentful that no critic ever registered our existence. In retrospect, and distant as those days seem, I am grateful that the critics so ostentatiously ignored us, we authors of the lesbian pulps. It gave us license, in a sense, to write as we willed, to cover the territory forbidden to 'respectable' novelists, to speak candidly about real, physical, emotional, consuming love between women. Looked at that way, it was a gift."

Another gift was what the readers got out of the books. The reader feedback Ann received from writing her novels touched her heart, even as those books touched so many women.

"As for the reaction from the lesbian readers, it was intense. I received carton after carton of letters from women all over the country. You would be amazed, if you could read them today, at the outpouring of relief to see themselves mirrored in fiction, at the sudden rainbow of hope the novels inspired; but also the litany of fears, at the despair of isolation and bewilderment. The portrait they paint of that era when gay love was illegal and there was no sense of community would stun young woman now. The impression they made on me is indelible. And the contrast they would have provided to all the freedoms now taken for granted is striking."

Ann's writing continued into the early 1960s, going from strength to strength with strong and interesting females like Laura and Beebo, as she told stories of their lesbian lives in popular paperback originals. In *Women in The Shadows* (GM #919, 1959), we have a darker novel of break-up and interracial romance, as well as an early look at gay and lesbian parenthood. *I Am A Woman* (GM #833, 1959) gives us her heroine Beebo Brinker older and wiser. In *Journey To A Woman* (GM#977, 1960) she continues the story of Laura and her lover as Beebo enters the picture. Her most popular book however, was *Beebo Brinker* (GM #1224, 1962). This one, written last, was actually a prelude to the stories in her other novels as Beebo arrives fresh from the hayfields of Wisconsin to Greenwich Village and enters the scene of the early 1960s. The book was an instant hit and has become a classic. It seemed Ann had really hit her stride as a writer.

Then in 1962, Ann Bannon stopped writing.

"My children were young, but old enough to start reading and to wonder what I was doing shackled to the typewriter all day. I had tried to write a 'straight' novel, *The Marriage,* but it flopped. My heart wasn't in it, I guess. And I just thought, if I couldn't write something I wasn't too self-conscious to show my children, I should be doing something else."

Ann returned to graduate school and put all her energy into a career as a college professor and administrator, and does not regret the experience and success she found there.

Today, Ann's novels are kept continually in print in attractive paperbacks from Cleis Press. The cover designs by Scott Idleman recreate classic lesbian pulp paperback covers of the 1950s for these new editions. They are stunning books and avidly read and collected by Ann's many fans.

Julie Ellis has written many fine books, under so many names, but many fans and collectors may not know her name or her work. Her current fans may not know of her early soft-core adult books written for Midwood Books in the 1960s as Joan Ellis and Linda Michaels. Julie had an incredible and successful career. She was a petite woman and a very charming woman. As a guest at my book shows in New York City, she was always a big hit with fans. Julie was always impeccably dressed and wore wonderful large hats. She always had a big smile for everyone she met and was a lovely charming lady.

Julie Ellis wrote in a variety of genres and styles, but her soft-core adult books for Midwood were ground-breaking and pioneering for a woman in that field of publishing during that era. She wrote sexy novels about adventuresome young women who enjoyed all life had to offer. Her work examined the sexual taboos and presaged the sexual revolution in relationships between men and women, couples, and women with other women. Sometimes she mixed crime and mystery into her books, for instance she wrote some fine books in the juvenile delinquent genre where high school and college age youths became entwined with crime and sex. Her female characters are often strong but also very passionate.

Originally Julie began writing one-act plays, then three-act plays produced Off-Broadway. Then she got into the paperbacks at Midwood Books.

"A friend of my husband was a literary agent with several clients (including Mike Avallone) who wrote for Midwood Books. I was astonished when he clucked at my insistence that it would take a year to write a book – and Midwood wasn't paying the kind of money to allow me to do that. I was in the midst of a first novel – put aside many years and just recently completed. 'As fast as you are, you'll knock one out in a month,' he insisted. It was kind of a challenge. 'Okay, I'll give it a whirl,' I told him – and 28 days later delivered *Lana*. Later I would work almost non-stop and turned out a book in 7 to 10 days. Those were hectic days…"

Lana (Midwood #54, 1960) is the story of, as the cover blurbs proclaim, "The youngest member of the world's oldest profession." Lana is only 15 years old in this searing novel of lost youth, as she begins her career with "The face of an angel…the morals of an alley cat." It's a good story with strong characters.

Julie's books were passionate and exciting and Midwood sold them as fast as she could write them. It didn't hurt either, that most of her books had stunning cover art depicting beautiful and sexy young woman by master artist Paul Rader. Nevertheless, the sheer amount of books Julie Ellis wrote for Midwood from 1960 to 1966 was nothing short of amazing. It is estimated she wrote over 100 books for Midwood and may have written as many as 150 books in total!

Julie always placed these stories among interesting backgrounds. The record business was an important part of *Pleasure Girl* (1961); the apartment house management racket was a key part of *Liza's Apartment* (1961) and segregation and racial tension in a small Southern town form a major part of *Mulatto* (1961). In *Numbers Girl* as by Linda Michaels (1961), we have a novel that goes inside the policy racket and mixes that criminal world with the story of a woman "looking for love *or* money". I think she was mostly interested in the money!

The story of how one of her most popular books came to be written for Midwood began with a painting. Julie said, "Harry Shorten, Midwood/Tower publisher, brought me into his office, showed me the artwork he had on file and said, 'Write a book where we can use this for the cover.' The artwork showed a pretty young girl with an ice-cream cone – so I worked that into the book."

That book was *Talk of the Town* as by Joan Ellis with a truly exquisite Paul Rader cover painting. It's the story of a young girl who would do anything to become the most popular girl in town – *and did!*

Julie adds, "Harry told me once that I was their best selling author – that they had standing orders to ship a dozen or more copies of each title to certain companies (including a group of engineers at Dupont down in Delaware)."

Some of Julie's books dealt with college life, and books like *Campus Life* went through many printings. Most were just sexy stories about young woman exploring their sexuality, in an era when the euphemism had not yet been replaced by explicitness in the written word. Books such as *Hold Me Tight*, *Country Girl* (1965), and *Snow Bunnies* (1966) were just cute, sexy, fun. Others dealt with lesbian themes: *Girl's*

Dormitory, or *Forbidden Sex*. In fact, Julie's work in this area had been discovered and praised by Katherine V. Forrest for her anthology, *Lesbian Pulp Fiction*.

Still more of Julie's novels combined crime and juvenile delinquency with young people and sex, *Girls in Trouble* as by Linda Michaels (1962), is a brutal novel about the black market business of selling babies. The very popular and collectable, *Gang Girl* (1964), mixes raw sex with sudden violence in a gang world as a young girl is lost on the streets. *High School Hellion*, as Joan Ellis, is another classic in the JD sub-genre.

The Hot Canary (1963), is a classic of sorts. With an intriguing title, and a simply gorgeous Robert Maguire cover painting that shows a hot redhead in a too-tight dress, it is a perennial favorite among collectors. It's the story of Donnie, a sexy lounge singer who has no voice but somehow has been able to make it as a singer. The blurbs on this one let on what Donnie's secret to success might be. They are priceless: "she sang for supper, but did something else for her midnight snack," and "...so started her climb to the top, but to get there she had to spend a lot of time on the bottom."

Of those early days writing such books for Midwood in the 1960s, Julie added, "There was a kind of club-like feeling among the writers. I can't remember all the names — one was also writing plays. There was Morris Hershman, Mike Avallone, a sister and brother who became close friends also – she wrote as March Hastings, I believe – I don't recall Ronnie's pseudonym. Also Luellen Davis, I believe her Midwood name was Ort Louis or something like that. And yes, there was a kind of stigma to writing these books. This didn't bother me."

In 1966, Julie stopped writing books for Midwood. She stopped because the books were becoming much more explicit. There was also talk of censorship problems on the horizon. So she moved into writing Gothics, romantic suspense, and historical novels. Since 1974, she had written only original hardcovers which were later reprinted in paperback and always under the Julie Ellis byline.

When I asked Julie what she thought about the fact that people collected and cherished her old Midwood original paperbacks today, she smiled with that impish grim of her's and said, "I'm absolutely fascinated! And grateful!"

Julie Ellis passed away in 2006 and this article was dedicated to her memory.
Marijane Meaker sadly passed away in early 2023.
Ann Bannon is still active in the writing field.

Lion Books:
Noir Paperback Icons

It is the smell of death... The Oxman Hotel stank with the stale odor of cheap whiskey, cheap two-bit racketeers, cheap unwashed women. But behind the rotting-front, behind the peeling-plastered walls, a big time syndicate did its filthy business. The payoff was in the millions.

Edna Loomis — and there was nothing cheap about her — set out to get it all. Her method was simple...she used the weapon of her flesh. But she made one mistake. His name was Peone, of the drugged eyes and the slender knife. Edna Loomis was a beautiful, ambitious woman. Peone was a coked-up killer!

It comes right out at you, noir, hard-boiled, a crime and corruption furious ride on the hellbound train, and Lion Books, in the above example from *Blondes Are Skin Deep* (Lion Book #62) by Louis Trimble, sets the locomotive on the tracks and stokes the furnace up high for the reader.

Noir and hard-boiled writing plunges us down to the depths, and during the 1950's tiny Lion Books was the undisputed king of noir and hard-boiled paperback publishing.

Today Lion is mostly forgotten, an obscure publisher of yesteryear, but in the 1950's it was big stuff. It began publishing in 1949, coincidentally the same year that its chief rival, Gold Medal Books, began publishing; but Lion published all these cool, incredibly hard-hitting paperback originals (PBOs) by some of the biggest names ever. Many Lion books have since become acknowledged classics, and as such been reprinted — but these are the originals!

Today, Lion Books are heavily collected by fans of classic hard-boiled and noir fiction. The original series of 225 books, (numbered from #8-233 and published from 1949 to 1955) includes such big-money items as the eleven Jim Thompson PBOs, including Thompson's hard-to-find classic first novel, *The Killer Inside Me* (#99). In nice shape this book can fetch upward of $500-1,000. The other ten Thompson's are each valued in the hundred dollars+ range, always depending on condition.

Thompson really epitomized the feel and mood of Lion's noir paperbacks. People on the skids, down in the lowest depths, going only lower and deeper into it in spite of how they tried to save themselves.

There's no salvation here, only despair and gloom. No hope, no quarter, and these books told it all true, where every single character often portray situations where not even one single character is a normal, well-adjusted human being. It's a rough ride through hell, a hell of their own making. Jim Thompson was the best practitioner of the art in the Lion stable of writers, but he wasn't the only one. There were others, and some of them wrote books for Lion as good or better than Thompson.

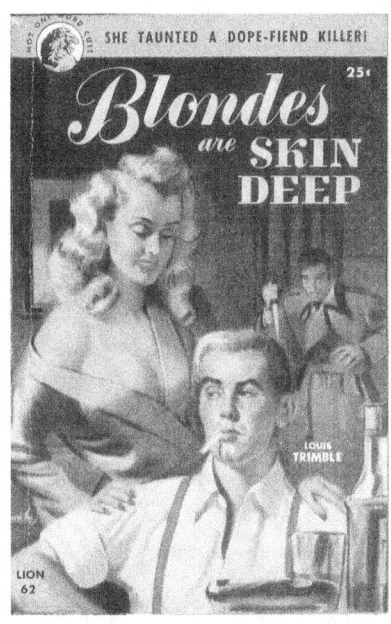 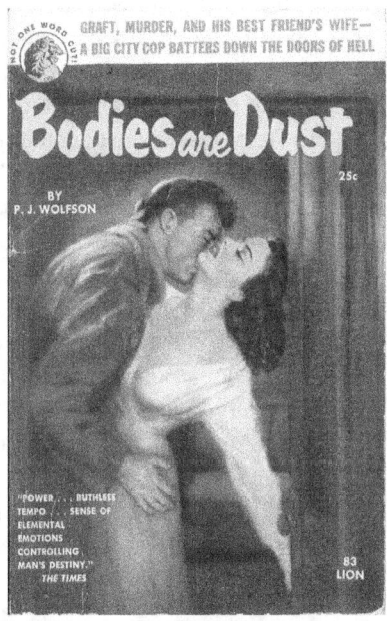

David Goodis knew despair first hand. His personal life was a noir disaster, and it came through in his books, including the four PBO's that he wrote for Lion. All Goodis books are excellent, with perhaps the most interesting being *The Dark Chase* (#133), a great tale of non-stop rage and revenge. The most difficult to find is *The Blonde on the Street Corner* (#196), "The story of men and women on the skids!" This last one in fine condition can fetch a nice bundle — or cost it. It features — as do most of the Lion Books — incredible noir and hard-boiled cover art, tough gals, sleazy girls, bad guys, thugs, violence, and crime images, all suitably atmospheric in the best 1950s noir style. These books really are noir icons, and with their cover art herald a time when we all thought the world was a better place. But it wasn't — not for the people in these books! Not for a lot of real people living back then either. Another reason why these books were so successful was that they held truth and power in the writing on their pages. They told it like it was. And like it still is.

Of course, Lion published all types of books in its main series — two nonfiction books on baseball, quite a few Westerns, World War II novels, and even some science fiction. However, its mainstay was noir, hard-boiled crime, and Lion did it better than anyone.

Even Lion's other genre books had definite aspects of noir and hard-boiled attitude in them. For instance, its three science fiction end-of-the-world disaster novels: *Doomsday* (#148) by Warwick Scott, *The Deluge* (#233 by — and get this — it is credited to Leonardo DaVinci [but actually written by Robert Payne]); and *False Night (*number 230) by Algis Budrys all feature tough-minded survivors as heroes who battle in the ruins of a hostile and destroyed world merely to exist one more stinking day. Now, you can't get any more noir than that!

Lion's Westerns, with such outrageous titles as *Eat Dog or Die* (#103) by C. William Harrison (which, by the way, shows an incredibly gruesome and sadistic cover of a man being hung), indicate its interest in — and one might even say obsession with — violence, war, crime, greed, corruption, and loss — many of the overriding themes of the noir and hard-boiled genre.

Nevertheless, it is for noir and hard-boiled crime that Lion Books is best remembered today, and we'll take a look at some of the best they had to offer now.

"Graft, murder, and his best friend's wife — a big city cop batters down the doors of hell." So proclaims the blurb on the cover of *Bodies Are Dust* (#83) by P.J. Wolfson, and let me tell you, this book does not disappoint. For sheer noir despair and hopelessness, for the all-

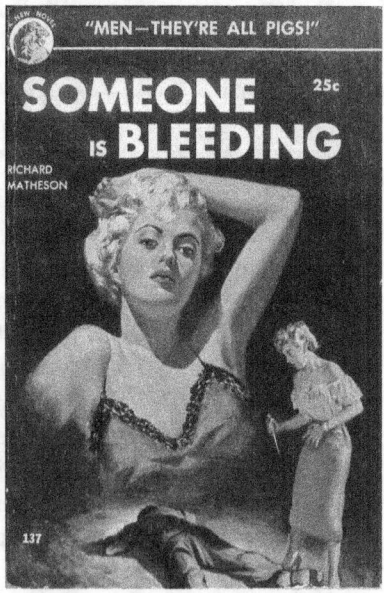

constricting feel of the rope around the throat, this book delivers. A crooked cop who thinks he's such a smart guy and knows all the answers, loses it all over a woman. It's a hell of a ride. And it ends with a slam.

In the same vein, though even darker and more twisted, if that can be possible, is the incredible and sadistic novel of an honest cop torn apart by a depraved woman, *Sin Pit* (#198) by Paul S. Meskil. This one's a chilling twisted story that you will not be able to put down. It is a classic novel I love so much I reprinted it under my Gryphon Books imprint years later when I got to know the author. I even used the same Lion Books cover art!

The Outward Room (#26) by Millen Brand is a love story of despair in which a man falls in love with an insane woman. She's an escapee from a mental institution. A dark love story that actually has a happy ending, it's an early noir influence. No later Lions will ever have happy endings again.

G.H. Otis (pseudonym of Otis Hemingway Gaylord) wrote two brutally intense novels for Lion, *Bourbon Street* (#131):"A loot-mad thug takes New Orleans apart," and *Hot Cargo* (#171):"They carried 129,000 tons of explosive oil — and a TNT woman!" These two are tough and gritty noir-hard-boiled at its best, in the James M. Cain tradition, with characters out of Thompson, and full of corruption, crime, greed, double-dealing, and betrayal, all wrapped up in a nice sweet bouquet of lies. Must reading! Years later I would write the introduction to the omnibus trade paperback edition published by Stark House. A book not to be missed! More on these two elsewhere in this book.

Meanwhile, in *Sin People* (#159) by George Milburn, we see the lovely Mamie, bad-girl town harlot go berserk. Let me tell you, what this little gal does to this town…The cover blurb proclaims: "Scandal, booze, and race hatred turned the townsfolk into raging brutes," and that's only the good news! It's a searing novel.

Lion published books by a lot of perennially favorite authors, many from the pulp magazines, and others who are forgotten today. It also published fiction by big-name authors such as the two brutal noir crime novels by Richard Matheson, *Someone is Bleeding* (#137) and *Fury on Sunday* (#180); and one by veteran horror master Robert Bloch, *The Kidnapper* (#185), a noir crime horror masterpiece.

Veteran pulpster Day Keene has two fine books in the series: *Sleep with the Devil* (#204) and *Joy House* (#210), and his buddy Fletcher Flora has *Strange Sisters* (#215), a kind of lesbian-noir novel. R.V. Casill, known today on the literary high-end, slummed a bit with an early book in the Lion series, *Dormitory Women* (#216), and crime writer Jonathan

Craig stepped in with a nasty little shocker, *Alley Girl* (#206).

Famed crime author Richard Prather, before he created Shell Scott, wrote two books for Lion in his early career: *Lie Down, Killer* (#85) and, as Douglas Ring, *The Peddler* (#110), a nasty novel about a low-life monster. Crime author Howard Browne had his classic noir novel *If You Have Tears* published by Lion as *Lona* (#94 under his pseudonym, John Evans). Veterans such as Gerald Butler, *The Lurking Man* (#81), and Gerald Kersh, *Prelude to a Certain Midnight* (#98), also had excellent books representing them in the Lion series, the Kersh book with a stylish fog-enshrouded cover by Rudolph Belarski that captures the mood of noir perfectly.

Other Lion noirs of note are *The Hoodlum* (#161) by Elaezar Lipsky, a re-titling of his classic *The Kiss Of Death*. Then there are the three fine hard-hitting novels by Benjamin Appell: *Brain Guy* (#39), in which a tough crime boss has all the answers; *Dock Walloper* (#166), about crime on the New York docks; and *Hell's Kitchen* (#95), a tale of youth gone wild on crime. A noir icon himself, author A.I. Bezzerides even steps in with *Tough Guy* (#153) and Federick Lorenz has some worthy noir entries with *Night Never Ends* (#193) and *The Savage Chase* (number 223).

David Karp wrote some incredible books. He's largely forgotten today but remembered by those who love great noir and hard-boiled work. He had four novels in the Lion series: *The Big Feeling* (#93), *The Brotherhood of Velvet* (#105), *Hardman* (#119), and *Cry Flesh* (#132).

These are all worth reading.

Lion Books also tackled tough social topics, such as racial problems, usually in its own characteristically noirish fashion. Interracial love, sex, suspicions, and race hatred got an ample going-over in such Lion Books as *How Sleeps the Beast* (#45) by the so under-rated Don Tracy. The cover blurb tells us all in three simple lines: "The man- NEGRO, The girl- WHITE, The Payoff-LYNCH!" Another book dealing with an interracial affair, or just plain lust, is *Luther* (#114) by Roy Flannagan. There are also three interesting Curtis Lucas novels: *Third Ward, Newark* (#80), whose cover blurb loudly proclaims: "A negro girl gets the jolt of her life" (some white men rape her); *Angel* (#162), with a nice cover of an attractive interracial couple walking down a city street and getting "the look"; and *So Low, So Lovely* (#91), a noir novel of despair among black people of the 1950s.

Almost every book that Lion published bubbles over and seethes with the style and mood of noir — it is always there somewhere. It is there in the text, in the cover art, in the title or blurbs, in the very look and feel of each individual book. Lion Books is not remembered today as it should be, the novels and authors it published certainly are. And that's a hell of a fine legacy for any publisher.

A Trio of Lions:
Classic Crime Noirs: Book Two

There was a time many years ago when a publisher of what were considered lower-end magazines, pulps and comics books named Martin Goodman, also wanted to expand his line by producing a series of paperback books. Goodman's overall publishing line was called Magazine Management, and one of the iconic lines he published through them was Marvel Comics. His paperback book line was called Lion Books, which began in 1949. It was a small publishing outfit that only lasted 9 years, from 1949 to 1957, and therein we begin our story of these three classic novels.

Goodman's first editor for Lion Books was Arnold Hano who was hired as editor-in-chief in 1950. Hano was a hard-boiled guy, a World War II vet — as were many of the readers of these early paperbacks — most of whom were male. He knew the kind of violent action and passion his readers wanted in their books and he gave it to them. Hano had previously been an editor at Bantam Books for two years and came to Lion with a large 'backlog' of manuscripts Bantam had declined to publish — but he liked them. Goodman gave Hano the green light to published what he wanted to publish. So Hano did just that, published books that he liked and that today are recognized as some of the greatest crime noir novels ever written. Thus the Lion Books line was born and thrived.

The Lion Books series today is remembered fondly by those in the know for publishing many genuine masterpieces of hard crime noir. Works by such masters as Jim Thompson (who they showcased in 11 original novels!); but also criminous noirs by Richard Matheson, David Goodis, Robert Bloch, Day Keene and many others.

Those 'many others' are what we are concerned with here. That is because the Lion Books list of 233 paperbacks, offers a deep mine of treasure — at least two-thirds of which are hard crime noir novels. And most have been out of print for decades — in some cases the Lion Books paperback is the *only* edition of some of these very collectable and desirable books!

A Trio of Lions: Book Two from Stark House Press (the 2nd in their *A Trio of Lions* series *), presents three of the best, rarest, and much sought after novels from the vintage era heyday of noir paperbacks.

SIN PIT by Paul S. Meskil; *THE DEVIL'S DAUGHTER* by Peter Marsh, and *DARK THE SUMMER DIES* by Walter Utermeyer Jr., offer up a delightful feast of crime, murder, betrayal, shock, depravity and twisted hungers that lead men and women into their own worst versions of noir Hell. The original editions of these charming small size vintage paperbacks would be hard to track down today, some can be quite expensive in nice condition, but Stark House has done all the work for you, and now all you need do is sit back and enjoy reading this omnibus containing three of the best Lion noirs you may never have known about.

SIN PIT by Paul S. Meskil (July 2, 1923 - Oct.11, 2005), was originally published as Lion Book #198 in 1954. In it, you are going to read a long-lost classic written by a master craftsman. *Sin Pit* was Meskil's only novel — but what a novel! Meskil had a four decades long career as a newspaperman on such papers as the *St. Louis Dispatch*, and the New York *Daily News*. He had been an investigative journalist for many years, writing books on organized crime, the Mob, Nazi war criminals, and other crime subjects. Some of these books have become classic reference works, but it is with *Sin Pit* where Meskil gave us characters and a story that plunge the reader into the low world of crime, crooked cops and dread femme fatales in a poisonous brew. All that, and a surprise ending you will surely savor.

You know you just gotta read this one when from the back cover of the Lion edition, the blurb loudly proclaims a statement by the book's hero, Sergeant Detective Barney Black:

"SHE WAS DIRT...and hungry and cheap and demanding. But it didn't matter. She was all those things, and I knew it, but she was much more, too. She was fire and ice and fury, and when she came up to me — that first time — her mouth making little squirming noises, I knew she was all I ever wanted.

"I was a cop. An honest one. Tough, but honest. And she was the wife of another man. Maybe she was a killer. Maybe she was a — a kind of person even tough cops don't talk about except in dirty whispers.

"But I didn't care. I had to have her."

I met and got to know Paul Meskil in 2004 when he saw an article I had written praising this book. Paul and I, with his son, Brian, became fast friends. They were even guests at my annual book show in New York City. Back then, I published a short-run 100-copy edition of *Sin Pit* for my show (using the original Lion Books cover art), in an effort to get it back into print after 50 years. By then, that original Lion paperback had become prohibitively expensive and there were no other printings. Today, that 2004 Gryphon Books edition is out of print and rare. The Lion edition is rare too. In fact, it is almost impossible to find any copy of this book — so thank you, Stark House!

Sin Pit is one of my favorite crime novels. Knowing it was Paul Meskil's one and only foray into crime fiction, one wonders what might have been had he continued writing fiction in the genre. For surely he had it all down right and true — he could sure tell an interesting and brutal crime story. No doubt, had he written more fiction this novel would have already taken it's proper place in the ivy halls of great crime novels.

Or as Paul himself wrote in his afterward to that 2004 Gryphon edition, "I was sitting at my desk in the city room of the New York *Telegraph* one day in 1953 when I received a phone call from literary agent, Berthina Klausman. She had seen some of my crime articles in the newspaper and wanted to know if I could write a crime novel in a hurry. I said yes, and she sent me to the paperback publisher, Lion Books. An editor there, gave me a contract and told me I could write anything I wanted as long as the locale was other than New York City, Chicago, or Los Angeles — which were then the sites chosen for most crime novels.

"That was fine with me because I had come to New York from St. Louis, where I worked as a crime reporter/writer for eight years. I knew St. Louis and East St. Louis very well and used this area as a scene for my first and only novel, though I wrote several factual crime books and about one thousand magazine articles on organized...and disorganized...crime.

"*Sin Pit* got little publicity except for a plug in Walter Winchell's column and a review in the magazine of the Missouri Bartenders Association. My original title was "Blood Lust" and they changed that title without my knowledge. I also originally wrote the book in the first person.

"After the book came out an anonymous reader sent me a key to the hotel room where the last chapter took place. I'm proud to have this book appear in print again after 50 years and I hope you have enjoyed it."

Paul would have been pleased to see this newest edition of his hard-hitting crime classic. He was a fine writer, and class act; a real gentleman, with a good sense of humor.

Of the other two novels in this volume, each is something truly special about it and offers stark and brutal truths in twisted noir settings. I love these books and know that you will too.

THE DEVIL'S DAUGHTER by Peter Marsh (Lion Book #16, 1949), is an author I could not find any information about. It seems that he may have only written the one book. In it, Marsh gives us one of the earliest Lion noir reprints, of the pricey and collectable 1942 hardcover first edition. As a Lion Book, it has all the trappings of the femme fatale noir, the cover blurb boldly proclaiming, "She destroyed six men — would he be the seventh?"

It is the story of a woman who *chose* to go by the name of Laura, who was on a hell-bent revenge mission to kill the men who had murdered her husband. She had already killed six of them! Now the seventh man came into her web, Mike Peruzzi, and the two fell into a turbulent doomed love. Was he a devil, a demon? She had mixed emotions about him. She knew she should plunge the knife into him as he slept, but she only kissed him very gently. But he awoke and felt her looming presence, even as she felt his demonic power over her. They don't write nasty noir better than this, but don't let that stop you from diving hip-deep into the muck — then swim for your life!

DARK THE SUMMER DIES by Walter Untermeyer, Jr. (Sept. 19, 1924 - Feb. 15, 2009), Lion Book #138 from 1953. This is a classic dark noir, by a talented author, who wrote a book that many crime aficionados rate highly. Untermeyer, Jr. is a rather elusive Lion author and not much is known about him either, although we do have a photograph of him on the back cover of the Lion edition. According to Hubin, he wrote only two crime novels — the other is *EVIL ROOTS* — and both were paperback originals for Lion Books.

This is a dark twisty tale of a young man and a manipulating older woman named Vicky, who has a scheme and a shame. As the back cover blurb warns us, Vicky:

"...had time on her hands...so she picked on the boy. She turned him and twisted him and made him do her bidding. She didn't think it was dirty; she didn't guess she was ruining the boy, making him hate himself. To her, it was just a game.

"But she didn't know what was going on inside the boy, the torment in the secret pits of his soul, the dark urges storming to the surface, the hate and love and lust and madness. She didn't know what she was doing. And that was the greatest shame of all."

One wonders about the authors of these three noir masterpieces. How they could write so convincingly of these dark subjects. What they must have seen, or experienced in their lives? I know Paul Meskil saw crime in real life, as it was evilly committed, and he wrote about it. So I wonder what each of these authors must have seen or gone through to reserve their own ring-side seat at the arena in the depths of human Hell. No one can know for sure, but they left us these books, and for that we thank them.

With the three novels that make up *A TRIO OF LIONS: BOOK 2*, you will fall into the *Sin Pit*, find yourself overwhelmed by dark desires, view deep depravity, brutal betrayal and vile corruption that you can not imagine. Prepare to be shocked, awed, and overjoyed as a noir crime fiction aficionado. These are wonderful reads. Oh, how I envy you first timers! Enjoy!

* The first Stark House Press book collection, of *A TRIO OF LIONS* appeared in 2016. It contained *Hero's Lust* by Kermit Jaediker; *House of Evil* by Clayre & Michel Lipman; and *The Man I killed* by Shel Walker, with introductions by Gary Lovisi and Dan Roberts.

Hard-boiled Paradise: Books to Remember

Paradise can be a tough place for some people. Hard-boiled crime fiction is paradise for many of us who like to read the hard stuff, no-frills, no nonsense, *no crap*. Don't tell me there ain't a lot of good stuff out there to read. I don't wanna hear it! Hard-boiled is a tried and true literary genre and has been practiced by the greats, near-greats and quite a few ingreats, but while there's some good *new* stuff around that always gets all the ink these days, there is also a lot of great cool *old* stuff that's been too-long forgotten. Even neglected. That's a shame. It's time some of this classic material gets a bit of ink. Let's start remembering now! Let's take a trip to hard-boiled paradise, with your tour guides…

Gutsy guys like Bruce Elliott, Elliott Gilbert, James D. Horan, Al Fray and Paul S. Meskil. They're not exactly your household names today. In fact, they were hardly known in *their* day, and they're not remembered today at all. That's a shame. They should be. They wrote some outstanding crime novels. *They damn well should be remembered!*

One is a Lonely Number is by Bruce Elliot, "an escaped con seeks refuge – finds jail bait!" or so the cover blurbs proclaim. It's a paperback original from Lion Books, #100, from 1956; there's also a reprint from Macfadden Books in 1968 that's easier to find. It's one fascinating, tough novel you'll not forget.

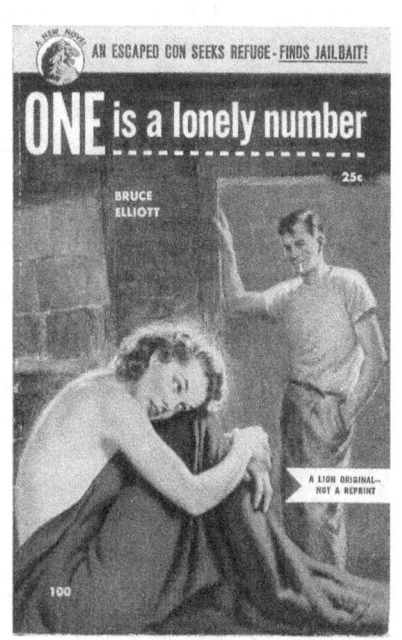

"It was stinking hot, Chicago hot, tenement hot, whore house hot."

The opening lines of Elliott's mini-masterpiece really set a mood and style. The writing and dialog are tough and the noir mood is downright chilling.

Escaped convict Larry Camonille is on the run and not going back to

Joilet. At the beginning of the novel he's hiding out in Chicago, while the other nine escapees who he masterminded out of prison are getting caught one by one, their photos in newspapers and descriptions flashed on radio news. Soon they're all caught, but one. Now everyone's out on the lookout for Larry.

He hasn't been with a woman in years, so he picks up a whore he sees and...

"He should have remembered when he picked her up on Division Street that the ones that looked so good in clothes, that stuck out like a bureau drawer, were the ones that fell to pieces when the brassiere came off. But there were so many things he was going to have to remember."

A broke-up guy, with one lung missing and the other bad, he can't drink, can't smoke and can't have sex. He knows he'll just rot and die in prison if he goes back, never making parole, especially now after escaping.

Larry mulls over the harsh truth, fact is he's *"32 years-old and dead. A corpse looking for a place to lie down and pull up the earth around it."*

This quintessential noir is full of sharp hard-boiled attitude and brutality.

Larry leaves Chicago and begins a noir odyssey that has him traveling on the run, a hunted man, trying to get to Mexico. He never makes it. Along the way he gets involved in small town passions and plots, and falls for a 14 year old slut, named Jan who just happens to be the love of his life. Jan falls for Larry also and with this imperfect union, for just one short noir minute, the black veil of his life is lifted from Larry's eyes. But only for a minute. This is, after all, hard-boiled noir.

In the end, Larry's story of hope and redemption with Jan is crushed by the evil forces surrounding him, he seeks revenge. He tries to justify his failure by saying to himself:

"Besides, what would have been the alternative? A dull nine-to-five job, a nagging bag of a wife, smelly brats, stinking apartments, getting drunk on Friday in the neighborhood bar where most of the men drank beer, not because it was cheaper but because they feared the loss of control that came from hard liquor; the interminable bar-room discussions, the endless baseball, wrestling, prize-fight talk; the cheap little reaching lies the men told about their nights on the town? The broads that were supposed to have fallen into their laps. The cabbies, all of whom looked like gargoyles yet maintained they got more loving

than Don Juan...

"*Camonille had heard all that talk. Knew that the broads that were supposed to fall like ripe peaches into the waiting hands of the working stiffs were, if real, hustlers or worse. He knew about the stinking stags the men's clubs put on, the tired old bags that showed up and showed all and who cared?*

"*He'd been to a couple of those smokers, seen the painted faces, the slack mouths of the 'girls.' Who were too old to pound the pavements, too scared of the fuzz to make it on their own – so now they were strippers, 'exotic dancers.' And when the sleazy show was over they did what they had to do for a lousy five bucks, or three bucks or two bucks. Or took on all comers, three for five dollars. Ten for ten dollars.*

"*Better to ride his own particular nightmare in his own particular way.*"

And Larry does just that! In his own way. You gotta admire him, though. This is grim stuff.

The name Bruce Elliott is not remembered today at all. He wrote some minor science fiction in the 1960s, but in the 1950s he wrote much better pulp magazine and paperback crime. ***One is a Lonely Number*** is a neglected little masterpiece, a taut, spell-binding, hard crime story, with an interesting protagonist whose warped morals fit the warped world that he inhabits perfectly. Larry never made it to Mexico, but you'll be glad you went along for the ride with him to his final destination.

Get this one and read it. It's a keeper!

Someone even more obscure who labored in the hard-boiled vineyards for a time and who wrote an even better novel is Elliott Gilbert, the author of ***Vice Trap*** (Avon Books #T-266, PBO 1958). This is a brutal, tough and frank hard-boiled novel of a twisted sex triangle between Nick, the Greek, the hopped-up dark hero; crooked ex-cop Dave Madrid, and the beautiful and playfully wicked Lona.

The narrator uses a great pseudo-Chandler style to tell his story of being trapped in a bee-bop deluxe of sex, drugs, crazy cats and slick chicks... and one really nasty ex-cop who just never quits. Your worst nightmare.

"*I pulled into the Desert Star Motel, off the highway leading into Cuesta, around four o'clock There were half a dozen big palms lining the gravel driveway back to the motel, which had five cabins on each side. It was a run-down place, with a café that served beer and wine in front and had benches and a horseshoe throw around the side.*"

The book even has a cool glossary in the front of the book with 50s jive and hip words. Most of them have found their way into our mainstream language today, but they were not mainstream in the 1950s.

Nick, the Greek jive-talking hard-boiled narrator, has Los Angels ex-cop Dave Madrid married to his Lona, while he was sent away to prison. He doesn't like it and wants her back. Madrid wants him and his two punk boys Sand-o and Graemie to pull a bank job for him. They don't want to. They don't like it. It looks funny. Nick just wants the ex-cop off his back and to get his beloved Lona back, but he ends up getting involved.

That's when all hell breaks loose! You see, Nick would do anything for Lona. Early on he thinks about her, seeing her again, remembering…

"She was on horse, then. All right, yourself too. Who wasn't hooked on something? Just this little, anyway, with her. Because not the big scene, the main line, only skin pops. But thinking she was chippying on somebody was so funny, and pretty cute. Hell, you could be blind. Her always catching cold; running-nosed, itchy colds. But telling me no, then coming in, and straight, forgetting, asking me to please come turn on. But I'd never gone that route.

"But she got off the stuff. If you didn't goof heavily, you could make yourself come off it. But those needle scratches didn't go. The heat busted you just for marks these days, too. But not a cop's wife. Nobody would touch her. Only that Madrid. But never the way I had."

It's an incredible hard novel and very underrated. It also has some surprises because there's a passage that tells us Nick is, of all things, in some kind of early incarnation, a paperback book collector! On page 78 we read:

"I stopped by the phone company and cut off the service, then I left my collection of paperbacks and magazines at the Goodwill."

Yeah, he gets rid of them, but he obviously had a 'collection', and he takes time to see to it that he finds the books a good home when he leaves his place. He doesn't just throw them out. I think this is the earliest example (1958), I've been able to find of the beginnings of some awareness of this particular 'hobby'. Interestingly enough, years later, Philip K. Dick would write of paperback collectors in the future in his early and groundbreaking science fiction novel, *Do Androids Dream of Electric Sleep (aka, Bladerunner)*. Another, by the way, incredible hard-boiled novel, though it is science fiction.

Vice Trap is raw, a brutal dive into the amoral world of drugged-up punks, dirty sluts, and back-stabbing slobs. I enjoyed it. Just take a shower afterwards.

Come Back for More (Dell First Edition #A161, PBO 1958) by Al Fray is another underrated and unacknowledged minor crime classic that deserves to be kept in print and read by new generations of crime buffs. It is a 'rock-hard' story of one man who fought the syndicate with every dirty trick they'd taught him."

This is a revenge novel. The hero is a former bank clerk who witnesses a murder and now has a vendetta to get the criminals responsible. Years later, overweight Swede Anderson becomes hero, Warner McCarthy, a tough guy trucker who joins forces with Gail Taylor, a beautiful and feisty women who has just inherited a trucking business from her murdered husband. She is trying to make it work for herself and her young daughter. Similar in many ways to the standard hard-boiled western where the widow will loose the ranch unless the tough gunslinger with a heart of gold helps her stand up against the evil cattle baron. Okay, it is similar, (shades of *Shane*) but it is also a real good book. And who's to say a classic like *Shane*, translated to the hard-boiled crime genre, might not make an equally effective novel. This one sure does.

So the bad syndicate guys want to buy Gail Tyler out, but she won't sell. They start putting pressure on her. She's got pluck and is determined to run the business for herself and her daughter. The mob puts on more pressure. She's about to throw in the towel when along comes McCarthy. He works for her, takes things in hand, and starts to turn things around. The mob takes all this rather badly, so what we have is a cool hard-boiled novel that screams toughness and attitude with every word. This book made me want to check out all the other Al Fray crime books. Which is a good indication of the strength of this minor classic. You will see more about the books of Al Frey further on in this book.

The Mob's Man by James D. Horan, Bantam Book #H3190, 1st pb printing, July 1966, has a classic tough guy cover by the great James Bama. This is an excellent expose of the underworld and the guys that make it work. It's fiction based on fact, as we follow a contract killer through his career as he tells us about his various jobs, thoughts, and punishments. He lives in a brutal world of his own making, a noir prison, and he's just getting older and more and more alone.

Horan is an underworld expert and he gives us a hell-bound tour of crime and criminals. This one was tough and reeks of reality and truth. It's an exciting, cool read.

I've also included a more contemporary book because I think it is *soooo* good. The book is *Oh No, Not My Baby*, by British crime writer Russell James. James is a really good hard-boiled writer. I've read a few of his other books, all good stuff I can recommend. This one, published in the UK by Do Not Press, PBO 1999, is a real twisted beauty. Nick is a rock musician, his band is looking for a contract and that big break. He's getting close when an old girl friend, the lovely Babette, an animal rights activist, gets herself killed when she asks him to drive her to a meat processing plant. He waits outside, she goes inside to take some photos, there's an accident, but it's *not* an accident. Something went terribly wrong. Nick gets involved. Now Nick falls into a dark mystery of corruption and murder, corporate cover-ups, goon-squads, an animal rights kill team you'll never forget, health cults and more. The characters here are real, each of them rings true, I find that very refreshing and so will you. It's an excellent read, a first-rate noir thriller that stands right up there with all his earlier classics. Russell James is a writer every American hard-boiled fan should be reading!

"She was dirt...and hungry and cheap and demanding. But it didn't matter. She was all these things, and I know it, but she was much more, too. She was fire and ice and fury, and when she came up to me – that first time – her mouth was making little squirming noises, I knew she was all I ever wanted."

So says tough and occasionally honest cop, Barney Black, about the girl of his dreams, Grace Trudo. He meets her when he investigates the murder of her 17 year old friend Randy Harding. Randy was shot with a .32 slug in the head and her body was found whipped. From that point on begins one of the toughest, most twisted, hard-boiled police procedural novels you'll ever read.

The book is, *Sin Pit* by Paul S. Meskil.

I've saved the best for last. I know I've mentioned this book elsewhere in this book, but I can not stop praising it.

Sin Pit is Lion Book #98, a PBO from 1954. There was no other printing until many decades after it was first publsihed. It's an extreme hard-boiled novel, a major underrated and unacknowledged classic of the genre. It stands up with the best of Jim Thompson, David Goodis and Chester Himes for hard-boiled attitude, noir despair and hopelessness; the dialog is worthy of Raymond Chandler and Dashiell Hammett.

This slim paperback has 127 pages of gut-churning crime intensity. Cop Barney takes us on a journey through the *Sin Pit* – better known as "Sin City", aka East St. Louis, Illinois. A city so corrupt that everyone is on the take, for sale, or running some kind of scam. Even the cops. *Especially* the cops! He also presents us with one of the ultimate femme fatales in the guise of Grace Trudo. The first time Barney sees Grace he describes her like this:

"She wasn't beautiful, like the movie dolls are beautiful, but she had more of what it takes to be a woman than anyone I had ever seen before. She was pure, raw sex. And I wanted her, just like that."

From then on life is downhill for Barney as he pieces together what turns out to be a case more twisted than you'd think tiny Lion Books or any 1954 crime paperback would dare publish. I don't want to give away the ending, but you will be surprised.

Meanwhile Barney investigates the murder of the girl as witnesses keep getting killed and his superiors on the police are watching him and getting increasingly suspicious that *he* may be the killer! In the meantime to solve this case, and to make Grace his, he has to find her and clear her. What he ends up doing is going way over the line, placing his career, freedom and even his life in dire jeopardy.

Sin Pit is a fine novel. This is the first novel by Paul Meskil, and his only book for Lion Books. Meskil lived on Long Island in the New York area, I saw him interviewed on a TV show about the police a few years back. He wrote some other books also, one was a mob autobiography for Playboy Press back in the 1970s. I'm still looking for *that* one. You should be looking for *this* one.

Meskil understands cops and crime and the hard-boiled attitude oozes through in *Sin Pit* and rings true. It's a great read, an outstanding and underrated novel. It would make one hell of a film noir.

Hard-boiled paradise is not for the squeamish. Not the usual thing people think of when they consider their own form of 'paradise'. But hard-boiled crime fans wouldn't have it any other way. It's a world of noir, brutality, hard attitude and danger; any woman can be a femme fatale, every man a killer or a sucker, all lost, surrounded and squeezed little by little as their doom approaches. It's not pretty, but life can be like that sometimes. These books all capture something of that noir spirit, fear, despair, they're generally unknown, but they deserve to be remembered, read, collected and talked about. Let's start all that talk here now.

Crime & Mystery One-Shot Wonders

When talking about crime and mystery authors who have written only *one* novel, the greatest of these one-shot wonders must surely be Margaret Mitchell with her classic Civil War romance-historical *Gone With the Wind*. The book was an instant bestseller, not to mention a popular film starring Clark Gable and Vivien Leigh, and it made Mitchell and her book the one-shot wonders of our era. Unfortunately, for crime and mystery readers, Mitchell did not write a mystery, crime, or private eye novel — which is what this article is all about. However, *Gone With the Wind* is a good example of what I mean by an author who only wrote *one* book, and then, for whatever reason, never wrote another novel.

There are various reasons for this. For Mitchell, it may have been impossible for her to produce another work of equal power, not to mention surpassing that first book. How do you surpass *Gone With the Wind?* Perhaps she wrestled with the notion, like many authors have done with their own work, and perhaps in the end, finally, it overcame her. Some authors may have only one book in them. Once they tell that story, they have done their work. They may have nothing more to say. Other authors become turned off to fiction or genre work by publishers

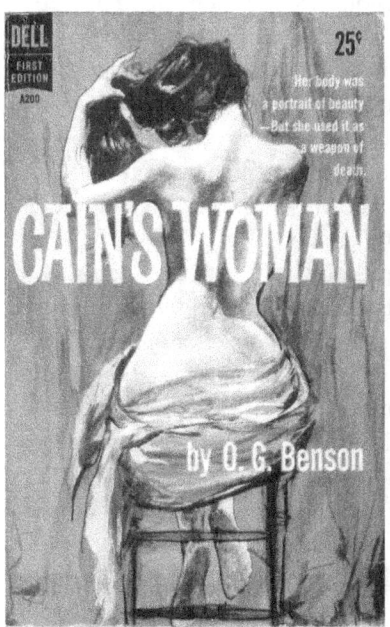
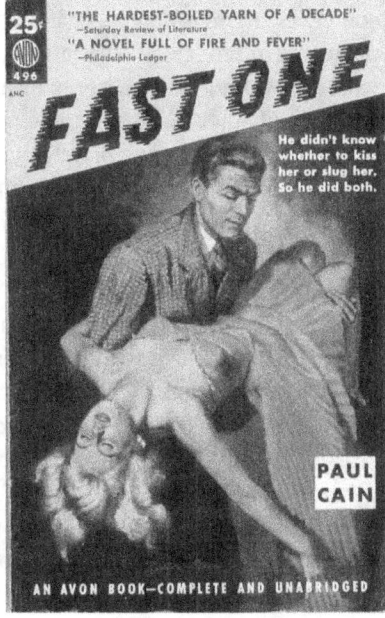

and editors who treat them shabbily. They sometimes decide to call it quits. The writing process is difficult, demanding, unforgiving, and too often goes without reward. Some authors also move on after a time to something more satisfying or lucrative. In still other cases health problems or unexpected situations, including early death, can interfere with a newer author's career plans and make him or her a one-shot wonder, whether they want to be or not.

In mystery, crime, and private eye fiction there are quite a few good authors with fine novels who fall into the one-shot wonder category. One way or another, we'll look at a few of them here.

Fair warning, I have broad definitions of what I consider a one-shot wonder. While some of the authors listed here have written only *one* book in their life, and thereby adhere strictly to the letter of the definition, I have listed others under a far broader interpretation. There are also authors listed who have written only *one* novel (but may have also had published a non-fiction book, or a short story collection). There are also a couple of examples of writers who wrote only *two* books, then wrote no more. Two-shot wonders? Sometimes an author was a one-shot wonder in the mystery field, but he may have written books in other areas, or in other genres, or under other names. Obviously this opens things up quite a bit, and only scratches the surface of this subject, but it allows me to clue you onto some great books you might not be aware of . And that's the *real* reason for this article. To share good books with good friends.

I'll explain this further as I run down each author, their work, and why they belong on this list of mystery, crime and noir one-shot writers. The list is in alphabetical order by book title.

A Taste of Brass by Robert Donald Locke (Dell First Edition, #A136, PBO 1957, cover art by Al Brule) is actually the first of two books by Locke. Two books, and that was it in the mystery crime field from him — but he did write at least 13 science fiction books aka Roger Arcot. This one is a fine novel about a Los Angeles private eye, he's a redheaded OP in the great Shell Scott tradition, name of Pete Brass. Simple, clean, and a good read. Locke only wrote one other crime novel, a soft-core crime sleaze novel *The Restless Lovers* for Monarch Books (#209, PBO) in 1961. Two books and that was it!

Cain's Woman by O.G. Benson is one of the best private eye novels I've ever read, a great and true one-shot wonder. Benson was a pseudonym for a Midwest author who only published this one novel. Benson's true name is not known and it seems he did not want it to be known. *Cain's Woman* originally appeared as a paperback original from Dell Books (Dell First Edition #A200, 1960, cover art by Darcy) and was later reprinted under the author's original title as *Cain's Wife* by Perennial Books (P773, 1985, with a great blood-red tears cover by Thomas Sperling). The book did not sell well, probably because the artwork on the original Dell edition by Darcy, while quite lovely, did not indicate the book as a mystery or P.I. novel. It looked like a romance. Nor do the cover blurbs indicate the book was a mystery. Certain death to a paperback in the vintage era when cover art indicated genre, and reaching the reader was everything.

The story itself concerns Max Raven, a down-and-out private eye who ends up falling for his client, rich seductress Naomi Cain. His job is to untangle a web of lies and betrayal to recover some dirty photos of Naomi so her rich old hubby doesn't see them. Max's problem is that he falls for Naomi, but his real problem is that Naomi has her own plans. There's a lot of great hard-boiled dialog here, a clever story, fascinating characters, and some excellent insights into human behavior. And while this book was written about six decades ago, in most respects it could have been written yesterday. It's a cult classic and screams to be reprinted.

Benson only had this one novel published. He eventually turned away from fiction because of problems with his publisher Dell Books, and his frustration with the unprofessionalism of certain publishers and editors. Ironically, there is a rumor that there is a completed 600 page sequel to *Cain's Wife* just itching to be published. Somewhere.

Fast One by Paul Cain (no relation to James M. Cain) is this author's only novel. Cain is the pseudonym of George Sims, who also wrote some scripts as Peter Ruric. He was the mystery man of hard-boiled fiction for many years, unknown, disappeared, found only upon his death in 1966. His novel is classic hard-boiled crime, a tale with machine-gun pacing, a great gangster epic about a killer named Gerry Kells. Cain's sharp and sparse writing style influenced almost all crime writers who have come after him. The book originally appeared as a serialization in *Black Mask Magazine* in 1932 and in a hardcover first edition from Doubleday and Doran Co. It was reprinted in a scarce pricey digest paperback from tiny and obscure Bonded Books (#10) in 1943; later reprinted by Avon Books (#178, 1948; and #496, 1952 with new cover art). There was also a Popular Library paperback reprint (#045264, 1980) in their Lost American Fiction Series.

Cain's other book was his *Seven Slayers*, a collection of seven hard-boiled crime stories also from the pages of *Black Mask*. It was originally published in a true first edition by obscure Chartered Books (#21) in 1946, and later reprinted by Avon Books (#268) in 1950. More recent reprints of both of these fine books appeared in paperback from Black Lizard Books (1987), and in the UK from No Exit Press (1988-1989). The thing about Cain was that even though he wrote only one novel, to many it is the ultimate hard-boiled crime novel of all time. His other book, the *Seven Slayers* is a collection of a bunch of his best short stories. A total of just two books, then.... But what books!

Eventually, a third book, also a collection of stories was published. Appropriately titled *Seven More Slayers*, this book collected the remaining Cain stories in a third volume.

Final Score by Emmett Grogan is the only novel by this Brooklyn born author. He was a hustler, junkie, burglar, and later on in life a writer and filmmaker. He also spent a considerable amount of his life in prison, so his book speaks with cold hard-boiled truth about crime — committing crime and capers. Grogan's novel is an acknowledged classic of the crime caper school, and was first published by Holt in 1976. There was a paperback reprint by Ballantine Books circa 1978.

Grogan only wrote one other book in his life, *Ringolevio*, but that was nonfiction, his amazing autobiography. I've read that one also and it's even more fascinating than *Final Score!* Grogan was intimately involved with the 1960s counter-culture movement in San Francisco called The Diggers. He was eventually found dead on a New York City F train at 35 years of age of an apparent heart attack. However, some think he might have been murdered, or died from a drug overdose. His cause of death does not seem to be all that clear — but the fact that he died so young is truly tragic. He had massive writing talent.

The Kiss Off by Douglas Heyes is another fine private eye novel, featuring Steve Mallory, a Los Angeles hot-shot who begins a missing persons case that ends up in "murder in a love nest". It's a good crime novel and Heyes is a good writer. The book was originally published in 1951 by Simon & Schuster, and then reprinted in paperback by Signet Books (#949, 1952; 2nd Signet printing #1329, 1956, with new cover art that is uncredited).

Heyes spent most of his time writing and directing motion pictures and TV so for a time he *was* a true one-shot wonder. In fact, as far as I know this was his only novel all through the 1950's, 1960's and the 1970's. Only in 1985 did he come out with a new novel, a paperback original, *The Kill* (Ballantine Book #32501). This is an excellent mystery set in LA in 1938. It also won the 1986 Shamus Award for Best Private Eye Novel in paperback. To be totally truthful, Heyes also wrote one other mystery *The 12th of Never*, but I have never seen this one, and have no information on it other than I assume it came out sometime before *The Kill*. How far before *The Kill*, I have no idea. The thing is, I just wanted to include Heyes here because his books are so damn good. You'll enjoy them.

Let Them Eat Bullets by Howard Schoenfeld is another of those kind-of cult classics that whenever hard-boiled paperback fans and collectors get together they usually bring up. It's a one-shot wonder from a one-shot author, and a great private eye novel from the golden days of Gold Medal Books. *Bullets* tells the story of Jerry Nelson, a tough-guy P.I. who gets involved in a fun and exciting adventure — as Anthony Boucher told back then — "complete with gangsters, blackmail, corpses galore and a nympho-sadist with arrested development….the funniest caper since S.J. Perelman's *Farewell, My Lovely Appetizer…*" Unfortunately, this was Schoenfeld's only book. However, with praise like that from Boucher, and two additional reprints from Gold Medal, it appeared Schoenfeld was on his way. One certainly wonders why this one-shot wonder did not follow up what appeared to be a promising writing career. *Let Them Eat Bullets* originally appeared as a paperback original from Gold Medal Books (#378, 1954; 2nd printing #586, 1957, 3rd printing #870, 1959), and all copies feature the same Barye Phillips cover art. It was Phillips on one of his better days.

Years later I was able to get to know Howard and his charming wife 'Duffy', and found him a very wonderful old fellow. He was a guest at my annual New York City book shows; I interviewed him for my magazine *Paperback Parade*; and under my Gryphon Books imprint, I even published his second book — over 50 years after his first! — *True And Almost True Stories*. This was a 2004 trade paperback that collected his science fiction and crime stories, but also contained some amazing autobiographical material about his youth growing up in Hot Springs, Arkansas. If you ever read the incredible crime novel *Hot Springs* by Stephen Hunter, well, Howard and his older brother were the template for the actual events back then in the 1930s. Howard talks about, how as a kid, he would walk down the street and see gangsters like Owney Madden and Al Capone. Hot Springs was the mob's 'Disneyland' back in the 1930s.

The Low End of Nowhere by Michael Stone is one that I stuck into this survey because it was Stone's first book (and at the time, he was a newer writer and this book had just been released) so at the time I figured he qualified as a one-shot wonder — but I knew that would not last. His first book is so good I have to let you know about it. Stone's private eye hero is called Streeter, no other name. He's a bounty hunter operating out of

Denver who gets involved in a treasure hunt for a dead drug dealer's hidden cash. On the way he meets up with two psycho P.I.'s, a crooked lawyer (perhaps just a *bit* of an oxymoron?), a bent cop, and two fast-talking hustling women. It's the first of a then new series and Stone was working on the next book at the time this one came out. Stone was, by the way, an actual working private eye in Denver. His first novel was released in hardcover from Viking Books in 1996, and in paperback by Penguin Books. There would eventually be four more Streeter novels: #2 *The Lonely Reach*; #3 *Token of Remorse*; and a fourth that is around here somehwre, but somehow, as things usually go when you have too many books — I could not find! But you should find them, and read them!

No Business For A Lady by James L. Rubel (Gold Medal #114, pbo, 1950; 2nd printing #765, 1958; 3rd printing #K1520, 1965) is an interesting discovery. It's a true story about Eli Donovan, former female marine, and now private eye. It's the first mass-market paperback I know of featuring a female P.I. and is significant for that reason alone. Rubel did write a few other books, at least 40 western novels, and three soft-core sex books, but this was his only mystery and P.I. novel. However he was a prolific western writer from the 1930s to 1960s and was said to write over 100,000 words per month!

The Rim of the Pit by Hake Talbot is a true classic. It's a whodunit that bridges the significant gap between the supernatural and gothic horror story and the private eye and crime puzzle story. It's a tough thing to accomplish, but this book does all it sets out to do. It's a disarming book and keeps you guessing, but it plays fair with the reader. There's a large dose of John Dickson Carr whodunit mixed in with spirit-possessed murder at a séance at a snowbound mansion. The book was originally published in hardcover by Simon & Schuster in 1944. It was reprinted in paperback by Dell Books (#173, 1947, in a lovely mapback edition), and later by Bantam Books (F#2922, 1965, also with a back cover map and introduction by Douglas G. Greene). It's the only book Talbot ever wrote. But what a book!

They always say it's good to save the best for last. This time it just worked out that way. *They Don't Dance Much* by James Ross is the last one-shot wonder we'll look at here. Ross only wrote one book, this novel, and that was that!

They Don't Dance Much is a great hard-boiled crime story about the goings-on and eventual robbery, murder, and utter betrayal and chaos in a roadside honky-tonk in Carolina in the 1930's. It's very well-written, a down home, hard-bitten look at Southern life and people. There's more than a taste of James M. Cain (though in a more regional vein), and a title that seems right out of Horace McCoy, that actually fits the book.

They Don't Dance Much has only four states that I am aware of. It was originally published in hardcover by Houghton Miffin in 1940, which is hard as hell to find. There was a 5,000 copy printing if which 1,200 were remaindered, but the book is a rare collectors item today.

The Signet paperback reprint (#913, 1952), though also scarce, is more accessible and inexpensive, but unfortunately it is *abridged*. I have no idea what the abridgement was. It might have been for length purposes. There was also a 35-cents Canadian Signet paperback edition.

Though I've not seen it, there was also a hardcover reprint from Southern Illinois University Press in 1977, part of Matthew Bruccoli's Lost American Fiction Series. There was also supposed to be a Popular Library paperback reprint from 1980. There is a U.K. edition but I have no information on that. Any version of this book is worth the search, if you can find one. It's a fascinating read, a generally unknown classic of crime fiction that deserves attention.

Ross (1911-1990) only wrote this one novel. He was 29 when he wrote it. However he did write a few short stories that were published and he was a newspaperman for many years. He did write one other novel, *The Red* — but it was never published — and it seems to have become a lost book. More on Ross and this novel in my article on it and him elsewhere in this book.

James Ross passed away in 1990, but not that much was known about him when this article was written. What I do know is that he was a mighty talent, and one can only wonder what his second book would have been like. While we'll never know that, at least he left us his great one-shot novel — just to keep us wondering.

2023 Update: After this article appeared in *Mystery Scene* #55 in December, 1996, I received a letter from famed editor and literary agent

Knox Burger written January 6, 1997 about my article. In his letter Knox wrote:

"I write as a voice from the past, though not your past. But I read your piece on one-book writers in Mystery Scene with interest. I was the founding editor, I guess you'd say, of the Dell First Editions paperback line, and had to do with some of the books you mentioned. Later, I ran Gold Medal Books.

"I wish I could remember more about Cain's Woman. I spoke and corresponded with 'Benson' and may even have met him. But I forget the story. I do remember having to change the title because 'wife' isn't as good a title-word on a paperback as 'woman'.

"Howard Schoenfeld, who was married to a somewhat monied woman, lived in a brownstone three or four doors away from mine in the later 50s, early 60s. My predecessors at Gold Medal Books bought that one. By the time I took over the line, in 1960, Howard had, indeed and alas, written a number of other books, and he kept sending them to me. But he'd lost it. Everyone had really liked Bullets, and we all wanted a successor. But the writing talent just seemed to have evaporated or something. I recall my discomfort at having to pass Howard on the street...

"There were some other good one-shot writers, but I haven't the time or inclination to look them up. A guy named Danials from Rhode Island wrote a thriller involving a linoleum knife as a weapon, and when he sent the manuscript in (it was slush), he accompanied it with just such a knife. It caught our attention.

As to Jim Ross, I published his short stories when I was the Boy Fiction Editor of one of our leading defunct magazines, Collier's. I enclose s copy of one of the stories ["Zone of Interior", ed.] taken from a collection called Collier's Best, published in 1951 or 52.

"It was I who brought the Houghton book to the attention of Victor Weybright, the founder of New American Library [as a Signet Book, ed.], just about 1952. I dropped a copy of the book off at his office, and the next morning he called and asked what he had to do to buy reprint rights. I was only a friend of Ross' at the time, not his agent or publisher, and I sent Weybright to Houghton. Later I was Jim's literary agent, and have sold film options to Dance Much about five or six times. Rights are presently held by the screenwriter Pablo Fenjves, who achieved brief fame when he testified about the mournful howling of the dog Kato on the night Nicole Brown and Ron Goldman were murdered. Jim did write another book — about a corrupt legislator in a southern state capitol, but it never really worked. He was a marvelous man, and I'm still in touch with his widow.

True Crime Mob & Gangster Paperbacks

They say the back of the mob or the 'Mafia', has finally been broken. John Gotti lies dead of cancer, other bosses are in fear of the feds. Most have died in prison. The mob just ain't what it used to be.

Organized crime, the Mob, the Outfit, the Mafia, La Cosa Nostra, whatever you want to call it — gangsters and gangsterism hold a place of fascination and sensationalism in the American psyche – and in the American mass-market paperback. People love to read this stuff, and by and large, it all makes incredibly compelling reading. *The Godfather*, although only fiction, was based on fact, and the phenomenally successful film was based on Mario Puzo's earlier phenomenally successful book of the same title.

But what of the true Mob and gangsters? Over the last five decades there's been an interesting group of paperbacks that have used the Mob and gangsters as their subject matter. Some of the books, like *The Valachi Papers* were runaway bestsellers – others are obscure and scarce today. Most are forgotten today also. Until now! I've read most of these, but not all of them, but I hope this article gives you a taste of these 'Mob hits' and clues you onto what's out there to look for. We'll look at 20 of the best and worst of them now. Some of these are first paperback printings, reprints of hardcovers, but many are paperback originals (PBOs), true first editions in paperback.

The Valachi Papers by Peter Maas (Bantam Books #04849, 1st pb 1969) is one of the most compelling and the first of the true "inside the Mob" books ever to appear by a real insider. Joe Valachi was a Mafia soldier, he ran numbers, shylocking, narcotics, burglary and slot machines for one of the five New York crime families from the 1930s into 1950s. They say (the Feds), that he was responsible for 33 murders – Mob hits. In the early 1960s he turned state's evidence and ratted on his associates in the Mob. Needless to say, this did not make him popular with his former bosses and criminal associates. He testified against the Mafia, or the Cosa Nostra, detailing what he knew of organized crime – and he knew a lot! His testimony was devastating and so is this book. Up to that point the FBI and J. Edgar Hoover had denied the existence of actual 'organized' crime. The 'Mafia' was thought to be a myth. Any Italian could have told them otherwise.

Valachi detailed an extensive, well-organized national crime organization with ties to other criminal enterprises. Valachi's testimony was a fountain of information and Peter Maas (who has since passed away, but also collaborated with Sammy 'The Bull' Gravano on his excellent tell-all Mafia book, *Underboss*) put all of Valachi's words and thoughts together into a coherent story that is one of the most compelling reads ever. Valachi tells his story in a wry narrative style with a down-to-earth gritty realism. I think this is still one of the best true Mob books ever written and it deserves a special place on any Mob paperback hit list.

Gangland U.S.A. by Richard Hammer (Playboy Press #16292, 1st pb 1975) is a scholarly but gritty look at criminal gangs in the US from the earliest days even before the Mafia. The book begins with a look at 1800s gangs, such as the Wyos, The Bowery Boys (not the quaint 1930s group of dead end kids in film, but vicious thugs of a century before), and the Madison Avenue Marauders. These are stories of the street gangs even before The Black Hand and the Mafia began and goes up to the era of Meyer Lansky, Lucky Luciano, and Frank Costello in the 1950s and 60s. This book is loaded with info and photos, a fascinating historical look at organized crime and its deep roots.

The Chicago Underworld (aka *Gem of The Prairie*) by Herbert Asbury (Ace Star Book #K-148, about 1962), is a lurid and cool story of the city of

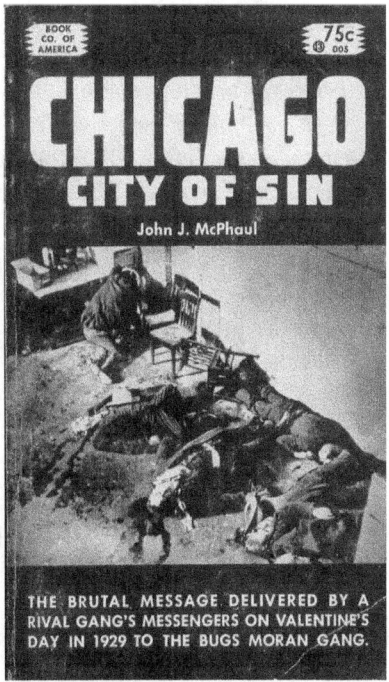

Chicago's century of criminal leadership in the nation since the 1830s. Incredible gang and crime history that unlike most Chicago gang books does not begin with Capone. No photos, but heavily referenced and with many footnotes. A fascinating and not often told story of pre-Capone era Chicago, the original prairie hell town of crime.

Meet The Mob by Detective Frank Mullady and William H. Kofoed (Belmont Book #L507, PBO 1961), is an excellent book about Mob leaders from Capone to Dutch Schultz, Albert Anastasia and Mad Dog Coll. It has great 'mobsters with machineguns' cover art and 16 pages of cool photos, some of them of dead guys killed in hits. Brutal but fascinating. Concentrates on the mob of the 1930s with Capone, Shultz and Murder Inc., a good read and a tough book to find. Worth the search, if you can find it.

Captive City by Ovid Demaris (Pocket Book #77201, 1st pb 1970), is an incredible book. Demaris is a crime writing pro with many fine books to his credit. This book's premise would be expanded upon later in *Theft of a Nation*, by another author, but Demaris was there first telling of how the Mob was stealing our country and freedom and buying off our politicians and corrupting our political system. *Captive City* tells how Capone's Chicago was bought and paid for by the Mob. Demaris gives us a compelling story and names names. The book also has 30 pages called "The Antisocial Register" which lists facts and info on the most famous and vicious Mob killers and bosses. It chronicles corruption and control of the police, prosecutors, judges and even Congressmen and the brutal and sadistic murder that the Mob uses to enforce their domination. This is Sociology as hard-boiled crime history.

Not Everyone Died by Danny Stephens (UK Consul Books, PBO 1964), is the author's own story of how he grew up in Chicago, became a reporter, and associated intimately with all the big names in the Chicago underworld. He knew and hung with Capone, Dillinger and others, and this is his story of crime and gangsterism as he saw it. It's a good book, written almost as if it were a novel, but it is not fiction. There are a lot of inside scoops here and the taste and feel of 1930s Chicago and the gangster bosses comes through in this book. This is a tough UK edition to find but worth looking for. There's a cool 'machinegun drive-by' drawing on the back cover that would have fit better on the front cover of the book. Chicago gangsters not only invented the 'rub-out' but they invented the 'drive-by' killing too!

Chicago Crime (aka *Rattling the Cup on Chicago Crime*) by Ed Sullivan (Collectors Publications, no #, no date but about 1964, from a California porno publisher. Were *they* Mob related?). This is a very obscure book. It tells the story of Chicago under the heel of Capone and organized crime. The back cover of the book has gruesome photos of the Saint Valentine's Day Massacre with bodies torn by machinegun fire. This

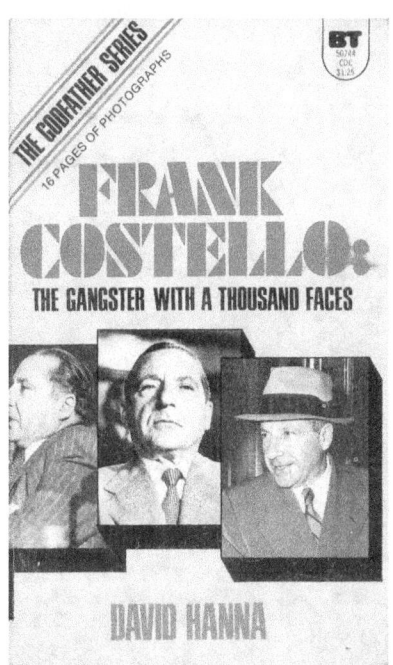

is another bloody and gritty history of Chicago during the Capone era and one worth reading from an uncommon source.

Chicago City of Sin by John J. McPhaul (Book Company of America #5, 1st pb about 1965) has an absolutely lurid cover photo of the Saint Valentine's Day Massacre showing murdered bodies on the cover. From there on it gets worse…better? This incredible book tells the story of what led up to the massacre rub-out of the Moran gang in 1929 and the story of how Capone planned it and the aftermath. The book features information and observations from some of the best writers of the era incorporated by the author into the text that gives a good picture of just what Chicago and the key players of the era were like. Good book!

Al Capone by John Roeburt (Pyramid Book #G405, PBO 1959) has a great gangster cover by Harry Schaare and is a novelization of the excellent film starring Rod Steiger as Capone. Not exactly true crime, this fictional novelization does capture much of the mood and atmosphere of Capone – he was charming and vicious, and you can get a real feel for the Chicago gangster terrorism of the era. It's a good book to read and I liked the film, and if neither are entirely accurate, they're a lot more accurate than they get credit for. Roeburt was a good hard-boiled crime writer of the 1940s and 50s era. I think you'll enjoy the book and the film.

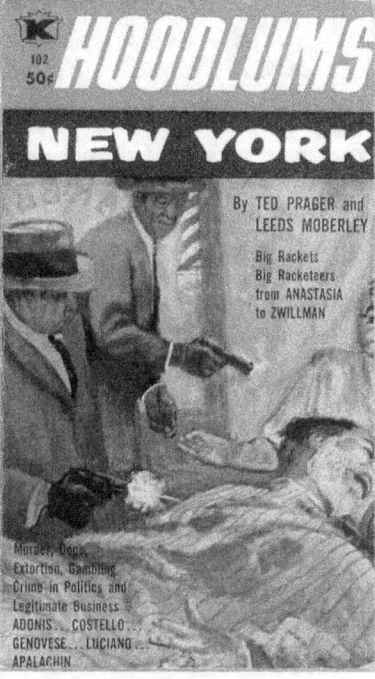

From Capone, to the guy who drove for him. *They Called Me Devil* by George H. Meyer (Acclaimed Book, PBO 1979) is one of those books put out by religious publishers written by newly converted Christian cons who've 'seen the light' – praise Jesus! – but don't let that mislead you. This is a hell of a good book! It is not to be passed by lightly. The religious element and proselytizing is kept to a bare minimum as Meyer tells his own twisted and nasty story of a youth gone bad in the 1930s and how he spent more than half his life in prison. He pulls no punches. He's a smart guy who keeps making stupid choices and while religion could help him, he can't escape his criminal mind. In the end George wins…when he's about 70, but his long criminal career and interactions with key historical Mob figures like Capone make for fascinating reading. This is a must book. It's hard-boiled and Meyer has a 'take no prisoners' attitude. It has some great photos and while hard to find it is definitely worth finding and reading. Great story!

Newspaperman Oscar Fraley met a fellow in a bar one night in the 1950s and he turned out to be the crimefighter Eliot Ness. After a few drinks Ness told Fraley his story and the two later became friends and began to write it up into one of the most legendary books about crime fighting ever written. *The Untouchables* by Eliot Ness with Oscar Fraley (Popular Library #G403, 1st pb 1960) was an instant hit and spawned the

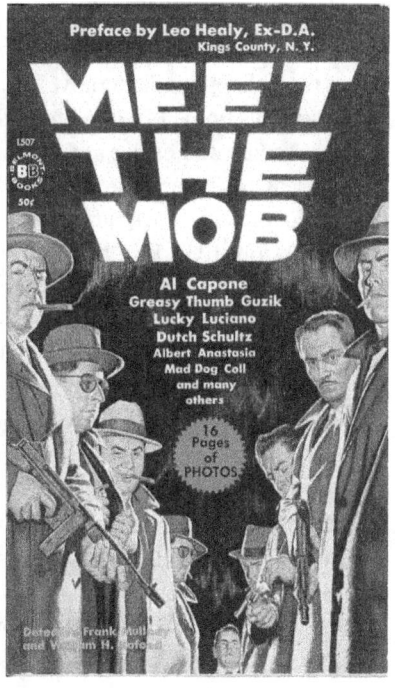

famous Robert Stack TV show. This paperback was issued to tie-in to the hit TV show *The Untouchables*.

This is one of the most incredible and fascinating crime books ever written about the bootleg era in Chicago and Ness's fight with Capone. Ness's story is compelling history and great hard-boiled crime-fighting adventure, true crime memoirs that make compelling reading. Films and some critics have downplayed Ness's role in bringing down Capone but this book tells it true. By raiding Capone's stills, breweries, speakeasies and underworld booze shipments, by confiscating Capone's trucks and warehouses, and locking up his brewers, employees and hoods – Ness caused the tens of millions of dollars flowing into Capone's Outfit to dry up. This is actually what brought down Capone, he could no longer pay off all the politicians and police. Capone had practically every city official in Chicago on his payroll – but as the money got tighter and payoffs smaller, he and his organization lost their clout. They could no longer buy the courts, prosecutors or the police, nor pay off their friends on the newspapers for positive press. It was Ness's work that allowed the tax evasion case to proceed and succeed. Ness's story of the Untouchables is a detailed account of his numerous raids – the real war that was waged against Capone. The parade of dozens of captured trucks driven by Capone's hotel to tweak the gangster boss. The toll-free telephone number that was set up to make reports – this was after all, in 1931! Each side had such set-ups to get info on the other! Don't miss this one. Ness's own story is incredible and a great read. This will open your eyes about what really happened and how it was done! The Kevin Costner film was based on this book, but don't hold that against it. This is a hell of a book!

More recent and easier to find editions of *The Untouchables* are also available. One from Award Books (#AD1484, at least three printings from 1975) has cool car cover art. There is also a Pocket Books edition (#64491) from 1987. Probably many more editions since then.

Eliot Ness and Oscar Fraley joined forces again a year later with *4 Against The Mob* (Popular Library #G512, PBO 1961), another incredible memoir of Ness's involvement in what appeared to be an early serial killer case in Cleveland. This one has Ness going up against the dread Mayfield Road Mob, disciples of Capone, who in the period of 1935-41 controlled Cleveland and most of the state of Ohio. Ness, with three agents (one a former Untouchable) smashed this crime organization much as he did Capone's years before. These Mayfield Road Mob guys were nasty, stone-cold killers and this is Ness's true account of what really happened. Ness and his work are underrated and have been debunked lately but they should not be. This is a fine crime novel.

After all this stuff about Capone and Chicago, you'd think things in the rest of the country were just going along hunky-dory. No way! After Capone, there's a flurry of tough-guy gangsters that had books about them published in paperback. One of the most interesting was *The Dutch Schultz Story* by Ted Addy (Tower Book #44-129, 1st pb 1968), all about a homicidal, paranoid, vicious genius known as Dutch Schultz (actually Arthur Flegenheimer, not Dutch at all but a tough New York Jew criminal). Schultz or "The Dutchman" controlled the numbers racket and bootlegging in Harlem, was a double-crosser and a lunatic psycho known for his often-instant violence and murder. He even scared other mobsters and they pretty much left him alone, until Luciano finally had him killed. The book has 16 pages of incredible and rare photos; some are the brutal murder photos of Schultz and his Mob associates. The back cover of the book has a famous photo of The Dutchman blown-away face down on a restaurant table. The book is a powerhouse of 1930s gangsterism history.

"Baby Face" Nelson by Steve Thurman (Monarch Book #MA313, PBO 1961) and *"Mad Dog" Coll* also by Steven Thurman (Monarch Book #MM607, PBO 1961), are two interesting books about 1930s crime and gangster legends. The first book has a charming (sic) cover photo of Nelson's dead body on a slab in the Illinois morgue being examined by two cops. Nelson robbed banks and killed two FBI agents and was one of the most dangerous wanted public enemies of the era. This book tells that story to the fateful day when he was gunned down. "Mad Dog" Coll

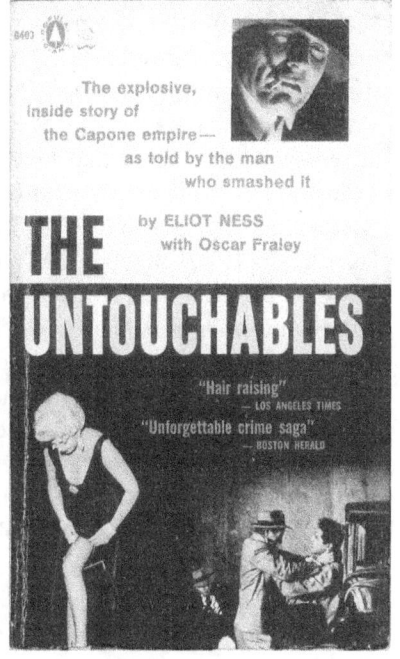

was a psychopath who used a Tommy gun to murder his way into organized crime. He was one of the best and most feared specialty contract killers of his day. It's said he was the gunner at the St. Valentine's Day Massacre but it was never proved. This book features a garish photo cover and ties-in with the obscure Columbia Pictures film starring John Chandler. By the way, Steve Thurman is the pseudonym of top pulp and crime writer Frank Castle.

In the 1940s and 50s a new breed of more "intelligent" and "suave" organized crime figures rose to the front ranks of crime. Just as vicious as their predecessors, but low-key. One went by the name of Lucky. *"Lucky Luciano* by Ovid Demaris (Monarch Book #MA302, PBO 1960) was one of the most famous of these new era gangster 'businessmen'. The vice overlord and dope peddler ran 'The Commission' in the 1940s and 50s. The book cover shows 'Lucky' in a photo being led from court after he was convicted and sentenced to 30-50 years in prison. Luciano was cold, his charming smile masked eyes as dead as a snake's, and he was tough and smart. Demaris made his bones as a writer on books like this in the 1960s, in-depth, undercover Mob exposes. It's a wonder he wasn't made a target of a hit himself. All his books are excellent reads and this early one is no exception.

After Luciano left the scene (prison took him out of circulation), his underboss and chosen successor took over. *Frank Costello: The Gangster With A Thousand Faces* by David Hanna (Belmont Books #50744, PBO 1974) was a more behind-the-scenes player. A millionaire crime boss who controlled many politicians, he modernized the Mob. But the suave businessman on the outside hid a hardened thug inside and he was not to be underestimated. This book takes a good look at Costello, an underrated Mob boss, and it has 16 pages of great photos.

An outfit called Retail Distributors published two Mob paperbacks of note that have a place here. *Hoodlums Los Angeles* by Ted Prager and Larry Craft (#101, PBO 1959) and *Hoodlums New York* by Ted Prager and Leeds Moberley (#102, PBO 1959) have cool covers and great information. *New York* has a cover illustration of the infamous Albert Anastasia hit in the barber shop, the Lord High Executioner of Murder Inc., and examines Costello, Luciano, the famous Apalachin meeting and Vito Genovese. The *Los Angeles* book has a cool thug cover showing a Buggsy Siegel type and features info on Mickey Cohen, Virginia Hill, Buggsy Seigel and the Kefauver Committee on organized crime in America. These are pretty cool books and they make a good set but they are tough to find. But don't let that stop you!

Los Angeles Mob boss Mickey Cohen always said, "I never killed a guy who didn't deserve it." *Mickey Cohen: Mobster* by Ed Reid (Pinnacle

Book #00257, PBO 1973) has an amazing 32 pages of great photos and is a fascinating book. Reid, like Demaris, is an old hand at writing books on the Mob and knows his stuff. Mickey Cohen was a LA Jew (originally just another Jewish hoodlum from Brooklyn) who went out west to make his fortune and his bones. He ran LA in the 1940s and tried to hold onto it in the 1950s. This book tells his entire story from his young hood days in Brooklyn up to his release from prison in 1972. It brings in Buggsy Siegel, Johnny Stompanato and Lana Turner and Johnny's murder by Lana's daughter; also Mob hits, assassination attempts on Mickey and a lot more. A fascinating story about an interesting individual who mixed Hollywood with crime...like the two weren't always connected anyway!

In a more modern and British vein, there is *Murder Without Conviction* by John Dickson (Sphere Books, 1st paperback 1988, UK) about the brutal Kray twins. Throwbacks to America's violent gangster heyday, the Kray's 'Firm' terrorized London in the 1960s and 70s. Dickson, a close trusted henchmen of the Kray's tells the inside story of the Kray rackets, murder, protection, gambling and Mafia connections. The Kray twins had grown increasingly erratic and senselessly violent and scared everyone in London. Dickson tells the inside story and it's a doozy. The book also has some cool photos of the twins.

There are many more great books on the Mob and gangsters and a lot of them were published in paperback. Some are paperback originals and only appeared in paperback. A lot of good stuff to choose from. I hope this look at 'Mob hits' whets your interest.

Crime To Die For:
Five Authors You Just Gotta Read!

I'm a big fan of hard-boiled and noir but I've read most everything by the classic guys. Luckily there are more recent writers carrying on the tradition. One of the best of these is **Daniel Woodrell**. What can I say? The guy is simply terrific. He's written what I consider to be *two* modern classics. Real stand-the-test-of-time type classics. His best book is *Give Us A Kiss* (Pocket Books, US). It's a fascinating mix of his stylized back country, rural brutality and poetry – what he calls "country noir". It's a magnificent hard crime novel that you'll enjoy taking a deep dark dive into. If, as they say, you *can't* "go home again" – *here's why you shouldn't!*

His other classic is a bit "off trail" which is an apt description since it is a western novel. *Woe To Live On* (Pocket Books, US, 1999, aka *Ride With the Devil*, the title of the film made from it) is one tough ride. You might be wondering, "Why is Lovisi bringing a western into this?" Well, don't let the western part of this baby fool you. This one is hard-boiled and gritty and fits perfectly with Woodrell's rural crime mythos.

I just finished one of his Ron Shade novels, *Muscle For The Wing* (Pocket Books, US, 1998). This one is also outstanding. "The Wing" is a prison gang of psychos out to take off big-money card games in the Louisiana town of St. Bruno. But the city is protected territory and no out-of-town "cowboys" need apply – and therein lies a crime and caper tale to warm the heart of any reader of nasty, low-life noir! Let's just say these boys may have made a serious mistake. Let's just say...

Woodrell's latest at the time of this writing was *Winter's Bone* and I'm sure it will be another "charming delight" not to be missed. Woodrell is quickly proving to be a master of the genre and if you are not reading him you are missing some true classics.

Don Winslow is a California writer who writes about the people and politics of that state and the surrounding area, including Mexico. His books are hard and stylized noir masterpieces – here we have good guys who go bad, bad guys who go good, while all around them everything in their life falls to hell in a handbasket. *California Fire and Life* (Knopf, US, 1999), has all that and more. In *The Power of The Dog* (Knopf, US, 2005), drug dealers and drug cops do a dance of violence in a blockbuster generational look at the history of the American-Mexican drug trade. It's an epic to stand with Mario Puzo's *The Godfather*. Then there is *The Savages*, a Mexican crime cartel masterpiece, also made into a hell of a fine film under the same title.

I also liked an earlier effort, *The Death and Life of Bobby Z* (Knopf, US, 1997), where the DEA forces a low-level bad guy to impersonate an even badder guy because they look so much alike. The resulting story gives the reader a wild romp through the southwestern drug scene and the brutality that smothers all who fall into that dark web. I like Winslow's characters, they're cool, tough, and ring true; and sometimes being a bit too smart by half they get in way over their heads. That's when this master writer has his fun and makes them squirm.

Winslow's earliest books include five Neal Carey mysteries about a grad student/private eye that began with *A Cool Breeze on the Underground* (St. Martins Press, US, 1991). While not as intense as his latest work, all of these are worth seeking out and reading as well.

Allan Guthrie is a noir aficionado and fan who ran a popular web site on the topic and eventually gave us a damn good first novel with *Two-Way Split* (Point Blank, 2004). Ed Gorman raved about it and he was spot on. However, it's with his second novel that Guthrie really hit his stride.

In *Kiss Her Goodbye* (Hard Case Crime #8, US, 2005), Guthrie gives us a minor noir classic. In it we follow a low-level crim and tough guy from

Scotland who goes on a rampage after the creature who murdered his daughter. He's a bad guy with bad associates, and a lot of terrible things happen to him and everyone around him before it's all over. The book was also nominated for a MWA Edgar Award this year. It didn't win – but it should have! You'll win though, when you get a copy and read it!

Look for other Guthrie books, there are more, and they are all excellent noir romps.

Martyn Waites is a writer I'm less familiar with but I was very impressed with his novel, *Mary's Prayer* (Piatkus, UK, 1997) when I read it. His books often explore the link between crime and various forms of abuse, including child abuse. He also uses newspaper reporters and journalists as his heroes or protagonists. It makes for interesting observations and compelling stories. Some of his books include *Born Under Punches* (Simon & Schuster, Ltd, UK 2003), *Little Triggers* (Piatkus, UK, 1999) and *Candleland* (Allison & Busby, UK 2000). *Mary's Prayer* and *Candleland* are stories about Newcastle journalist Stephen Larkin. His other protagonist is Joe Donovan, a once renowned investigative reporter now on dark days since his kid went missing. These are tough and stark books. Other Waites books include *The Mercy Seat* (Pegasus, UK, 2006) a Joe Donovan thriller and *Pretty Little Dirty* (Vintage, US, 2006). He has probably written more since this article first

appeared and I am sure they are worth tracking down.

Jason Starr hails from the UK but now makes his home in New York City which gives him an excellent duel culture perspective on the crime and mayhem he shows us to devastating effect in his work. In *Bust*, another Hard Case Crime original (#20, US, 2006), Starr teams up with Ken Bruen in a crime caper full of nasty characters who will cold-bloodedly knife their way into your ever-lovin' heart. This one twists and turns as everyone plays everyone else. It's one that I couldn't put down and the team are reportedly working on a sequel. In fact, since this article appeared I believe there are three more books in what has become an incredible, and damn funny, crime series.

However, on his own, Starr – dare I say it – shines brightly. I really liked his *Tough Luck* (Vintage, US, 2003), where poor Mickey Prado can't seem to do anything right. Mickely's small life seems on track and then he puts in a bet for a Mafia wannabe, which begins him on a downward spiral that will chill your heart. I liked Mickey and rooted for him, but… you'll just have to read it to find out! In this novel Starr also perfectly captures the Brooklyn neighborhoods and people of the 1970s and 80s when the book takes place. Being a Brooklynite who lived through those wild times, I can tell you Starr got it scary damn right!

Starr tells twisted noir tales. He has believable characters who because of greed, lust or other flaws get involved in apparently minor or harmless acts, which invariably lead to major-league weirdness, danger and violence. In *Nothing Personal* (No Exit Press, UK 1998, US 2000) he gives us another twisted noir as two couples live their dirty little lives of betrayal and dysfunctional chaos – which he adroitly shows us comes back to bite them all in the end. It's a very well-crafted and readable shocker. His first hard cover, is *Lights Out*, which many are touting could be his big breakout novel. Jason has been a guest at my New York City books shows and is a fine fellow, and a hell of a terrific writer!

So there you have five guys everyone should be reading. Look for their books. But please don't die trying…

A Closer Look at *Falcon Books*

To the untrained eye they appear to be just another series of digest-sized paperbacks featuring sexy pin-up cover art. But a closer look reveals a treasure trove of original crime and private eye fiction from key 1950s writers who would become legends in the genre. There's some great stuff hidden here and more than a few surprises as well.

Falcons are digest-size paperbacks, bound with staples. Books in the series change format slightly becoming a bit shorter – about a half inch shorter than the standard digest size. There seems to be no logic or order to this sizing, probably just the use of a different printer. Falcon Books were published by the same outfit that published similar sexy digest series: Exotic Books, Ecstasy Books, and Rainbow Books, but none of those had the accent on mystery and crime that the Falcons did.

The series begins for no apparent reason, with book #21, the sleazy crime drama, *Season For Sin* by Anthony Scott in 1952, and ran for a total of 24 amazing books, to end with #44, *Honky Tonk Girl* by Charles Beckman, Jr. If possible, an even more searing hard crime sleazer. Cover blurbs on this one proudly proclaim, "It was the last stop for the scum of humanity on the road to hell!"

Well, it doesn't get any better than that in the pulp crime genre of the 1950s.

As collectables, Falcon Books are coveted acquisitions and usually sell for a premium, when you can find them. These days they only seem to be listed as auction books, and hence go for auction-type prices. Nevertheless, almost any book in the series, in about Fine condition, could set you back close to $100. They're that popular and in demand. Some sell in excess of many hundreds of dollars!

Like everything else, some books are more common than others. With some elusive titles downright impossible to find today. A key reason for collector demand is all the gems in the series: hard-boiled crime, rare drug books, key juvenile delinquent novels, outrageous campy sleaze, all topped off by incredible sexy girl pin-up cover art. For many collectors, what could be better?

Each of the 24 Falcon Books is unique in that they are hard crime and noir that was given the ultimate sexy gga treatment. You could call them hard-boiled sleaze, though published at least a decade before that genre would meld into the soft-core adult paperbacks of the 1960s. The cover art in the Falcon series was superior to most other digests. Those covers were well-drawn, lurid with garish colors, all with sexy good-girl, or bad-girl pin-up cover art using bright reds and yellows. The covers offer a femme fatale feast for the eyes. Sleazy in some respects, but these girls were no victims, they were 'happy' to be bad girls. They're naughty, and they're enjoying it! Cover art was done by George Gross, Rudy Nappi, and others. All covers feature very sexy woman prominently displayed on the cover in provocative pin-up poses. They're stunning and a main reason for the collectability of the books in the first place. The back covers are often just as interesting, with amusing and campy black and white photos, always duly noted as being, "posed by Professional Models." Usually showing bad girls being...*bad*.

However, it's not only what is *on* the covers – as nice as that may be — that makes this series collectable. It's what's *between* those covers. That means the novels — the writing — the actual stories themselves. Almost every book was written by a top professional crime and mystery pulpster. These were men who could tell a hell of a good story and they did. Their stories ring true, their characters are memorable. There's some real sleepers in this series.

The Falcon Books series is also important because 20 of the 24 books are paperback originals. Aside from a prime drug book by Evan Hunter (aka Ed McBain), and Richard Prather's first book, there are no less than 13 books written under pseudonym. Of that number 7 were written by the same author under still more different names. That author is the prolific and professional pulpster, Norman A. Daniels.

So let's begin with Daniels. He wrote seven books in the series under pseudonym, all paperback originals. Daniels wrote four books as by Mark Reed (#22, *The Scarlet Bride*; #26, *Lay Down and Die!*; #32, *Sins of The Flesh*; and #43, *House of 1,000 Desires*); two book as by Norma Dann (#27, *Lida Lynn* and #34, *Shack Girl!*); and one book as David Wade (#35; *Raise The Devil!*). Norman Daniels under his own name also wrote book #29, *Mistress on a Deathbed!*, and #38, *Sweet Savage* both paperback originals from 1952. Daniels all by himself had a total of nine books in this series!

One Daniels sleeper of interest is #35, *Raise The Devil* as by David Reed, a very dark early serial killer novel reminiscent of the brutal Black Dahlia murders and with a tough cop protagonist. It's a minor classic and generally unacknowledged.

Another novel hiding under a pen name is #25, *The Case of The Cancelled Redhead* by Hamlin Daly, a paperback original from 1952. This novel was actually written by veteran pulp author, *Weird Tales* contributor and Oriental scholar, E. Hoffman Price. Another sleeper under pseudonym and generally unknown even by his many fans.

Lion Books crime author, Fredric Lorenz, also contributed one book for the Falcon series under a pseudonym. That book is #37, *Woman Hunter*, by Laura Hale. For years thought to be yet another Norman Daniels pseudonym, this book was discovered to be written by Lorenz and was a paperback original from 1952. It's a searing crime novel.

Of the many interesting books in the series, one of the wildest is #28, *Girls Out Of Hell* by little-known Brooklyn crime and sleaze author, Joe Weiss. A paperback original from 1952, this scarce and very desirable juvenile delinquent girl-gang and woman-in-prison novel is very hard-boiled. It also has incredible bad-girl cover art by George Gross. One of his best covers in the series. Even the back cover is outstanding on this one – collectors love it. The photo and blurbs here talk about reform school girls and tough gang girls. This book has become tougher to find. It used to be seen quite frequently at shows and on dealer lists, but not any more. This is one of the best JD novels by a writer who wrote gritty crime and JD fiction for Avon and other publishers in the 1950s (and in hardcover for The Woodford Press). Joe Weiss was a cantanterous fellow all told, but he was an underrated author who is avidly collected by those in the know. These days this book has become one of the key Falcons, highly in demand, so it can be very pricey.

Perhaps the most sought after book in the Falcon series is #36, *Junkie* by Jonathan Craig, another paperback original from 1952. Cover art is signed by Ketor Seach. This is one of the two prime drug books in the series and very tough to find. It sports the same title as Ace #D-15 (*Junkie* by William Lee — however, this Falcon book has absolutely nothing to do with the Ace Book or Lee/Burroughs). In fact, this Falcon Book is much harder to come by and is probably worth almost as much in nice condition! This is one of the scarcer and most desirable drug-related crime paperbacks and in pristine near Fine condition can easily sell for up to $1,000!

Three important big-name masters of mystery, crime and private eye fiction appear in the Falcon series with one book each. One of the most important is Richard A. Prather, with Falcon Book #30, *Dagger of Flesh*, from 1952. It features cover art showing a great sexy gang moll by Ruddy Nappi. This is Prather's first book and his first novel. Prather told me he was not very happy with the title, nor the cover art — he didn't like the sexy girl on the cover. It's ironic that one of the reasons why collectors like the book so much is the exact reason why the author disliked it so much. Also, the book was *not* a Shell Scott novel originally, but had a different hero named Mark Logan. Logan transformed into Shell Scott in later reprints. This book is also hard to find, especially in better condition and can be quite pricey.

The second important mystery and private eye writer in this series was Anthony Scott, who kicked-off the series with the first Falcon, book #21, *Season For Sin*. Scott was actually Brett Halliday (who was actually, David Dresser), the famous mystery author and creator of the Mike Shayne private eye series. This was an early Halliday novel under yet another pseudonym and generally not known.

The third important mystery and private eye author is Evan Hunter (aka Ed McBain, but born Salvatore Lombino, who sadly passed away

soon after this article was originally written). His book, #41, *The Evil Sleep*, is also a paperback original from 1952. This was Hunter's first book and it is very much sought after. However, this is not only a crime novel, it is a very valuable drug book about heroin addiction, and collectors are eager to get their hands on the scarce number of copies available. *The Evil Sleep* is probably the rarest and most expensive Falcon Book. An about Fine condition copy could be worth from $400-1,000! The book was never reprinted under this title. It was reprinted only once as *So Nude, So Dead* (Crest Book #139, 1956), under yet another Hunter pseudonym, Richard Marsten, and that revised edition is scarce and pricey as well. I believe these are the only editions of this scarce book.

Someone with the unlikely sounding name of Hodge Evens also wrote books in the Falcon series. For a long time some collectors assumed Hodge Evens was also Evan Hunter. This was because Hunter used so many pen names, the similarity of the names (Evens/Evan), and the fact that Hunter had already written one book in the Falcon series — much like Norman Daniels who also used pseudonyms in this series. Also in some early reference books and lists, Evens name was incorrectly shown as Evans, so some assumed this was just another Evan Hunter pseudonym. Collectors (but especially book dealers) would have loved there to be three sleeper Evan Hunter digests discovered in the Falcon series. However, this was not to be. Hodge Evens is NOT Evan Hunter. He never was. They are totally different authors.

Hodge Evens wrote three books in the Falcon series: #24, *Three For Passion*, "An emotional whirlpool of crime, passion and love!"; #33, *Yellow-Head*; and #40, *Whip-Hand*, "a seething turmoil of passion, violence and hatred." This last of the three Evens titles seems to be a very tough Falcon to find. All are paperback originals from 1952. It turns out that Hodge Evens is actually veteran genre author, Dudley Dean McGaughy, better known as Dean Owens. Owens, writing as Hodge Evens, also wrote books for Beacon and Rainbow Books and was another prolific pulpster.

There were also books by lesser mystery and crime authors who were mainstays in the crime digests of the 1950s and 60s like *Manhunt, Pursuit,* and *Hunted*. One, already mentioned above, was Jonathan Craig with his book #36, *Junkie*. Two other crime genre authors with a book each in the Falcon series were Bryce Walton with #42, *The Long Night*, "a novel of hasty marriage…and hastier death", and Charles Beckman, Jr. with #44, *Honky Tonk Girl* (more on this book and author elsewhere in this book). These last two books might be first novels for them, as both wrote almost exclusively in the short story form.

Three other books offer fodder for further investigation: #23, *Mabel and Men!* by George Boltari; #31, *Slave Girl* by Tom Roan; and #39, *Joy Street* by Chet Kinsey. These seem to be the author's actual names but it is hard to tell for sure. Tom Roan wrote many western stories and novels in the pulps and paperbacks, and he also wrote under the name Adam Rebel, but whether Roan was a genuine name or a pseudonym is still a mystery. Obviously, there are still questions that need to be answered about some of these books.

Unlike most sexy digest series with the prerequisite girly pin-up cover art, Falcon Books also offer finely written hard-boiled crime and mystery novels. They're good books in and of themselves — good to actually read. The best of the pulp paperbacks. They offer crime and suspense fiction by quality authors who really know how to tell a good story. What could be better!

I'd estimate a complete set of all 24 Falcon Books in at least Very Good condition could be worth in the area of $2,500! In about Fine condition, like new, perhaps as much as $10,000! So with that kind of dollar value, sexy cover art and collectable authors, Falcon Books really do deserve a closer look!

Sex and Savagery in Pulp Paperback Crime Cover Art

In the cover art of the pulp crime paperbacks of the 1950s, sex and savagery often went together like peanut butter and jelly. Paperback cover art from the late 1940s, 50s, and 60s relished the sexy, the lurid, and often the sleazy to make a sale. Mystery and private eye novels especially were packaged by combining crime with sex.

Paperbacks evolved from a pulp magazine heritage. Not only were many of the writers and artists originally from the pulps, but so were many of the editors (Leo Margolies, Sam Merwin) and publishers (A.A. Wyn of Ace Books and Ned Pines of Popular Library). Paperbacks of this era had a particularly strong connection with sex, mostly images of scantily clad women in pulp-inspired cover art used to sell copies. The 'sex' was risque, but never overt. Nevertheless, they sold to a predominately male book buying public at the time. Publishers knew what book buyers liked back then and gave it to them. Today, these old paperbacks often send modern feminists shrieking in anger while 'sophisticated readers' shake their pointy heads in dire disapproval. But to those who understand and appreciate them, the cover art on these old crime paperbacks is amazing, beautiful and always fascinating.

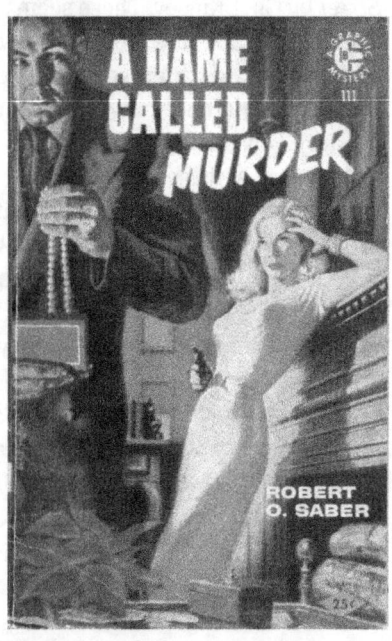

Some of the most egregious examples of sex and savagery in pulp crime paperbacks also turn out to be some of the most hotly desired and collectable paperbacks today. No surprise there. Covers showing so-called 'bad girls' (you can tell who they are because they almost always are blondes holding a lit cigarette), and femme fatales (dangerous homicidal women) are inextricably linked to noir, hard-boiled and tough-guy private eye mysteries. A beautiful woman with a gun is a pulp and

A MYSTERY, CRIME & NOIR NOTEBOOK

paperback staple, and if she's scantily clad – all the better for most male book buyers of the era.

Interestingly enough, even traditional mystery novels suffered from this packaging. For instance, *The Doll's Trunk Murder* (Popular Library #211) by Helen Reilly received the sex and savagery treatment with a particularly brutal bondage cover by pulp art great Rudolph Belarski. Here we see a beautiful woman bound with rope, her mouth taped, and her dress open to strategically expose as much breast as was permissible in the era. As if that's not enough, she's also menaced by a man's gloved hand holding a knife at her throat. This was an extreme example, but even mainstream mysteries were given the sex and savagery cover art treatment to make them more saleable. This cover, like many others, was re-used from an earlier pulp magazine for this paperback book.

However, most books just had the generic sexy girl, or femme fatale cover without the savagery of bondage or violence. The violence was implied, not shown on those covers. One good example is the Veronica Lake look-alike on *A Dame Called Murder* by Robert O. Saber (Graphic Book #111). This is an outstanding cover by Walter Popp. Here we see a doll get the drop on a two-timing jewel thief. Somehow we know she's not playing, and that she will very efficiently shoot the man in the back. A classic sexy femme fatale on a crime paperback cover.

To be sure, certain authors, or certain publisher runs, had a near lock on sex and savagery in the paperbacks. They seemed to specialize. Mickey Spillane's hard-boiled Mike Hammer paperback reprints from Signet Books showcased some brutal bondage cover art by Lou Kimmel that oozed sex and violence. In *One Lonely Night* (Signet Book #888) Hammer fights commie spies in the 1950s and comes upon a woman stripped naked, tied and hanging by her wrists. Luckily, Hammer is there to save her. On the cover of *The Long Wait* (Signet Book #932) it is Mike Hammer himself, bound and beaten, shirt torn and tied to a chair with a disheveled women in the foreground. What is her connection to the scene? Is she Hammer's captor or companion? Other crime authors like

Jim Thomspon, David Goodis, Charles Willeford, Bruno Fischer, Richard Prather, John D. MacDonald and more in their early books for Lion, and later Gold Medal, benefited from sexy cover art. Sometimes violent art as well.

In England, James Hadley Chase (beginning with his savage and violent opening opus) *No Orchids For Miss Blandish* (a 1950s paperback reprint from Canada's Harlequin Books, #108), set the tone early in the 1930s and 40s. When these books were reprinted in the 1950s, the sex and violence oozed out of the cover art based on events in the story. For instance, in *No Orchids*, we have the story of Slim Grissom – homicidal maniac and kidnap rapist of the innocent Carol Blandish. It's a brutal crime novel with a high body count. The book horrified the critics of its day in the 1930s and 40s; much as Spillane's Mike Hammer would do so with critics in the 1950s. Well, what do critics know, anyway?

Chase continued with many other hard crime novels, including a sequel, *The Flesh Of The Orchid* (Harlequin Book #111), where the 'bad seed' from an unholy rape becomes a beautiful and sexy female homicidal maniac. Chase was a staple of the UK tough-guy and violence crime school that imitated American hard-boiled private eyes – specifically Spillane's Mike Hammer — even though his work pre-dated Spillane! In American and Canadian reprints Chase became popular on this side of the Atlantic in the 1950s and churned out numerous tough crime novels. Many of these had the prerequisite sexy girl with a gun on the cover or the female victim being menaced by a male criminal with

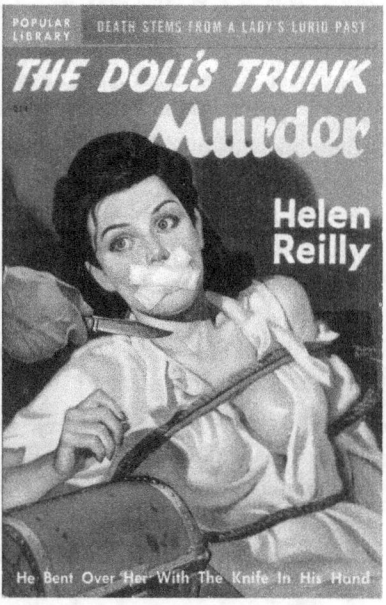

murderous intent.

However, the genre reached its nadir of sex and savagery (or it's heights according to some collectors today) in England with the cover art on the early Hank Janson crime digests. These were digest-size paperbacks, written by Stephen Frances with cover art by Reginald Heade. Heade's exquisitely sexy women were pin-up art supreme, such as the cover he did for *Lola Brought Her Wreath* (Gaywood Press, 1950). Later the books became so hot the publishers were raided by the police and some copies were actually banned. Other copies were destroyed.

Heade himself went into hiding for a period, and afterwards did paperback cover art under a pseudonym, as by 'Cy Webb'. By that time about 50 Hank Jansons had been published and more would come later – albeit toned down in context and with cover art by different artists. One of these later Jansons with an excellent 'bad girl' crime cover is *Come Quickly Honey* (Roberts & Vinter, 1960).

Meanwhile, all the Hank Janson sales success spawned an entire genre of imitators, called today 'British gangster digests.' They were written by a host of authors under tough-guy, Americanized pseudonyms and with great campy titles. Examples are: *Unhappy Hophead, Floosie On The Run, I Like My Women Tough*, and *Rebecca Of The Snatch Racket*. They featured sexy, often slightly dressed women, sometimes violent content cover art by a host of Heade wannabes, mostly pros such as Perl and Ferarri. Ferrari on a good day: *Tomorrow – The Chair* by Ross Angel (Scion Books), with the typical half-naked girl with a gun. On a good day the gangster artists could turn in an adequate cover. On a bad day, you had to wonder what they'd been drinking.

Back in America, the digests there also contributed to the crime scene. Phantom Books published an excellent private eye novel by Joe Barry, *Homicide Hotel* (Phantom #500), but the cover art shows one of the most brutal sex and exploitation scenes ever. On it we see two double-Y-chromosome thugs chloroforming a woman tied with rope to a chair, as they pull her hair and terrorize her. You know she's a goner. I think it's one of the most brutal covers ever to appear on an American paperback. Just as a side note, the image on the cover has absolutely *nothing* to do with story in the book, a situation not uncommon between the text and cover art on many of the books of this era. A runner-up in the violence-against-women category would be another contribution by British author James Hadley Chase and his American publisher Eton Books (#E112, which was an imprint of Avon Books). It had the charming title of *Kiss My Fist*. It shows a man giving a roundhouse punch to a woman in the face, literally knocking her block off. It's a cover that packs quite a wallop. Guaranteed to get all kinds of people upset today for all kinds of reasons. But don't get too riled up about it, the book was publised in 1952 — over 70 years ago!

Not to leave it with the girls always getting the rough end of things, there were also various American crime digest magazines in the 1950s and 60s – lesser sisters of *Manhunt* and *Ellery Queen's Mystery Magazine* – *much* lesser. They went by names like *Guilty, Trapped, Two-Fisted, Hunted, Saturn Web,* and *Sure-Fire*. On the covers of many of these the women turn the tables on the men, showing they can be just as violent and brutal. The cover for *Guilty* (July, 1958), shows a woman garroting a police detective from behind as he tries to make a report at a street call box. An incredible scene. More savage yet, the cover of *Trapped* (August, 1960), where we see a disheveled, almost stripped naked woman getting the drop on her attacker with a particularly long pair of nasty scissors as she tries to push him out a window. Many of these magazines had particularly sexy and savage art. In fact, one cover art motif on most issues seemed to be to show ever more violent and imaginatively graphic ways for a woman to kill a man. Or vice versa. Covers showed femme fatales, or 'wronged women' getting their revenge by garroting, death by stabbing with a knife, ax, scissors, ice-pick, shot with gun, pistol whipped, whipped with a whip, choked, and more. Liberal doses of sex and flesh were thrown in the art. Some covers had girl fights with the inevitable cat fight tearing of clothing. Some showed two girls ganging up to kill a guy.

These were all lower rung magazines full of crime stories, but sex and savagery were the selling points. In truth, crime is a nasty, violent business; and murder, often committed from reasons of passion or jealously inevitably has a sex and savagery angle to it. However these digest magazines, and many of the most egregious examples of the books in this article in their cover art only exacerbated and exploited the situation for a quick sale. It's all crime sleaze. It's also avidly collected today.

Falcon Books, another 50s digest outfit I have already mentioned, mixed hard-boiled crime with outstanding sexy cover art. Books like *Girls Out Of Hell* by Joe Weiss (Falcon #28) told the sordid story of girl-gang crime – a classic of the juvenile delinquent genre. In *The Evil Sleep* (Falcon #40) by crime legend Evan Hunter and *Dagger Of Flesh* (Falcon #31) by Shell Scott creator Richard Prather, we have two early crime novels by modern day legends in the field. This entire short-run series of two dozen books is a collector's dream with something in content or cover art for everyone.

In the US many mainstream paperback publishers also specialized in crime, such as Lion Books, Monarch Books, Graphic Books, Gold Medal, Popular Library, Avon, Eton Books and Ace Books with their 'double novel' books. All featured very sexy cover art, updated images based on the old pulps. They even used covers painted by pulp greats like Rudolph Belarski, Earle Bergey, Rudy Nappi, Walter Popp, Robert Maguire, Norman Saunders and others.

Signet Books, the company that boasted it's motto, 'Good Reading For The Millions' (which translated to the more proletarian 'good books for the masses'), was nevertheless built on the sex of their Erskine Caldwell early paperback reprints (*God's Little Acre*) and the savagery of the early hard-boiled Mickey Spillane paperbacks (*I, The Jury*). They also published a long run of hard-boiled crime in the Spillane mould with sexy and sometimes violent cover art. Writers such as Adam Knight, Charlie Wells, Jack Webb, Sam S. Taylor, Mike Roscoe and more gave us Spillane-like classics, many with glorious sexy cover art by veteran paperback master Robert Maguire. Two good examples of Maguire's art: *So Cold, My Bed* by Sam S. Taylor (Signet #1247): a bad girl does in a guy; and *Slice Of Hell* by Mike Roscoe (Signet #1216): a guy gets a drop on a girl. Maguire's women stand alone as pulp noir femme fatale icons on the paperbacks of the 1950s. He did many great covers in this style for Signet Books, Berkley Books, Pyramid Books and others. They're exquisite.

In fact, the sex and savagery shown in the cover art of these early crime paperbacks of the 1950s and 60s is what mostly sold these books. It's what helped make some of these authors successful, and in some cases, household words. It ensured publisher sales and company success. It got the books noticed! It's also what has made the books so avidly collected today – in a world where no contemporary mainstream books offer anything to rival this incredible artwork.

The best examples of these covers are just wonderful, showing very sexy and beautiful women often involved in the height of passion or crime. The worst examples are savage, brutally sadistic images of violent crime. Each is a snapshot frozen in time of our collective historical tapestry, from an era of less pretensions, no political correctness, and few if any sensitivities. That's the way it was back then. Sex and savagery in paperback cover art often mirrored life. The anger, the hatred and passions were all there, displayed as colorful images to entice the reader and book buyer. These covers, for the most part — for better or worse — showed crime as the ugly and nasty business that it truly is. Today, we can enjoy these books in our more enlightened era for what they are. They are history. The cover art is outstanding, well rendered, and often fascinates us. These books are interesting and fun. Sometimes, they're even *cool*.

Rediscovering: The Wages of Fear

The Wages of Fear by Georges Arnaud, is hard-boiled suspense at it's very best, a novel loaded with hard-luck characters and dripping with intense atmospheric terror.

It is 1952 and the white riff-raff living in a small Guatemalan port town — all ex-patriot Europeans and Americans, lonely and lost after trials endured during World War II — find themselves trapped by despair and poverty, just like most of the locals. Each man has his own sad story and each one is lost in a dead-end existence. These men are not of the local native Indians — they are despised foreigners unable to leave the country without the proper cash stake, unable even to afford a ticket home. Their story is as dark a tale of noir desperation as has ever been written, but that background merely sets the stage for an even more haunting story of tense pulse-pounding suspense that is to come.

Georges Arnaud was a French writer whose books were originally published in his native France, but *The Wages of Fear* was his masterpiece and it has been translated into English and published in America and the UK. The first English-language edition was a British hardcover from the Bodley Head in 1952, translated from the original French edition. Both editions are scarce and pricey today. The first U.S. edition was the hardcover published by Farrar, Straus and Young in 1952. The first U.S. paperback edition was published by Avon Books (# 531) in 1953; reprinted by Avon in 1958 (#804) under the new title, *Flesh And Fire*. The first UK paperback edition was published by Guild Books, (#469) in 1953. There are many later paperback reprints which can be found on internet book sites. This book is well worth seeking out.

Many fans will remember the book because it was made into two fine films. It was the basis of the 1953 film *The Wages of Fear* with Yves Montand, made by Henri Georges Clouzot. This is a taut classic noir, a black & white film masterpiece, sadly not shown these days on TV as much as it used to be. I still remember being riveted by this film when I first watched it on late night TV in the 1960s. Years later, *Wages* was the basis of the 1977 film, *Sorcerer*, starring Roy Scheider, with a screenplay by Walon Green, produced and directed by William Friedkin. While the films capture much of the raw intensity and suspense of the story, reading the book offers so much more depth to the lives of these desperate men that is missing in the films. The book really fleshes out these men as men, starkly illustrating their dire situation, and the intense pressure each one is under.

The story concerns this motley crew, hopelessly stranded in a foreign land. There's Gerard the Frenchman, Liugi the Italian, Johnny the Romanian, and Juan Binba the Spaniard. These four men form the core group, who along with their fellows live a hap-hazard existence of whoring, gambling and drinking themselves into mindless oblivion. They dream of escaping the heat-infested swamps and claustrophobic jungle of these Central American villages, but are trapped from ever going home. Some are wanted men. Others are too wasted, too far gone to even care. There seems to be no way out, no salvation, for any of them. So they rot away, some slowly dying of syphilis from the wretched whores of the town, others drinking themselves to death on poison rot-gut rum, some murdered in the dark of night by the Guatemalan military or secret police whom they fear and who hate all foreigners with a passion. These are men without money, without position or power, and they are all fair game. Arnaud's characters are hopeless and desperate, existing hand-to-mouth at the lowest level of this dirt-poor, bloody-violent alien society.

On the top of this Dantesque world and controlling it all, is the all-powerful Crude Oil Corporation which owns the oil wells in the country and most of the people and wealth. And sitting atop the corporation is O'Brien, their man in Guatemala, who runs it all like some banana

republic despot. Gerard and his fellows exist at the largesse of O'Brien, occasionally doing odd jobs for him. Some legal, some not so legal. There's is a story as dark as anything Jim Thompson or David Goodis ever wrote.

At the time of publication in 1952, *Time* Magazine called this book, "Brutal, violent and good storytelling. *The Wages of Fear* makes a lot of hard-boiled writers look like children writing for their maiden aunts."

The *Time* reviewer hit it pretty close. However, this is no Dashiell Hammett or Raymond Chandler clone, and certainly not a private eye novel. It's hard-boiled, but more in the style of James M. Cain's brutal, dark, noir. In fact, while there is a lot of crime committed, this is not a crime novel, per se. What it is, is a depiction of these men's lives as they live them on those mean alien streets, a dark desperate story full of atmospheric doom that hits its stride when four men attempt to change their fortunes. They do this by agreeing to drive two trucks full of volatile nitroglycerin over rough mountain roads to be used to put out a raging oil well fire.

DRIVERS WANTED. DANGEROUS WORK. HIGH PAY.

The job is actually a death sentence.

The corporation offers four men a wad of cash that is a princely sum for any man in their sorry situation. No man can pass it up. The money would be enough to pay for passage home, enough to start a new life. It's escape money and they all want it.

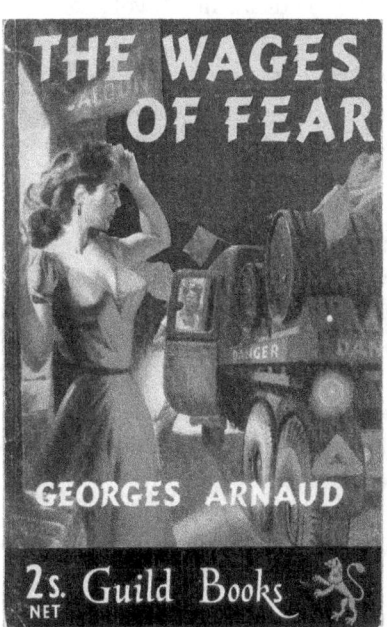

Every man seeks the job.

Four men are chosen.

O'Brien and the corporation men have a cynical plan. The nitro is necessary to blow out the oil well fire and end a serious emergency in the country. However, they dare not hire local Guatemalans because the natives and Army would come down hard on them for using local people in such an obvious suicide mission. Instead they use the riff-raff foreigners who are all expendable. So they make an offer to these men who have nothing to loose. They offer a thousand dollars per man for this dangerous job, which seals the deal as well as the fate of all four men.

Things get tense even before the trucks leave the town on their mission. Gerard soon discovers that his partner, Johnny — the man he relies on most and must trust with his life — is an utter, abject coward. Johnny looses his nerve and is a wreck. Then when the first truck goes up in a ball of fire killing Luigi and his partner, Gerard realizes that they're not only hauling explosive nitro but that the trucks have been sabotaged by one of their own fellows. It seems someone else wants to take their place on the next run should this one fail — and get all that cash.

Gerard drives with desperate care over the broken roads, fearing every pothole, each crevice and bump which could mean instant death — catastrophic obliteration in a huge explosive nitro fireball. Arnaud's writing puts the reader in the front seat right beside Gerard; hearing his thoughts, seeing his growing tension, feeling his unbridled terror. Just when it looks as if things could not get any worse — they do.

Johnny's fragile reasoning, which so far has held together by mere threads from the intense pressure and fear, is eating him up. He has become a useless wreck. Gerard knows he needs his partner to hold up his end, in frustration he beats Johnny mercilessly to force him to pull himself together. This works, for a while.

When the two men encounter a field of quicksand, it is Johnny who notices that the dark mud is actually oil — oil that is highly volatile, easily ignited — possibly even ignited by the exhaust of their truck. Johnny, who has been injured tries to hang on as Gerard bulls his way forward — lurching the truck dangerously through the oily quicksand before they finally end up getting stuck. Now, after all they have been through, the truck gets stuck in the quagmire and even Gerard finally admits defeat.

At that point, at their darkest and most desperate moment, Johnny suddenly remembers that similar situations were dealt with when he worked in the oil fields back home in Romania. He tells Gerard he knows a way he can get them out of their mess. However, Johnny is severely injured, he is going into shock, losing his memory, so Gerard is frantic to get the information out of him before he dies. Johnny fights to stay conscious and at the last moment tells Gerard what to do. The suspense and tension never flags in these desperate scenes.

Using the information Johnny has given him Gerard gets the truck safely through the quicksand field. He delivers the nitro and becomes a hero. Johnny doesn't make it. Gerard is given a thousand dollars for his part in the nitro delivery as well as another thousand that was Johnny's share. So Gerard is now up two grand and planning to make a new life. Things are looking good.

This is always the most dangerous point in any noir story.

The nitro delivered, Gerard is naturally more relaxed on the lonely drive back to town. He is finally free of the monumental stress experienced driving this very road a short time ago when making the nitro delivery. Now he is making plans for a new life. He has some money and is thinking about how to spend it. He's going to buy that boat he's always wanted, then get out of Guatemala leaving this life behind him forever. He sees himself living in Paris, enjoying the good life.

The previous run on these roads had been a nightmare, done at an infuriatingly slow pace, only five miles per hour — with the threat of a nitro explosion over his head every second. Now the winding mountain roads call out to Gerard. It's a far different ride going back. It's even pleasant. He's relaxed and can drive faster now. Gerard opens up the engine of the truck, increasing his speed. He's in a rush to get back to town with his cash so he can get out of Guatemala forever.

The mountain roads loom ahead, steep and winding, narrow and always dangerous. On the way down Gerard knows he must slow his speed, but becomes frantic when the brakes do not answer his footfall. The brakes don't work! In desperation he quickly tries to downshift the truck, to slow it any way he can. The transmission moans and groans and then suddenly locks at high speed. The truck is now speeding downward out of control towards a curve. It hurls through a fence — then shoots over a cliff.

"Gerard is still at the wheel, victim of his own obstinacy, his obstinate resolve to live"

And so ends this classic and very dark noir novel. No one wins in this gloomy tale of dead-ender desperation — no one, except readers and fans of tough, unadulterated noir suspense. This one is well-worth a revisit — or if you have never read it — what are you waiting for?

A Giant Passed Our Way

Mike Avallone had a long and successful writing career that began in the pulp magazines. After World War II — he'd been a tank commander in Patton's 3Rd Army fighting Nazis — he returned to civilian life and began to write professionally.

Mike wrote and sold anything and everything to the pulp magazines in those days to support himself and his family — mysteries, science fiction, and even sports short stories. But the pulps were on their way out in the early 1950s, while paperbacks were coming on strong. Mike was ready.

In 1953 Perma Books reprinted Mike's first book (originally a hardcover edition), and the first in his acclaimed tough-guy, wise-cracking Ed Noon private eye series, *The Tall Delores*. Over the decades 36 Ed Noon books would be published, culminating with *High Noon At Midnight*, from Paperjacks in 1988.

Avallone and Gene Kelly 1987

Mike was a big fan of the pulps; pulp heroes like The Spider, The Shadow and Doc Savage; and he loved classic Hollywood films and actors like Gary Cooper. Mike also loved musicals, and later in his life he and the famed dancer, Gene Kelly, became good friends. The photo accompanying this article shows Mike at his New Jersey home when Gene Kelly came for a visit him in 1987. Mike was overjoyed to meet one of his movie heroes. I tell you this because Mike included references to many pop icons of the silver screen and the old pulps in his Ed Noon books. Ed Noon was Mike's idealized fantasy version of himself, and in these very under-rated and idiosyncratic novels, Mike was set free to be at his creative best. His imagination ran rampant and knew no bounds.

"Avo" as his friends affectionately knew him, was the consummate professional writer and the quintessential 'paperback writer'. Known as 'the fastest typewriter in the East' and author of over 200 books, Mike's philosophy was simple: "a *writer* should be able to write anything at all — from the *Bible* to a farm seed catalog — and anything in between." Mike wrote a lot of the in-betweens. And he did it well.

Mike wrote in just about every genre, under a plethora of pen names, and his career spanned five decades. At his height in the 1960s and 70s, if an editor needed quality professional work fast, they always turned to Avallone. His energy was boundless. Mike never let them down. He always delivered — as a writer and as a friend.

Mike wrote dozens of movie and TV tie-in paperback novels and novelizations, including the highly successful first novel in the long-running *Man From U.N.C.L.E.* paperback series, *The Thousand Coffins Affair*. He wrote the first book in the revitalized Nick Carter spy and private eye paperback series that was to become a huge success. He wrote the *Partridge Family* TV tie-in series; *The Felony Squad*; *Mania*; *Hawaii Five-O*; *Karkatoa, East of Java* and *Friday the 13th* and many more tie-ins with TV shows and popular films. As Edwina Noon, he even wrote Gothics in the 1960s. Later in the 1970s as 'Sidney Stuart' he wrote books in the hard-boiled men's action/adventure series, *The Butcher*.

Avallone also wrote soft-core adult paperbacks in the 1950s for Beacon Books; in the 1960s for Midwood Books; and in the 1970s as 'Troy Conway' for Paperback Library. These 'adult' paperbacks are mild in their so-called 'adult' content by today's standards and are actually great fun and campy reads. These books are full of Avallone wit, charm and sense of humor. Mike wrote under many pseudonyms, though most of his books were published under his own name. Mike was always proud to put his name on his work, and did not want to hide behind a pseudonym, even on his 'adult' material, as so many other writers did. These so-called 'adult' novels are some of his best work. Real noir suspense stories! Try *The Doctor's Wife* (Beacon Books, 1963) for a hard-boiled noir; or *All The Way* and *The Platinum Trap* (Midwood Books 1960 and 1962 respectively, for sheer story-telling enjoyment.

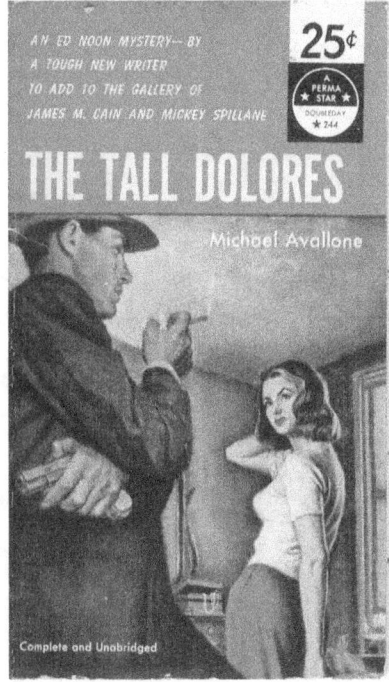

Mike Avallone touched a lot of lives. He was a good, gentle, generous man and a good friend. I knew him for many years. I published some of his work, and he was a popular guest at my New York City book shows for over a decade. He was a giant who passed our way for too short a time, and those of us privileged to know the real man will always miss his warm good humor and that wonderful "'Avo' charm and smile.

Michael Avallone passed away at his home in New Jersey, on Friday March 26, 1999 of complications from anemia and heart trouble. Mike had been ill for the previous year. Those who knew him will always miss him and think of him fondly — and still enjoy his many wonderful books. An under-rated writer — he was a giant who passed our way, and left us too soon.

Shanghai Incident & Others

Dan Roberts, a good friend and book collector extraordinaire who passed away in 2014, turned me onto this book and when Dan recommends – I listen!
And I'm glad I did.
The book was by a fellow named Steve Dodge who I had never heard of (he's not to be confused with the better-known crime author, David Dodge). Steve only wrote one novel – but it's a real good one. However, as I did a little research about this Steve Dodge fellow I discovered that there was a bit more to the story.
Shanghai Incident by Steve Dodge, Gold Medal Book #456, is a paperback original from January, 1955 with nice cover art by Lou Kimmel. The book is a hard crime and spy novel. It's worth reading. I enjoyed it. It's also the only novel I know of written by *this* author – but as things turn out – Dodge is actually the suspense and adventure novelist, Stephen Becker. I know this because *Shanghai Incident* was reprinted by Gold Medal Books (#994) in April, 1960, under the author's true name. This second printing also has the added bonus of being graced by beautiful Robert McGinnis cover art showing a gorgeous blonde dame – the femme fatale of the novel, shown more prominent and  stunning than Kimmel's cover for the first printing. There is also a back cover photo of Becker on this reprint – so Dodge is Becker.

Shanghai Incident is a fine spy novel. It tells the story of David Chapman, who is an old China hand and OSS undercover agent (Office of Strategic Services – the precursor to the CIA run by Wild Bill Donovan). Chapman parachutes into China in the closing days of World War II to 'fix' a few things. He's been 'fixing' things for his boss at 'the Agency' ever since. The story in the book takes place in 1948, a year before Mao's communists are poised to take over the mainland and steep it in glorious red revolution – along with war and death and murder and the loss of all freedom. But that's neither here nor there concerning

Chapman's story, just a bit of background. Chapman's been sent back to look for a missing scientist with a secret – the secret and the scientist have mysteriously disappeared. Chapman is a tough guy but thoughtful, an interesting mix in a pulp paperback spy hero, and the book really moves with intrigue and style.

What begins as a tough hard-boiled novel about murder turns into a spy story and eventually becomes a fine noir thriller, especially once the gorgeous and mysterious blonde femme fatale, Anne Nichols, enters the picture. Chapman, of course, falls for her, and apparently, she falls for him too – but I think it might be safe to say (and I'm not letting out too much here), that she may have ulterior motives. There are also a lot of other well-drawn characters in this book, such as 'businessmen' who are involved in politics and spying, and other unsavory acts such as in the black market.

There is also Cheng, a smart and tough Chinese cop who grew up before the war in Seattle, so he speaks English like a pro, and his relationship with the wise-cracking Chapman makes for some enjoyable moments and interesting banter. Cheng is a very engaging character, and the author lets on to us his love of China and the Chinese people through Cheng. In fact, I wouldn't mind reading a book with Cheng as the main protagonist at all. Sadly Becker never wrote one.

Cheng's relationship with Chapman put me in mind of the best scenes with Humphrey Bogart and Claude Reins (as Rick and Captain Renault) in the famous film, *Casablanca*. They make an interesting pair, and when you throw in the lovely Anne Nichols, you have all the ingredients for some interesting things to happen. And they do. Once Chapman leaves China (which he must, when Becker himself left in 1948) he tells us about it in this heartfelt passage on page 156:

> *I was almost crazy, my face like a kid's hot against the cold window glass, my eyes almost crossing, straining for a last look at the city, my city, at Shanghai, at the towers and hovels and*

colors and people, and the whole sprawling confusion of it, the specks moving and the lines dimming and the buildings smaller and smaller and then behind me, and somewhere among that was Anne, Anne, my God, Anne—

Stephen Becker was born in 1927 and died in 1999. He wrote this one novel under his Steve Dodge pseudonym. And while Dodge isn't a name to conjure with, Stephen Becker, it turns out, certainly is. In fact, Becker went on to write many fine novels, some of them about China, Asia, and various wars. All were popular and well received. However, *Shanghai Incident* isn't Becker's first book, four years earlier he had published under his own name, *The Season of The Stranger* (Harper Books, 1951), set during the communist takeover in China, just two years previously. In fact, Becker spent 1947 and 1948 in Peking, China, and like the hero in *Season*, probably left in 1949 when the communists took over.

Becker is also the author of *The Chinese Bandit* (Random House, 1975), the first book in his popular Far East Trilogy where a U.S. Marine in China turns bandit and seeks a black market fortune. The other two books in this trilogy are *The Last Mandarin* (Random House, 1979), where in 1949 adventurer Jack Burnham goes to China to track down a Japanese war criminal responsible for the Rape of Nanking in 1933. The third novel, *The Blue-Eyed Shan* (Random House, 1982), also takes place in 1949 as an anthropologist returns to China on a treasure hunt. John Irving said of this last book in the trilogy, that it is "…that rare book…a work of literary perfection and sublime entertainment."

Becker's other novels include *A Rendezvous in Haiti* (Norton, 1987), about a U.S. Marine in Haiti in 1919, fighting insurgents. *The Outcasts* (Athenaeum, 1967), a comic-tragic novel about an American engineer building a bridge in the tropics. *Juice* (Simon & Schuster, 1958), a novel about man's lust for power generated by money and politics and his refusal to be bought. *A Covenant With Death* (Athenaeum, 1964) is the story of murder in the American

Southwest in 1923. *Dog Tags* (Random House, 1973), is a heroic and ironic novel of what happened to Korean War POWs. *When the War is Over* (Random House, 1969) is a novel based on a historical fact, the execution of a young Confederate boy by a Union Army firing squad 32 days *after* the Civil War ended!

Other Stephen Becker books include the excellent *Comic Art in America* (Simon & Schuster, 1959) and several well-received biographies. One of these was about the politician and businessman Marshall Field III, and there were translations of two books by famed author and holocaust survivor Elie Wiesel: *The Forgotten* and *The Town Beyond The Wall*. There were also at least three uncollected short stories in 1964 for *The Magazine of Fantasy and Science Fiction*. Obviously Stephen Becker worked in many diverse areas in the writing field and left an incredible body of quality work.

Shanghai Incident turns out to be one of his most expensive paperbacks, but that's not saying much as most of his paperback editions sell for $10 to $20. This edition might cost a bit more, the Gold Medal Books paperback original (as by Steve Dodge) could cost about $25. The second Gold Medal printing under the author's true name and with Robert McGinnis cover art, could run about $35.

Becker's hardcover firsts are not out of reach for most readers and collectors, most go for reasonable prices. They're certainly worth looking for to read and collect. Becker was a fine writer and even became a Nobel Prize-winning author!

So from that rather humble and obscure beginning of a noir-spy novel for Gold Medal Books in 1955 under pseudonym – great things can happen to some writers. And they did for this one. Stephen Becker had a fine writing career and produced many excellent novels. Now that I know *Shanghai Incident's* Steve Dodge is Stephen Becker, I know I will be on the lookout for some of his other books. I hope this short article will peak your interest as well in his books. They're well worth your attention.

Charles Beckman, Honky-Tonk Girl, and I

Way back in 2011, crime author, famed editor, and good friend, Ed Gorman, asked me to write this article for his internet blog.

One of the great things about publishing *Paperback Parade*, my magazine about all aspects of collectable and vintage paperbacks, and paperback publishing, is all the wonderful articles and interviews it contains showcasing so many fine artists and authors. My writers, and I, do a lot of research to find vintage era artists and authors — but sometimes they find *me!*

Like when I received an email from Patti Boeckman, the wife of legendry pulp writer and Jazz musician Charles Boeckman, Jr., who wrote under the name of Charles Beckman, Jr.

When Patti asked me in her email, if I knew who her husband was, I just blushed with joy and told her — do I! Of course I recognized his name! In fact, I had many of his stories and books in my collection. From then on I had many back and forth emails with Charles, who then in 2011, was 92 years of age. I eventually interviewed him for *Paperback Parade* #77 and we became fast friends. He was a fine gentleman, a master Jazz musician for over six decades and a vintage era pulpster who has been writing for well over a half a century. That issue of PP also featured rare excerpts from letters to him from his pulp editors of the 1940s, all about him and his work that open a fascinating window into the pulp writing business of that long-ago era. Charles wrote westerns for the 1940s pulp magazines, crime stories for the 1950s digest magazines, and one early novel from 1953, *Honky-Tonk Girl*, which I feel is a minor hard crime and noir masterpiece, a classic crime novel.

Honky-Tonk Girl tells the tough story of Jazz musician Johnny Nickles and the members of his band set adrift in a crooked town where every hand is played against him and his band mates. Beckman gives us great characters all awash in his authentic Jazz background — then he mixes in murder, mystery, and not one, but three femme fatales! It's a furiously churning noir soup. A very cool and fun novel to read. After I read it I immediately knew this was a book that was ripe for reprinting and deserved a new edition so it could be enjoyed by today's noir and crime fan audience.

At that time, through the graces of Robert Reginald at Borgo Press / Wildside Press, I was able to get *Honky-Tonk Girl* reprinted in a new and attractive trade paperback. This was the first and only edition of this book in over 60 years! It features my introduction, as well as the classic bad-gal sexy cover art from the original rare Falcon Books digest paperback edition. This Borgo/Wildside edition brings back to life a very underrated crime noir novel at a very affordable price.

Update: Anyone interested in *Honky-Tonk Girl* can still order a copy from the Wildside Press website. It is still available today. Readers interested in the further fine works of Charles Beckman, Jr. will find books about him and his work available from Bold Venture Press.

Jazz Meets Murder — on Honky Tonk Street

Honky Tonk Street is a dark, lonely and sordid edge of town where doom and despair reign supreme. It seems that every city has such a section and in *Honky Tonk Girl* by Charles Beckman, Jr., we have a stunning example of paperback noir fiction at its best — and that means bleak and deadly. Beckman, a popular pulp author and well-known jazz musician, tells the tempestuous story of cool musician Johnny Nickles and his hot but ill-fated jazz band.

This book is not the usual crime novel with a music background. In fact a cover blurb from the original rare Falcon digest paperback from 1953 says some rather tawdry things about the book, telling us, "It was the last stop for the scum of humanity on the road to hell!" Well, that's a heck of a noir mouthful and promises a heck of a lot, but it's not far from the truth for Johnny and his boys. This steamy novel tells of the rise and fall of Johnny Nickles and the members of his band as they play hot sets in seedy clubs among the whores, winos, and grifters who make up the denizens of Honky Tonk Street. With all they have to put up with, they also deal with corrupt cops, and an evil politician, while mysterious deaths haunt members of the band. It's an explosive mix.

However, that's not all Beckman gives us, because what would any self-respecting noir be like without a femme fatale? Well, Beckman gives us not one — but three admirable candidates. Three interesting women form the basis of many of the problems perplexing young Johnny. Johnny gets involved deeper with each of them while seeking the killer of his friend, popular band member and drummer, Miff Smith. These three gals were also involved in various ways with Miff, and each one of these women knows something about what happened to him — but none are talking. The three gals include Raye, the unstable daughter of big shot political boss Sam Cowles; Jean a lovely Honky Tonk Street hooker with her own dark secrets; and Ruth, a young bobby-soxer jazz buff and dangerous jail-bait. Ruth actually saw the killing but she has blotted out the traumatic image from her memory. She can not remember anything about the murder, nor help Johnny in his quest for the killer, even though he tries to reach her hidden mind for clues.

In the meantime, Johnny finds himself trapped in a deadly game with local power broker Sam Cowles, his corrupt lackey Sheriff Botello, and a deadly professional thug for hire — so danger swirls all around him. What's worse, there is the band's mysterious "Ghost Album" which memorializes and recreates classic jazz songs by long-dead masters of the art. The only problem is, it appears a killer is stalking Johnny and the band, and the wonderful music on the Ghost Album has now become a curse to Johnny and his band members with each note they hear.

Beckman mixes jazz and murder, then adds big city corruption as a chaser, as only a pulp crime author who is also a long-time jazz musician could do so. He does it admirably. The book is a haunting noir. We feel the world closing in on Johnny Nickles and can almost hear the moody jazz riffs and cool music background tightening around his neck. Beckman's text beats a worthy accompaniment to the harsh tempo of Johnny's downward spiral. In this novel jazz is not merely a background to the noir setting, it is a flesh and blood thing rich with texture that runs deep and true throughout the story. Beckman knows his stuff and struts it as masterfully as any jazzman playing a hot solo to a packed house.

Honky Tonk Girl, regardless of the sleazy title, the sexy and provocative cover art, or the cheap digest-size paperback format of the original edition, is a classy, well-written novel. Generally unacknowledged until now, and totally underrated, the book in my opinion is a mini masterpiece of noir crime fiction.

This book, which was originally published in 1953 even presages certain aspects of plot and story used so effectively in films 30 years later. For instance, Johnny's tale of the stalking of his band, the murder of his band mates, even the haunting music of the secretly made 'Ghost Album', readily bring to mind the 1983 film *Eddie and The Cruisers* (based on the 1980 novel by P.F. Kluge). In that film there are similar mysterious happenings with Eddie, and his rock band, The Cruisers. There are even missing tapes of their second album 'A Season in Hell', the music of which still haunts the living band members decades after Eddie mysteriously disappeared in the early 1960s. I don't want to give too much away here, but a similar situation occurs in Beckman's novel. While Beckman's book is about the 1950s jazz scene and the *Cruisers* book and film are about the 1960s rock and roll era, both are effective and fun, however it was Beckman and his novel who were three decades ahead on this one.

In *Honky Tonk Girl*, Beckman also throws in an interesting minor character in the tall, slim, impeccability-dressed and well-mannered homosexual sadist, Gene Hargiss-Jones. Jones does dirty jobs for political boss Cowles but he reminds me of a similar character in the Coen Brother's 1990 noir crime film *Miller's Crossing* — and that is the cold-hearted homosexual henchman, Eddie Dane, called The Dane. Both Jones and The Dane are scary guys, as well as closeted homosexual sadists. Once again Beckman intuitively picked up on a certain aspect of crime and gangsterism in his novel used effectively in a film almost 40 years later.

Johnny Nickles in *Honky Tonk Girl* is a decent sort of guy, but he and his jazzmen friends are still reeling from the murder of Miff Smith even as he tries to solve that murder in a case with more twists and turns than a Coney Island roller coaster. Beckman weaves a rich and deep tale in this slim novel. Readers today might find it quite amazing that an author can pack so many characters, so much action, and all that sharp-edged truth about the worlds of jazz, crime and big-city corruption into such a small package. However the crime authors of the pulp era never padded their stories, they never allowed excess exposition to get in the way of a hot, fast-moving tale. They knew their stuff and strutted it like the masters they were and Charles Beckman in *Honky Tonk Girl* has given us a fine masterpiece of noir that has stood the test of time.

Honky Tonk Girl has always been an expensive, difficult to find digest-size paperback that was never reprinted. The book is an enjoyable read that still holds up well many decades after it was originally written. How many other pulp paperback novels from 1953 can do that? *Honky Tonk Girl* is a terrific book that should have a prominent place on every fan's 'must-read' pile of classic noir crime. I know you'll enjoy it. Now go get *a-reading!*

Update: After this review of his book appeared in print, Charles Beckman very graciously sent me an email on October 7, 2010 with his comments on it. Charles wrote, "Thanks so much for your splendid review of my Falcon book, *Honky Tonk Girl*. I'm supposed to be a writer but words fail me when I try to express what a fine job you did on this review. Patti and I have read the review and agree that you are one heck of a good writer. You captured the characters, situation, effect, etc., so well that even if a reader had not read the book, he or she would have had a very good concept of the story. I have always been a little unsure of how well the story went over, but your review reassured me that the book had some real value. You even called it a minor noir clasic. That's praise indeed, considering the number of top rate paperback suspense novels written in the 1950s era. (Maybe I should try to find a publisher who would consider doing a reprint of the story!) Do you have an objection to my sending a copy of this review to Bill Pronzini? He has always liked the story."

Of course, I was soon afterwards able to get *Honky Tonk Girl* published in an attractive trade paperback reprint from Wildside Press in 2011, using the same Falcon Books cover art. It is still in print and available today.

Angel's Flight:
Cool Jazz & Hot Murder

It is *soooo* good.
Soooo perfect!
Can a novel be so good you could say it was perfect? The answer is yes.
I can promise you that this book will give you a jolting experience you will not soon forget. *Angel's Flight* is a classic crime masterpiece of darkness and doom set to a jazz and a be-bop beat. It's not noir despair — because it goes even lower than noir — it delves into what you might almost call — anti-life! It's that dark, dismal, and it's that good a read!

Angel's Flight was crime and thriller novelist Lou Cameron's first novel. It was originally published in 1960 as a Gold Medal Books paperback original, (#S1047), with stunning sexy gal cover art by Mitchell Hooks. As far as I know this book had never been reprinted. In 2015, in my book collector magazine *Paperback Parade* (#90), I wrote an article in praise of this book. As a result, Greg Shepard the keen-eyed publisher of Stark House Press read the book and knew it deserved to be reprinted for a new generation of readers and fans. So was born the Stark House Press special Black Gat edition — and now after over half a century — it is now available, well overdue, and most welcome for crime noir aficionados and collectors.

The story begins in the Depression Era jazz world. What was called the 'Dirty Thirties'; then it moves to 1939 when Germany invaded Poland; then 1940 when FDR sends help to Churchill and England during The Battle of Britain and on to the close of World War Two. Later on the Korean War is the time setting. However, this is not a war novel at all. Cameron only mentions these then current events through his narrator Ben Parker, to put this decades long saga of the music business into historical perspective. Cameron is telling a grand story, an epic of sorts — a noir horror tale set to a hot jazz beat.

This is Ben Parker's story. Ben's a decent bassman who is one of only three white boys in Daddy Holloway and his Hot Babies jazz band. Daddy is a three-hundred pound black piano player and most of the band is African-American of various shades of black, but Ben fits in because he's a good musician and a real friend to Daddy whom he has known for many years and has great respect. Daddy's a cool cat, a leader and a talented musician — he coulda been a contender if not for his race. These are jim crow days, and worse. Daddy plays those piano keys hard and true as he travels the country with his band, with his gorgeous mixed race daughter, Blanche, in tow. Daddy has a lot of demons that cause him to pound those piano keys like a demon himself. He's made his band a jazz legend during the Depression and in him Cameron has created a terrific and fascinating character. But Daddy's not the only character who will ring true, or tug at your heart in this fine novel. In fact, the entire book is crammed with cool cats, fascinating guys and gals of all types, and a lot of really interesting jazz and jive talk of the era that makes it a compelling read. The language Cameron has Parker use to tell his story is vibrant and rich and it rings bold and true like the music itself. Cameron uses that language like a master craftsman as he builds this compelling tale of music, life, betrayal, and much worse.

    Ben Parker's life takes so many twists and turns you could get whiplash from reading this book. Those around Ben are shown effected by the times, by the changes in jazz and the prejudices of those times which Cameron chronicles so well; the pain, the anger, the deep hurt of betrayal. The chief betrayer of them all is a young punk name of Johnny Angel. He shows up one night at one of Daddy Holloway's gigs. He is introduced in this brief excerpt from the opening of the book:

We were playing a club in downtown L.A. the night Johnny Angel blew in. That is, the first time I noticed him. I never paid no mind to the savages when I was up there on the podium, but during intermission Daddy signaled me into the wings and pointed him out.

"Benny," he said, his eyes sort of narrow, "you dig that ofay punk in the George Raft shirt?"

I looked where he was pointing. A tall blond kid in a cream sports jacket and black shirt was holding up one of the pillars near the percussion end of the stand. He was about nineteen or twenty. Sharp and good looking. He knew it.

I said, "A punk, Daddy. What about him?"
"He taggin' us, Benny. He been at every date for the past month. What do you 'spose he want?"
"So what should I do, ask him?"
Daddy looked at his watch. "No use flappin' mouths with him Ben. Do we finish this next set, though, I wants you to watch him and Franky the Drum."
"You think he's a fag?"
It was no secret our drummer parted his hair on the wrong side. He was a little mulatto with eyes like a deer. The tall kid in the cream jacket didn't look the type.

And from farther along we read:

Either way you sliced it, I didn't like that punk in the cream colored jacket.

That punk is Johnny Angel, who will destroy everything and everyone he comes into contact with. Ben will fight him in a gallant losing battle. It is only because Ben is such a talented musician, smart and bold, and a true survivor that he is not destroyed like so many others. However those others are not so lucky and Johnny Angel leaves a mighty pile of misery in his wake. Daddy Holloway is only the beginning. Daddy's a character who is as real as you or I am, a man with deep passions and emotions, one of them guys — you know the type — stand up guys who only seem to get bad breaks. His race is certainly the reason for a lot of his bad breaks, back then it was a brutal world for African-Americans to strive and even survive, but that is not the only reason for Daddy's problems. He's a good man, a trusting man, but when a monster like Johnny Angel enters your life — beware!

Ben opens his story by telling us a little bit about himself to allow us to get to know him and a real feel for his story. Now remember, he's telling us about things that happened in 1939 — in a book that was published way back in 1960 — 63 years ago! It is a black and white world in more ways than one, and no one crosses the color barrier. Cameron does not sugar coat the racism of the era, nor the racial aspects of situations that often effect his characters — both black and white. In the book Ben regularly calls blacks spades, even blacks who are his friends, but never uses the "N" word — and when other whites like Johnny Angel use the "N" word in his presence he angrily calls them out for saying it. Meanwhile, Daddy and other blacks regularly use the words ofay and cracker to describe whites. In this book, because of the times it depicts, words like "spade", "ofay", "cracker", are not always the derogatory words we know of today, they are sometimes used merely as descriptive words. Crude certainly, but descriptive and not hateful among the jazz folk, as they were often used during the times among too many regular people. It was that kind of world. You dig? So here we go!

Before you get the wrong idea about yours truly, I'd better fill you in a little on Ben Parker. That's me.

At a very early age I discovered I was queer, for women. I've never had to fight the bottle too hard, and you couldn't get me to take a puff on a stick, or a shot of stuff, at the point of a gun. In some circles this makes me sort of a square. But I survive.

As far as spades go, I can take them or leave them. Some, like everybody knows, act like they ain't been down from the trees as long as the rest of us. Others have turned out to be right guys. One of the nicest spades I ever knew was Daddy Holloway. The other was Franky the Drum.

Sure, he was a junkie and a queer. But one time in Salt Lake City, when the depression was blowing hard and cold and I hadn't played a date for many moons, Franky got me third chair in a spaghetti joint down by the tracks. They paid me in minestrone, but it kept us off the streets during the winter of '32, and that was one cold winter, Dad.

Another time, when I was stranded on the Borsht Circuit, I wired a lot of people for a ticket back to the Big Apple. Franky was the only cat who sent me one. Later on, they told me Franky sent me his last skin and had to hit the blood bank before payday. Not many cats, black or white, will give a pint of blood for a guy. Franky was as queer as a three dollar bill but, like, a friend.

Another interesting factoid about this book, it contains what may be the earliest use I've found in popular fiction of the word "gay" for homosexuals. In one part of the book, the subject of the black drummer's homosexuality comes up. Ben and he are friends, but Ben uses the word queer to describe Franky's sexual preference. The drummer tells Ben that he doesn't like that word, that he prefers the word gay. This from a book in 1960. The word 'gay' was a term not used in the general culture at that time, but was used for years in the subcultures of jazz, drugs, race, and of course, the beginning gay culture. Just one little interesting part of this book that adds to the ring of truth. Franky definitely had his problems being a drug-using, gay, black man, in a jim crow segregated world, but his worse problem of all turns out to be Johnny Angel.

In *Angel's Flight*, Ben Parker narrates his amazing journey through the world of jazz and his battles with Johnny Angel over the years. It's a wild ride and one rife with deep emotional damage and titanic struggle as Ben plays his gigs, makes his records, tries to break through the crooked payola system to get his music heard. Ben even stoops to playing on risqué stag party records to put food on the table, but his boss Flannery, who owes him some big money for the work can't pay up. Then Ben takes over Flannery's dirty joke stag record business and begins a legit outfit called Summit Records with the dream to create platters containing real music, good music. Ben knows music.

Along the way Ben meets a gorgeous singer named Ginger Tracy who he has developed into a hit singer. She's the gal that Mitchell Hooks has depicted so well in his painting used for the cover of the original vintage Gold Medal paperback.

Ben gives us a description of Ginger's appearance and her singing talent:

The song was supposed to be funny. It wasn't. It left every male in the joint with an empty ache in the pit of his gut. Ginger Tracy was cruelty to animals.

Well, Johnny Angel tries to take Ginger down too, charms her with his good looks and promises of big contracts, but Ben gets in his way and saves her. Ben falls for Ginger hard, and even though she's got lesbian tendencies and their relationship is nothing if not turbulent, Ben is persistent. He plays her legit and for once it seems to work for him. Then, just when things appear to be going well for the two of them and their love seems to bloom… Well, you'll find out!

Ben is shattered, but he somehow picks up the pieces of his broken life, like he has done so many times before. That's because Ben Parker is a survivor. But so is Johnny Angel. Johnny Angel however is not only a survivor but also a user, a betrayer and a con man — not to leave out he's a prime louse and crook. Throughout this book the two men keep crossing paths until there is a final confrontation that will stun you with its utter viciousness and sheer…evil.

With all that fine story behind it you might assume the title of the book concerns Johnny Angel. It does not. In fact, Angel's Flight is an actual place, a scenic lift in Los Angeles, a place where Ben and Ginger meet for a date that turns to disaster. Four decades later top crime author Michael Connelly would use the title for one of his famed Harry Bosch crime novels *Angel's Flight*, which also concerns events at that historic LA landmark.

Meanwhile, Johnny Angel turns out to be anything but an angel. He has become the manifestation of evil in the music world and a destroyer of everything and everyone he comes into contact with. He is a user and a con man, a cheat and a liar who always seems to get away with everything. We all know people just like him. In the end, the book offers some stunning revelations.

The author, Lou Cameron (1924-2010), was a well known American writer, but he was also an accomplished comic book artist. As a comic book artist, he illustrated Classics Illustrated and horror comics before becoming a writer. Then as a writer, Cameron became the author of dozens of excellent Gold Medal paperback original crime and spy novels written from 1960 to 1992. He also wrote 15 books in The Stringer western series, and dozens of paperback original westerns in The Longarm series under his pseudonym Tabor Evans — he wrote at least 52 books in this series which defined the then new 'adult' western genre, in a series that eventually ran to over 400 books. The Longarm series was later continued by famed author James Reasoner. Cameron wrote many other books under many other pseudonyms including John Wesley Howard and Ramsay Thorne, and he wrote many film-to-book novelizations. In 1976, Lou Cameron won the WWA Spur Award for the best western novel of the year for his novel, *The Spirit Horses*.

Angel's Flight from 1960, was Lou Cameron's first book. Judging by this first effort, I am sure many of you will be on the lookout to read his other fine novels. In *Angel's Flight*, Lou Cameron created a be-bop jive jazz noir novel that sings loud and true with terrific characters, has real heart and is a joy to read. Without a doubt it is an underrated and unacknowledged noir masterpiece. So stop wasting your time with whatever book you are reading now, and take a deep dive into this classic story of cool jazz and hot murder. I tell you true, you're in for a real treat!

Fiction Too Tough:
James Hadley Chase

He was born Rene Brabazon Raymond in London in 1906, but the name familiar to mystery and detective story readers around the world is James Hadley Chase.

Chase wrote in the tough guy school of American type detective thriller novels popular in the pulp era, though he never set foot in America. He wrote over 60 books though not all are always available in paperback and many have multiple titles, which can make things difficult not only for the bibliographer, but the reader as well. Add to this the fact that he also had some of these books published under the pen-name Raymond Marshall (not to mention Ambrose Grant and James L. Doherty – which I will mention anyway) and you can see things could become a bit confusing. We're going to try and keep things simple here, concentrating really only on one book – the one that made his name notorious, and it's sequel – but first a bit of overview and other stuff about Chase.

James Hadley Chase had been a door-to-door encyclopedia salesman.

He took up writing with the intention of making money – and he wrote for money. He began writing when he worked for a large firm of book wholesalers, and during that time he wrote his first book, *No Orchids For Miss Blandish* (aka *The Villain and The Virgin*). He wrote it in just six weeks of white heat in the Summer of 1938. It was published in 1939 in hardcover in the United Kingdom and became an immediate sensation.

No Orchids is the violent and bitter story of the terrible kidnapping of a young millionaireess by a group led by a madman criminal and his vile mother. Other critics said it was modeled somewhat on William Faulkner's *Sanctuary*. Nevertheless, it was a tremendous success. It was said that five years after its publication it had sold 500,000 copies – this is in a British hardcover before there were paperback reprints. Sales figures I have seen listed for it from years back show that more than 13 million copies were sold. This was Chase's most famous and successful book – though not his most bizarre nor most outrageously titled.

Among his many fans, the French have a high regard for Chase's work, and films of his novels have been made by the French cinema. *No Orchids For Miss Blandish* was also made into two films, in 1951 directed by St. John C. Claves (?) and in 1971, called *The Grissom Gang* directed by Robert Aldrich.

Like the Mike Hammer stories of Mickey Spillane, which Chase preceded by a decade, it seems the prime motive at work in Chase's books is the hard crime pulp thriller often with the theme of the pursuit and holding (or consolidation) of power by criminals. Many of these books seem to be elaborate power fantasies, pure and simple, and they were, and are, very popular because they reflect the frustrations and desires of many ordinary working people who read them. But there's more to it than that – which we will get to in due course. The main thing is that Chase knew his audience. In a sense he used the violence as a catharsis for our fears and frustrations, though some early

critics thought his books went too far.

Nevertheless, Chase's work is always entertaining and interesting, though his fiction can be rough and hard – some say it is purposefully cruel. And some of it seems to be, but then it's a cruel world and Chase was trying to tell it like he thought it was. He was amazingly accurate when it came to understanding the criminal mind.

Some of Chase's books show the hero as a criminal and critics denounced his books at times because of this. Other detractors do not like the violence and just plain brutality of his stories – many of these books once they came out in paperback often added outrageous and sexy cover art that strangely enough was not that far off the mark in depicting a scene from the actual story. The most outrageous of these paperback reprints which was oh *soooo* politically incorrectly titled is *Twelve Chinks and A Woman* – but then the brutal image of a woman getting her clock cleaned by a guy's punch to her face on the cover of *Kiss My Fist* is another real nasty one. Talk about violence against women! Then there is the shocking drug and white slavery novel *The Marijuana Mob* (aka *Figure It Out For Yourself*) which also has some interesting characters, the US Eton paperback reprint, with that cool title and some nice gangster cover art offers a classic hard-boiled image.

But it was with *No Orchids For Miss Blandish*, his first book, where Chase not only made his name, but became notorious in certain circles and it set the stage for the murder and mayhem to come in many more of his hard crime novels.

In 1939, the critic John Mair listed the casualties in *No Orchids For Miss Blandish*:
— Guys rubbed out: 22 (9 with gun, 6 with tommy-gun. 3 with knife, 2 with blackjack and, one by suicide)
— Guys slugged bad: 16 (15 in face or head, one in the guts)
— Guys given workover: 5 (3 with blunt instruments, one with a knife and one with burning cigarettes)
— Dames laid: 5 (3 willing, one paid, and one raped)

This critique was supposed to shock the reader and put them off the book. Today hard crime fans look at it as a beacon to good stuff they must read. A lot of stuff is happening in this book. A hard-boiled classic! And it is!

Mair was complaining about a book that was as tough and brutal as you could probably get in 1939 in a mystery crime novel, but this was only the beginning for Chase. He continued writing for many years, decades even, and his popularity had always been high and his sales steady.

More critics — damn them! — Boileau and Narcejac said that Chase created what they called "The formula of the cruel novel."

An interesting letter on Chase and Orwell from L.B. Hurst in the UK appeared in the UK mystery fan magazine *CADS* #32 from February 1998. In it Hurst says:

"Thanks to book searches by Jamie Sturgeon and Ralph Spurrier I now have the three editions of James Hadley Chase's *No Orchids For Miss Blandish*. Three, you ask, but Hubin (1984) lists only two – the infamous novel of 1939, published by Jarrolds, and the revised edition published by Panther in 1961. Yes, but that ignores the second edition which was published again by Jarrolds sometime between 1942 and 1945 (the copy is wartime but with no date of publication given), which was a novelisation of the stage play. And the 1961 edition seems closer to the novelisation.

"The Panther edition comes with a publisher's note, and I think it is worth observing a couple of things: firstly the reason for Chase's revisions. These are quoted as the author's 'who feels the original text with its outmoded dialogue and its 1938 atmosphere would not be acceptable to the new generation of readers who may be curious to read the most controversial, the most discussed and the best known gangster story ever to have been written.' Secondly, the author and the publisher were aware of critical studies of *No Orchids*. They mention George Orwell's 'Raffles and Miss Blandish' (published in *Horizon* magazine in October 1944) and *Persephone* by D. Streatfield (RKP, 1959).

"Now, I had read 'Raffles and Miss Blandish' long before the novel, and I read the paperback, which was the only one available to me back in 1972, looking for the quotations Orwell gave, and cursing Chase's 1961 revisions which cut them out. Now I can find them, and what have I found? That Orwell mis-quoted, and no-one ever seems to have noticed or bothered to comment.

"Orwell says that Chase has 'hundreds of thousands of readers who ... understand at sight a sentence like 'Johnnie was a rummy and only two jumps ahead of the nut-factory.'' Let's take that sentence as an example – it was not in the 1961 copy I read. It's not in the novelisation. And it is not exactly in the original. Orwell had quoted from memory, abridging a long paragraph, and misspelling the name. It is on page 33 of the first edition: "Johnny was a rummy. He lived for drink and looked it. He lived by hiding anyone on the run. His place was known to most of the hoodlums in the district, but the Federal Agents had not got on to him as yet. He stood looking at Bailey with watery eyes. Drink had rotted him, and he was only one jump ahead of the nut factory."

"From the novelisation onwards the 'nut factory' disappears, and in the paperback edition Johnny has been 'ruined' by drink, not 'rotted'.

Orwell says 'the book sold, according to its publishers, no less than half a million copies'. My copy of the novelisation, on its title page, says '510th Thousand'. Did Orwell have copies of both editions with him when he wrote, but ignored checking either when he quoted? Did the publishers keep the two editions in print simultaneously? Why have editors and critics not noticed the discrepancy between Orwell's essay and the text in question? Can any CADS readers enlighten us? And why did Chase change his novel so frequently, and to so little advantage?"

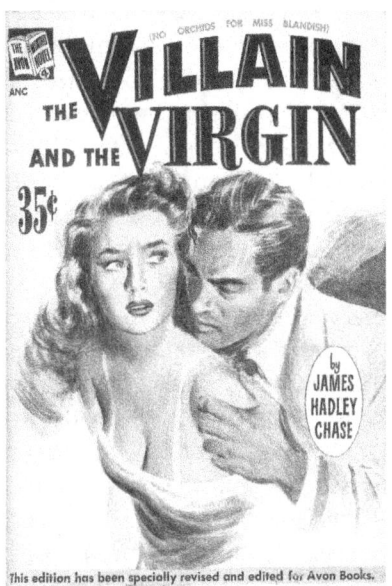

I would venture to say that the answer as to why nobody noticed Orwell's misquote is because he was Orwell – a literary god. Chase was 'just' a crime writer and one who was looked down upon by critics of the period, a man who wrote in a genre that was looked down at by critics of the period. Literary snobbery triumphant and no one would even question any quote by someone of the stature of George Orwell. I've just read Orwell's article – and quite honestly – he just doesn't get it at all. He was so wrong about crime and crime fiction and he had no understanding of the criminal mind. On the other hand, he did write *1984*, so...

Here is additional information form the "Publisher's Note" that appeared in the 1961 UK Panther paperback edition:

"In 1942 the play of the book, written by the author and Robert Nesbitt with additional dialogue by Val Guest, was presented by George Black at the Prince of Wales Theatre, London, where it ran for seven months. The principal players were Robert Newton, Linden Travers, Hartley Powers and Mary Clare. The provisional tour ran from 1942 to 1949. In 1945 Renown Film Company persented the film version of the book at the Plaza Cinema, London with Linden Travers and Jack La Rue in the star roles."

Here is an excerpt from a letter by scholar and researcher Steve Chibnal writing in *PBO* #5, Summer 1997 issue, and what his research had to say about Chase's novel and British soldiers in World War II:

"An early report in the *Daily Express* suggested that soldiers wanted only thrillers, 'the gorier the better', while the most popular novel with the troops, and probably the best selling novel of the whole war, was James Hadley Chase's pseudo-American story *No Orchids For Miss Blandish* published by Penguin's down-market rival, Jarrolds, of the Hutchinson Group. *No Orchids* was typical of what *The Bookseller* described colourfully as 'drunk and disorderly reading' and it's notoriety was sealed when George Orwell singled it out as a prime example of popular fiction's degeneration into a 'cesspool'. Describing books like *No Orchids* as violent power fantasies 'plainly aimed at sadists and masochists', Orwell deplores their atmosphere or moral ambiguity and glorification of brutality, and likens their psychological appeal to that of fascism and totalitarianism. Given the choice between the American 'jump on his testicles' school of writing and the refined snobbery-with-fisticuffs stories of E.W. Hornung's Raffles, Orwell will take Raffles. But the socialist critic's opinions found more favor among *Mass-Observaton's* largely middle-class panel of reporters than among working-class readers. As one panel member opined, 'I don't buy books of the calibre of *No Orchids* because I cannot bear the poor style in which they are written, and so far as the sexual experiences contained in them are concerned, I consider myself my own private life far more interesting.' But with sales in excess of half a million, it seemed more people preferred the private life of Miss Blandish. The book defined the borderline of pornography, and the less salubrious Charing Cross Road dealers could not keep up with demand. As one observer reported:

"'A young girl comes in a shop to sell an armful of second-hand books. Amongst them is a copy of *No Orchids For Miss Blandish*. She smiles rather shamefacedly at the assistant, 'It doesn't matter about that one if you don't want it,' she said (sic) nervously. Maybe we don't want it,' answers the assistant, 'but if you are not doing anything tomorrow morning come round here and watch the queue for it...there will be one.'"

Vintage paperback collectors have always shown a lot of interest in Chase's work because of the violence, sex, exploitation and political incorrectness. A Chase book usually is violent, may deal with a taboo subject, often has an outrageous title (this guy could really pick provcative titles), and usually had cover artwork which may also be very violent or illustrate a subject that may be sensitive today. That of course is all on the surface – they say not to judge a book by it's cover – but of course we all do. The cover and title are the first thing we see and they catch our eyes on any book. Chase's books usually have titles and covers that are always noticeable, they get your attention and some of them have been called offensive. Nevertheless, once away from the superficial packaging, Chase is actually a good writer who tells some damn good stories which have held up rather well over the years to become mini-classics of the mystery genre.

Today, eager collectors gobble up books by Chase – especially the older and scarce titles for which he is an author whose work seems to be disappearing and is increasingly difficult to come by.

Chase wrote novels about a variety of detective protagonists. The private detective Dave Fenner who appears in *No Orchids For Miss Blandish* appears only in one other novel, *Twelve Chinks and A Woman* (1940). The same is true of his other detective heroes. Vic Mallory, Mark Garland, Corrigan and Don Micklem all appear in only two or three novels.

It is said that Chase was never tempted by using a fixed character in a series. He regularly killed off his characters who threatened to become troublesome or limiting and he has said, "How can one possibly create suspense if the reader knows from the outset that the hero will survive?" So Chase kills the hero every so often so the reader can never be sure what is coming.

No Orchids For Miss Blandish stars private eye Dave Fenner, a former newsman, who is hired by the husband to find kidnapped heiress Miss Blandish, who is missing for 3 months. Miss Blandish was kidnapped by two criminals, Bailey and Riley, who heard she was rich and had a $50,000 necklace. They kidnap her to rob her originally, then think they can ransom her, but the Grisson mob kill them and take her from them to sell her back to her husband. Ma Grisson and her homicidal and sadistic son, Slim are two of a kind, as mean and deadly as Ma Barker and her brood. Or worse! There is an unhealthy relationship between Ma Grisson and her son Slim, and all the men in the gang. Ma was a terrible, fearful, dominating and heartless bitch – but smart. Though Chase never mentions incest or sexual abuse, Slim did not get the way he was by accident, and that is another way in which Chase's writing either by experience or intuition latches onto the truth behind violent and brutal crime examining the roots from which it springs.

No Orchids ends with the death of Slim. Ma goes down fighting and kills four cops with a Thompson machine gun. Miss Blandish is saved by

Dave Fenner. She has a child, Carol, the result of a rape by Slim Grisson. Or just maybe, it's not a rape – maybe it's one of the earliest cases of "Stockholm Syndrome" 40 years before Patty Hearst. Miss Blandish seems to lust after Slim and is both disgusted and attracted to him. It is obvious this inner conflict leads to her eventual suicide four months after the birth of her daughter, Carol. Miss Blandish commits suicide by jumping out of a window. By the end of the book almost everyone is dead except Fenner. This is a tough, nasty, unrelentingly bleak crime novel.

And just when you think there is some saving grace through all this with the birth of Carol Blandish, in the sequel we continue the violent and nasty noir darkness. You see, Miss Blandish's daughter, Carol, has now grown up, and it is feared she has taken most of her genes from her beast of a father, Slim Grisson.

The background of Carol Blandish in *The Flesh of the Orchid* conforms to the then popularly accepted stereotype that genes trump environment or upbringing. Carol Blandish is kept in a sanitarium for the criminally insane, she's thought to be a homicidal maniac, but she escapes and falls into the hands of the Sullivans. These are a duo of brutal killers as nasty and vile as anything Chase has written.

Here's the origin of Carol Blandish from Page 13 in *The Flesh of the Orchid*:

"*This is what you don't know: before she died she gave birth to a daughter. The father of the child was the kidnapper, Grisson.*"
"*And this child is your patient – grown up? Is that it?*"
Travers nodded.
"*The child, Carol, was exactly like her mother in appearance, and Blandish couldn't bear to have her near him. Carol was brought up by foster-parents. Blandish never went near her, but she lacked for nothing. The fact that her father was a mental degenerate made Carol suspect, but for the first eight years of her life she showed no signs that she had inherited anything from her father. But she was watched and when she was ten she ceased to mix with other children, became morose, developed violent tempers. Blandish was informed and engaged a mental nurse to watch her. Her tempers became violent and it soon became obvious that she wasn't to be trusted with anyone weaker than herself. By the time she was nineteen it was necessary to have her certified. For the last three years she has been my patient.*"

Steve, Carol's lover dies at the hands of the Sullivan's, another crime team right out of Ma Grisson and her gang. Carol blinds one of the gang when she escapes, then goes after two more (Frank and Max – the notorious Sullivans) to kill them for the murder of Steve. The last 30 pages of the book are about Carol's release into normal society. See, she's not crazy and she gets control over her money (Her grandfather's and mother's money from her lawye/guardian) who we find out kept her locked away in the sanitarium to control her wealth.

One really interesting character Chase gives us is Miss Lolly, the former circus bearded lady (who has a full beard down to her naval) who helps Carol Blandish to escape her kidnappers, Tex (Lolly's husband) and the brutal Sullivans. Miss Lolly is also a hero who kills Max as he tries to get to Carol's hospital room to murder her.

This is a wild book, a worthy sequel to *No Orchids* and Chase amazingly kept up the action, intensity and violence with some interesting characters in a good plot.

The Sullivans are just as brutal and sadistic as Ma Grisson and Slim. Here is Chase's brilliant description of them from page 42:

Two black crows.

The description fit the Sullivans. They were a sinister-looking couple in their black, tight-fitting overcoats, black slouch hats, black concertina-shaped trousers and black-pointed shoes. Knotted around each short thick throat was a black scarf.

A few years ago they had been the star act of a small travelling circus, and they had been billed as the famous Sullivan Brothers. But they were not brothers: their real names were Max Geza and Frank Kurt. By profession they were knife-throwers and trick marksmen. The finale of their act was to throw phosphorus-painted knives at a girl who stood against a black velvet-covered board. The stage was in darkness and the audience could see only the flying knives, which gradually outlines the figure of the girl as the knives slapped into the board an inch from her shivering skin. It was a sensational act and might have gone on for years only the Sullivans got bored with the circus and with the girl.

The Sullivans tried to get another girl, but for the money they paid they couldn't find a girl willing to risk the flying knives and also be accommodating after business hours. So they got fed up with the circus and told the manager they wanted to quit, but the manager refused to release them from their contract. Their act, he reckoned, kept the show together – and it did.

So one night Max solves all their problems by throwing a knife with deliberate aim and it pinned the girl through her throat to the board, and that finished the act, got rid of the girl and broke the contract. Max

couldn't understand why he hadn't thought of the solution, which was simple enough, before.
  It was Max's idea for them to become professional killers. Death interested him. Taking human life seemed to him to be God-like, and he liked to regard himself as a man set above and apart from other men. Besides, he wanted big money; he was tired of the peanut stuff they were making in the circus.
  Frank welcomed the idea.

Here is one particularilly chilling scene of the murder of Roy on page 53:

  "No!"" Roy screamed as the gasoline ran over his head. "You can't do this to me! Steve! Help me! No…no…no…!"
  Max fumbled in his pocket, found a match, struck it alight on his shoe.
  "Here it comes, ol' man," he said, and laughed.
  "Ever seen a guy burn?" Frank asked Steve. "Even when they're dead they jump and twitch… like a chicken with its head chopped off. We burned a guy a couple of weeks ago. He went up like a firework and the crazy lug ran right back into his own house and set that on fire too…burned his wife and kids." Frank shook his head. "Take a look at that," he went on, suddenly excited. "That's what I call a blaze. He's cooking fine now, ain't he? Now watch him run… they always run. There! Didn't I tell you?…Watch him!"
  Steve shut his eyes, put his hands over his ears.

  Chase's description of the Sullivans, once again either through experience, or pinpoint intuition, captures the essence of these killers. Modern studies of serial killers and mass murders tell us of the God-like narcissism of these evil people. How they feel above the law, society, and all other people, especially of the power they feel when they take a life.
  The sheer enjoyment at murder the Sullivans exhibit in this novel, their gruesome joy at the horror of setting people afire may seem extreme, but it is accurate. These are violent criminal misfits who look at other people merely as 'things' to be manipulated, or used. When you are no longer useful to them, they kill you.
  Chase knows these people well and shows them to us in these two books unfettered and true to form. Chase's observations of crime and criminals are brutal and violent, absolutely as his critics suggest, but that is only because he is spot-on accurate in his characterizations of these criminals and the way their minds operate. He knows them, almost too

intimately.

Critics like George Orwell had no idea of the grit and horror out on the streets. Orwell should have stuck to his political observations, which were where his true strengths lay. Instead it appears that Orwell's, and other, elitist's pseudo-informed observations about Chase and *No Orchids* probably led to Chase and the hard crime genre not taken as seriously as it should have been. Chase was not only telling powerful, exciting, brutal stories, he was warning us about the monsters who hide among us and showing them for what they truly were. It would take us, and FBI profilers, 50 years to catch up with him, and with what he knew so well.

However, it is Chase's readers who never flinched at the inaccurate barbs Orwell, and other critics of his ilk, threw so cavalierly. It was the 'people' who bought Chase's books, the people who read them, and the people who enjoyed them by the millions, for decade after decade. Much as Mickey Spillane would be vilified early on in his crime writing career by the no-nothings and the do-nothings, James Hadley Chase told brutal and violent stories that rang amazingly true to form, and you can't ask for better than that.

Sin Town:
Sleaze Noir at its Best!

When I read a novel that surprises me by the quality of the story and writing — whether it is a classic, or a low-down sleaze paperback — I can not help but write an article about it so as to share it with others. In fact, my enthusiasm for such books makes these articles sometimes seemingly write themselves. I guess it's the thrill of discovery.

A lot of 1960s sleaze (soft-core) adult novels are actually very well done crime noir novels and one of the better of these — while still being a prime sleazer with all that entails — is *Sin Town* by Dell Holland (Bedside Book #1233, 1962, pbo, an ass-kicker in just 192 pages).

Sin Town tells the torrid story of Eddie Chase, in a novel loaded with old-time ambience about the Brooklyn waterfront, the area around Red Hook and Sand Street at the Brooklyn Navy Yard, back in the day when that area was a rough sailor hangout, and a vital Navy part of the port of New York. It is also a novel of Manhattan's Greenwich Village which was a melting pot of wild beatniks, heavy booze and some very kinky sex — straight, gay and a lot in-between. This book is crammed full of accurate and pointed descriptions of that particular early 1960s 'scene' — but as was the law about books such as these, there is nothing at all sexually explicit here.

Into this heady mixture comes young 'sea-going tom-cat' Eddie Chase, who leaving his Navy career from the Fifth Fleet — with a thousand bucks of back pay cash burning a hole in his pocket, and lust and ego the size of Manhattan — now goes on a mission of booze, beautiful babes and brawls. He finds them all and more in Greenwich Village.

From page 13 we read Eddie noting the luscious women of New York in his own unique horn-dog description:

Marveling at the abundance of first-class quail to be seen, Eddie took his time. There were all kinds of women striding along the glistening pavement: tall, short, slender and bulging like a bag filled with cantaloupes. Some were apparently models: long slim made-up creatures with arrogant, aloof eyes, hurrying quickly towards their next appointment, heels clocking like castanets and hard little buttocks twitching from side to side with each step.
Even the working girls, the secretaries, receptionists, clerks and

typists were eye-catching, though they too had the city's look of don't-come-close-to-me in their eyes. Occasionally women with breath-taking beauty would pass by like beings from another planet in simple, clear-cut outfits that shrieked money. In any other city in the country all traffic would halt as they came by, smooth thighs shielding their precious treasures, breasts boldly jutting out against expensive dresses while their eyes, expressionless as a statue's, surveyed the shop windows.

Poon tang! Eddie was in the Poon capital of the world.

The story also involves Eddie's only friend, Chuck Huzak, who like Eddie is also a Navy quartermaster and still in the Navy. You see five years earlier Chuck was in college and had it going good with a doll named Kathy — but he couldn't hack the domestic life and he skipped out on her and joined the Navy. That action destroyed Kathy and set her upon a road of sexual degradation. Chuck has loved her ever since. Soon he shall meet her again and the dark noir twist of the knife will begin to cut deep.

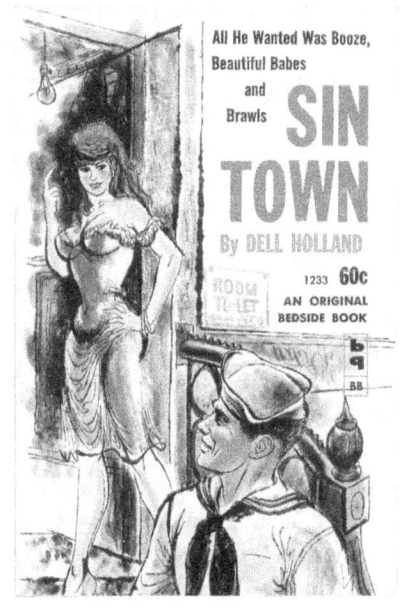

So now, five years later, Eddie is out of the Navy and looking to get together with Chuck and soon the two begin their downward spiral into the weird world of Greenwich Village, the wild women and the bizarre morality.

Eddie is a primitive type guy, down to earth, well-meaning but a fighter with a temper, a good-looking young stag chasing after every skirt that he sees and taking them all where he can get them.

The sleaze part of this novel is fun and campy being represented in the story describing some of Eddie's conquests with some great over-the-top writing that piles on the sexual innuendos and red-hot prose. Actually, the author was a master of the language when it came to the sleaze form describing sex without being explicit about it. For instance a sex tryst from page 115 between Eddie and his best friend Chuck's former gal, Kathy — who is now married to Hal who is sleeping in the next room — gives us this torrid description:

> They slammed together in feverish haste, joined and locked together in towering, upward-spiraling release, gasping and clutching each other as he sank deeper and yet deeper into her excited body.
> "Oh, Lord, yes, yes, yes!" she cried, her heated belly matching his quickened pace.
> Possessed by lust, they strained their rutting bodies together in an upward mounting, towering explosion of flesh that seemed to take them up and away from the entire universe in complete and mutual surrender.

Wow, they sure don't write 'em like that anymore! Actually, the author of this book, like many other writers of sleaze was obviously a competent professional writer.

Whoever Dell Holland was, he was a very good writer. He knew New York, the Navy, Brooklyn, the Navy Yard, the 8th Avenue hookers, and the Village and he saturated the book with the taste and feel of it all. It really makes this book stand out. He also knew how to tell a tough and sad noir story. Eddie and Chuck and the women they bed and betray — or who betray them — offer the doomed desires and twisted truths that are in the best tradition of noir novels. This one has it all.

Eventually, Eddie shacks up with Selma, a sexy hot artist in Greenwich Village. In one scene on page 122, Holland gives us a sarcastic but pointed description of some of Selma's hipster friends:

> They were a typical Village group. Most of them were gonna be artists of one kind or another. They were gonna write a book, gonna act, or gonna paint some time in the far-off future. In the meantime they devoted their energy to criticizing people who actually were doing something.

You can not get more accurate than that about a certain mentality and Holland nails it perfectly in less than 50 words. It is as true today as he wrote it then! In another brief passage on the same page, the author describes a typical Village beatnik coffee house of the era:

> Paul's Place was an old cellar beneath a tenement cleverly made up to look like an old cellar. Dust an inch thick covered the floors and tables, which consisted of raw planks laid over barrels. Some refugees from the junkie ward on Riker's Island made half-hearted attempts to force music out of their instruments, but barely were able to make themselves heard over the shrill gabbing of the packed crowd. Clouds of thick, yellow smoke swirled over bearded and pony-tailed heads.

Who was this guy?

Dell Holland must certainly be a pseudonym or perhaps a house name. Whoever he really was, he was very good! *Sin Town* is peppered with stark truth and sharp observations like the few examples I have included above, and they make the book worth reading in and of itself.

Hawks Authors Pseudonyms says that Dell Holland was actually William R. Coons (1904-1992), (verified by Lynn Munroe in his interview with Coons), who was a writer of many sleaze paperbacks in the early 1960s. Coons is an interesting fellow. He was also an instructor of English at Skidmore College, a liberal arts school in Saratoga Springs, New York. He also spent 15 months in Attica Prison, from March 1970 to June 1971, for possession of LSD. He was the author of *Letters From Attica* (1972), and was somewhat disdainful of radical policies because he saw them as naïve, but he anticipated a "Payback time."

That "Payback Time" may have come three months after he was released. In September, 1971, there was a revolt by 1,300 Attica inmates that began a five day siege of the prison. Three prisoners and one guard were killed in the riot; 20 inmates and 10 guards were later killed by the police and New York State Troopers when they took over the prison from the inmates under orders of New York Governor, Nelson Rockefeller. I rememeber that time well.

It was a hot political issue at the time. Politics aside — the fact that Coons was released from Attica three months *before* the riot began, and if you read the prisoner's manifesto — it is well written, logical, concise and stating some valid concerns — I wonder if it is possible that Coons, an incarcerated radical English instructor, at war with the "System", and a professional writer himself — might have offered his writing talents to the cons during his stay there. Perhaps even giving writing classes to the very leaders of the future revolt who would pen the Attica revolt manifesto?

While I have talked about Coons and the surprisingly good writing in *Sin Town*, the actual printing of the book — the text — has some interesting points to mention as well. Sleaze publishers played notoriously fast and loose with the text of these books. They often dropped entire chapters if the book ran too long, ended the book seemingly willy-nilly before the actual manuscript ended if it ran too long, or added extra stuff the author did not even write to fill it out, or sex it up more! *Sin Town* would not be a lower-end sleazer if it did not have some problems with the text, and it can be a challenge for the reader to decipher some of the sentences. For instance, there are quite a few paragraphs where at the end of a line — the sentence is continued two or three lines farther down on the page — with apparently unrelated sentences in between. Or there is no text at all! The text just ends in mid paragraph! The printer probably dropped the page a few sentences — or maybe even paragraphs! On page 118 the slipshod composition by the typographer has left in the book title, with "galley gutter", (instructions for the printer), printed after the third paragraph. However the strangest and most absurd example I have never seen on any vintage paperback, is on page 52, the third paragraph, where there is not only an unrelated line of text in the middle of the paragraph — the text line is *upside down and backwards!*

The above quibbles aside, and they are small in the overall quality of the book as goes the writing, *Sin Town* gives us a terrific story of Kathy's fall, and Chuck's descent into doom, all in a plot in the best noir sleaze tradition. Meanwhile, our tom-cat hero Eddie is caught in the middle of it all and is going down fast! Will he make it? He has some tough choices to make. Read this one and find out. You will not be disappointed — but most likely surprised and delighted!

A Look At
Marijuana Girl

There's nothing I like better than reading a vintage paperback in the original edition. Especially books that are 40, 50, or more years old. It's like going back in time — when that book was first published — you get a glimpse and real feel for those days and the people in reading such a book.

And such a book is *Marijuana Girl* by the enigmatic and mysterious N. R. De Mexico. It was originally published in a 127 page digest paperback by Uni-Books (#19) in 1951, and sports an excellent 'bad girl' photo cover. It's a real beauty and quite scarce. The book was reprinted a couple of years later in another digest size paperback, this time from Stallion Books (#204) with identical cover and contents, and that is even more scarce!

At the time I originally wrote this article, back in 1992, over 30 years ago, I had no idea who N.R. De Mexico was — perhaps only a pseudonym? However, he is credited as writing quite a few similar exploitation digests in the 1950s. Sex and drugs seemed to be a large part of this author's stock in trade and he seemed to know his stuff, especially around the drug and Jazz club scene of the early 1950s Greenwich Village in New York City. More about him later, in the mean time let's take a look at the book he wrote.

Marijuana Girl begins in the sleepy Long Island town of Paugwasset and is about a young high school girl, Joyce Taylor, a blonde bombshell ready to try new thrills and adventures in the big bad world of Paugwasset and beyond — and that eventually means New York City.

Joyce is a 17 year-old high school senior and begins her adventures when she is kicked out of her school for doing a strip tease in study hall. Study hall was never like that when I was in high school! I must have went to the wrong school. Anyway, Joyce is obviously a wild girl, but she gets more than she bargains for with cheap thrills, bad company, and *pot!* The cover blurb tells us, "Joyce Taylor would try anything…once!"

On the first page of the book, one of the high school boys notices Joyce, and he immediately calls out, "Hubba, hubba," and from there on she is on every red-blooded male's radar.

Joyce is on the fast track downward in this sleazy exploitation-titillation novel, and we all get to take a ride with her. And it's not a bad ride. The book is well-written, interesting, and seems fairly accurate in its limited delving into sex, drugs, and the Jazz scene of the early 1950s. A sleazy period piece, but enjoyable — and there is a good story told here as well. What more could you ask for? This is, after all, a sleaze digest on the lowest-end of the publishing scene in the 1950s.

One of the charming aspects of the book is an actual "Jive" glossary included in the back of the book that defines such enigmatic and hip words from long ago as "horse", "smack", "reefer", and other mainstays of the Jazz and drug culture back then. There's a lot of stuff here, much of it has since found it's way into our language today and is nothing special — but back in 1951 it must have been way off the beaten track for almost everyone.

Not too soon after the story opens there is an older guy who enters the picture. This is Frank Burdette, the 31 year-old city editor of *The Courier*, who loves Jazz, and as the blurbs tell us, has "…also brought the cult of the weed — marijuana." In this novel, as in a lot of similar books from this era, Jazz and drugs are inextricably linked — which is the way a lot of it was in those olden days.

Frank takes things as they come:

"he was conscious of wrong doing in indulging himself in a smoke now and then, though in Pauwasset he kept its use secret from everyone but Janice, his understanding wife. She knew that it was an almost inescapable part of his background, a product of formative years spent in the company of musicians, entertainers, and others who took "tea" smoking as much for granted as others take tobacco smoking."

But as things so often happen, when Frank's wife leaves with their son for a three month visit to Maine, Joyce Taylor comes into the picture. Joyce fascinates Frank when she comes to work on the paper as a copy girl and they go out for lunch together — then they go out to a Greenwich Village Jazz club — and then one thing leads to another, as it so often does, and then…you can guess the rest!

There are some decent descriptions of the early Village Jazz scene in this book that almost make it worth reading all by itself. Almost, but not quite, and there is the sex/drug angle which I have to admit is very mild and incredibly campy by today's standards. Or lack of them!

The Jazz club Frank and Joyce go to is on 8th Street in the Village. It's called The Golden Horn. I don't know if any place with that name ever truly existed. It's described in an interesting manner.

"The air-conditioning was insufficient, the seats were wire-backed and hard to the touch of spine or buttock. But the music was the best. Here, from time to time, came Sidney Bechet, Louis Armstrong, and other greats of native American music. Here had played such supermen as the immortal Bix Beiderbecke. Here was the temple of a noble art."

And further, *"Here they came to attend the important business of drinking, smoking and listening to music. In taxis, and afoot, by bus and subway and private car, they came to have their pulses speeded by the hammering rhythms, their minds diverted by a spectacular run of guitar or piano — to have their attention caught, breathless, by glittering arpeggios. Here, too, came Frank and Joyce."*

And, of course, there was the smell of marijuana throughout the club, *"an odd smell that clung to everything and damped down the atmosphere. It smelled a little like burning hay — old hay. But there was something else of the odor that made it different. It was a touch of sweetness that made the odor nearly pleasant..."*

Well, now...

So Frank and Joyce enjoy the club and the music, and eventually go outside near the NYU campus with two Black musician friends of Franks.

"Wait a minute," Frank said [to Joyce] as Jerry started to pass the case. *"You know what this is?"*
"No. I — you mean..."
Newspaper stories of Jazz musicians floated through her mind.
"Is it marijuana?"
Jerry said, *"That's right, honey. That's the grass. It's the greatest."*

And that's how it happens in this novel. Joyce is on her way down the marijuana road to a life of misery and sin and we all take a ride with her. It's hard with today's knowledge to take the content of this book seriously, since it may seem silly today. However, this book was looked at seriously enough at the time for it to be cited in Congressional committee hearings.

On a historical (or perhaps hysterical?) note, in May, 1952, the United States House of Representatives authorized a probe of paperbacks, magazines, and comic books for so-called "immoral, obscene or otherwise offensive matter". These were the notorious Gathings Hearings (named after their sponsor, E.C. Gathings, Democrat-Kansas) and one of the books they commented on was *Marijuana Girl*. They stated:

> "Other paper-bound books dwell at length on narcotics and in such a way as to present inducements for susceptible readers to become addicts out of sheer curiosity. As an example of how this subject is handled by current books, one need only read Marijuana Girl by N.R. De Mexico. A more appropriate title would be: "A Manual of Instructions for Potential Narcotic Addicts!" ...even the evil effects of drug addiction are made to appear not so very unattractive by artful manipulation of the imagination. While the analysis of this book has been directed chiefly to its narcotic phase, that should not be construed as implying that it is not replete with lewdness and vulgarity."

Come on, guys! This book wasn't that bad, even for the narrow standards of the 1950s, when you look at what was going on in comic books and the horror pulps at that time. (Of course, these guys did just that — they looked at comic books and pulp magazines as well. They put E.C. Comics out of business — but that's another story.)

I wonder if the committee members ever saw a copy of *Junkie!* by William Lee (an Ace paperback original actually written by Beat poet William Burroughs, which came out *after* these hearings), which also had a glossary of dope terms and was daringly subtitled "Confessions of an Unredeemed Drug Addict!" Unredeemed? I think their heads would have exploded over that one. As it turned out, others would notice that book soon after it appeared and write about it.

So *Marijuana Girl* has this bit of history and controversy behind it, and that makes it all the more interesting as a curio and collectable. It was pretty popular in it's day, and continues to be popular today among rabid paperback collectors. The book was reprinted as a digest paperback only once in a scarce Stallion Book (#204) a few years later. It is an almost identical edition, but seems even more scarce than the original Uni-book edition! *Marijuana Girl* was also reprinted twice in rack-size paperback years later. First by Beacon Books (#328, 1960), which was affiliated with Uni-Books, and still later on from Softcover Library (a continuation of the Beacon series) in #S75124 in 1969.

Many years later, sometime in the 2000's I believe, (because my copy has no publication date on it), it was reprinted in a facsimile edition in a small size paperback (4" x 5.5") by Fender Tucker's Ramble House Books. A lovely and scarce edition.

Most importantly, there was also a Stark House reprint in trade paperback, under the title *A Trio Of Beacon Books* from 2019 which contains a fascinating and important introduction by collector and scholar Jeff Vorzimmer.

In this book Jeff unearthed the true author behind the N. R. De Mexico byline and he gives us some information on the enigmatic pseudonym — and the real man behind the N.R. De Mexico name. It seems that De Mexico was a mystery until about ten years ago when Kim Bragg, the son of the author came forward to claim that the name was a pseudonym of his father, Robert Campbell Bragg.

Bragg, it turns out, was a writer who wrote many sleaze digests as De Mexico and under other names. He was also the editor of *Suspense* magazine. So he was a talented author and editor. Unfortunately he tragically died too young, at just 36 years of age in February, 1955. Bragg died in a Greenwich Village grocery store. Since the Gathings Committtee witch hunt was well underway in 1952, soon after *Marijuana Girl* was published in 1951, it is assumed Bragg did not want to draw attention to himself as the author of such a controversial book, and since he died so soon afterwards, his credit for the pseudonym had become lost in time.

A Trio of Beacon Books a trade paperback from Stark House contains *Marijuana Girl*, as well as *Call South 3300: Ask For Molly* by Orrie Hitt; and *The Sex Cure* by Elaine Dorian. Jeff's introduction to all three of these classic sleaze noirs, and the story behind them and their authors, is fascinating and important. If you can not afford the original Uni-Book, or the even more rare, Stallion Book digest of *Marijuana Girl*, this is the book you must get. *You will enjoy it — even if it goes against Congressional recommendations!*

Author's Note: This article is expanded and updated from one that appeared in *Paperback Parade* #28, March 1992 issue. For more information on *Marijuana Girl and* the Congressional investigation, see *Hardboiled America*, pages 116-117; *Two-Bit Culture*, page 235; and of course Jeff Vorzimmer's introduction to the Stark House Press edition of *A Trio Of Beacon Books*.

"Borrowed Love"
Romance as Dark Noir!

Sometimes you can uncover an interesting and very good book wrapped in the most unlikely of packages. Such a situation came about when I found myself casually perusing a group of hard-boiled 1950s UK gangster digest paperbacks, leering at the sordid cover art, and reading the racy titles. Enjoying the books entirely, and wondering just how each promise the book seemed to offer would be delivered in the story. My mouth was watering with the prospects of these delightful crime goodies.

I found one with rather nice sexy gal cover art by R.W. Perl that caught my eye, but it seemed to be more of a romance than anything else and that did not make me all that interested. I don't really like romance novels — even rare 1950s UK ones. I don't collect them and I don't read them, but there was something about this one that got my attention. The book title was *Borrowed Love* by Joel Johnson, who was actually British pulp author Norman Firth, (Grant Hughes, UK, no date, circa 1949, and just 96 pages) but it definitely looked like a romance. Kind of… In spite of what the cover blurb told me:

THE SHADOW OF DEATH STALKS MARSEILLES! A story of vile treachery and a terrible crime committed by a ruthless killer and how retribution eventually overtakes him.

Actually that sounded rather good to me. But the book really "looked" like a romance. Yes, there was a sexy gal on the cover drawn by the ubiquitous Perl, so that was a plus. Yes, she was a rather lovely gal shown in the throws of — something — passion? Despair? Whatever. Yes, she did have a rather languid, sorrowful look about her, though, enough to make me wonder — but there was no gun in her hand. That's a dead giveaway for a gangster crime novel. There was no tough gangster standing beside her, or behind her on the cover. But she was holding her hand over her breast, so I was in a bit of a quandary as to just what I had here. I was, in fact, mildly chagrined. Was this a romance? The title and cover art certainly seemed to scream romance, but like I say, there was something very interesting about this one.

I looked over that slim 96-page UK digest paperback, and the book intrigued me as I took a closer notice. I opened the book up as I do with many books to casually peruse it, and began to give the first page a read to see just what I had here. I don't mind admitting that it is not what I thought it was. At first, what it appeared I had was a rather gritty hard-boiled Foreign Legion novel! Or so it seemed. Well, the book was only 96 pages after all, so I decided to give it a read and see where it led me. It led me to what turned out to be a taut murder noir thriller and very well written. In fact, I was unable to stop reading it until I finished it. Here's the incredible story.

At the beginning of *Borrowed Love* we are introduced to Harold Mills, a French Foreign Legionnaire who is in prison for desertion. He's the black sheep of a well-to-do family back in England, the twin brother of Gerald, the white sheep, good-guy of the Mills clan.

Well, Harold, acting exactly as black sheep do everywhere, stole money from the family firm, caused great scandal, was about to be arrested, so he escaped the police and England and figured he'd hide out in the French Foreign Legion. Big mistake! In a dark tale somewhat reminiscent of *Beau Geste,* Harold finds out that the Legion is not his bag at all, so he deserts. That's another bad move because he is captured. Now he's in prison in Algeria for desertion. He escapes by accidentally killing his jailer, the kind-hearted fellow by the name of Swede. Accident or not, Mills is now a murderer! A death sentence — the rope, or the guillotine - awaits him if he is caught. He must get away. Through the help of the dancing girl Eta who he has met in a den of debauchery in

Algeria, Mills finds a way to freedom. Eta is described as a quintessential bad gal:

> She was Eta; she did not know her other name. Her mother had been a low caste Frenchwoman, her father a low caste Arab with a trace of negro blood in his veins.
> Strangely enough the product of their union was small and dark and lovely. Her taut brown body wriggled and writhed to the tune of the reed pipes. Her sole covering was a small girdle which circled her waist, and from which hung tenuous strands of silk.
> Spawn of evil as she was it was only natural she should be evil herself. And she was. (p8-9)

Eta helps Harold Mills get out of Algeria after he pays her all the money he has and gets him to the French seaport of Marseilles. Now Mills finds himself trapped in another den of darkness and in dire circumstances as he hides from the Legion, being a deserter and a murderer. His only hope is a response to a letter he has sent to his twin brother in England, pleading with Gerald — the good-hearted Jerry — to come at once and bring him money.

> He could only hang out and wait, and hope, and sweat and smother in the foul air which never left the building, in the narrow room where the fleas played leap-frog with the cockroaches, and which he dared not leave. (p16)

Meanwhile back in England, good-hearted Jerry is all set to wed the lovely Andrea but the letter from brother Harold, whom he thought dead, suddenly arrives and begs for his help. While Harold is a miserable lout and a nasty lowlife not deserving of any help, Jerry the good soul, immediately leaves for Marseilles to help his brother. In the meantime, he leaves his lovely and chaste Andrea in the hands of his good friend Barry, who looks out for her. Barry does not know the reason for his friend's trip to France.

In Marseilles, Harold waits for Gerald with growing alarm. Will his brother even show up? Harold admits he has been a nasty and evil brother to his good twin, there would be no reason for him to come to his aid now. He would certainly not do the same were the situation reversed. Harold is about to give up all hope when Gerald finally arrives in the disgusting flop-house flea-ridden dive where Harold is hiding out.

The reunion between the twin brothers is one of harsh bitterness. The brothers have nothing in common and have never liked each other.

Harold sees his do-gooder brother as an upper class prig who got all the breaks in life. Gerald sees his black sheep brother as nothing less than a criminal, a rogue he does not approve of at all and who is not to be trusted. Nevertheless, they are twins and brothers, so blood runs deep. Apparently, however, not quite deep enough.

Harold tries to reconcile with his brother somewhat, thanking him for his help even as he greedily grabs up the money he has brought him. Still in the guise of brotherly affection, he gets Gerald talking about home and family. He asks him what he has been doing? Who his friends are? When he hears about Andrea and the impending marriage he pumps Gerald for information about her also. Of course Gerald proudly shows Harold a photo of the lovely Andrea and Harold lusts quietly for her. After some time, when Harold believes he has learned all about Gerald's life in the five years since they have been apart, once he believes that he has caught up on all he has missed in his brother's life back in England — *he kills him!*

In a shocking scene, Harold a cold-hearted and evil man twisted with hate for his better brother and lusting for his wealth and good life, shows just the type of man he is.

A monster!

Harold murders Gerald in cold blood without any qualm, then assumes the identity of his twin brother. He puts on his brother's clothing, affects his speech and mannerisms and in essence, Harold has now become Gerald. Then Harold sets his dead brother up to be him — dressing Gerald's corpse in his Legion uniform substituting him as the deserter and murderer who has now apparently committed suicide because he has come to the end of his rope. Left behind is a convenient suicide note for the local Marseilles police.

Case closed!

Then Harold, now in the identity of Gerald, heads back to England and Andrea.

He had borrowed his brother's life and clothes, why not his intended wife? (p22)

Harold returns to England taking his place now as Gerald Mills — the good-hearted, very decent chap whom all like — the future husband of the lovely Andrea and the best friend of the adventurous and somewhat lecherous Barry Arnton. But Harold has a big problem impersonating his brother, especially interacting with Andrea, Barry and the family. The people who know him best. It is far harder than he thought for his dark and twisted nature to be good and bright, so hard for him to be Gerald true to form. Harold can not help but revert to his vile nature. Andrea and Barry notice something is very wrong. Andrea admits Gerald has changed since he has come back from Marseilles, but she does not alert Barry to the real reason for his trip, only asks his aid to help Gerald, his best friend.

Harold just gets in deeper as he tries to adjust, trying to hide his true evil nature without success. He makes excuses for his strange behavior by saying he's just 'not himself' since he got back from France. He hints he went through a stressful situation there, but will not explain any further. Okay, that will work for a while, and it does. Andrea loves Gerald, and Barry as his best friend wants to help, so the two work together to do what they can for their friend. But Harold keeps acting odd, and things do not add up.

At the same time Harold is surprised that he is now feeling some actual guilt for killing his brother, who after all, only came to help him. He had no such feelings at the time he had murdered his poor brother. Now he dreams dark nightmares of Death coming for him for what he has done, and he keeps seeing this strange apparition of a little grey man that begins to haunt him day and night. The little grey man has the odor of Death about him. Harold fears he is going mad and cries out in the night at the appearance of this fearful apparition. Andrea, staying at the mansion, and Barry always around now to help out, try to understand their 'sick' friend, but they are beginning to become suspicious.

Harold also lusts after the lovely Andrea — what's not to like, she's a dish! — so at first he was very keen on the marriage and consummating the relationship. And not necessarily in that order. However, he realizes that the whip welts on his back given to him for his desertion punishment from the Legion would give his impersonation away — then Andrea would know the truth. So the wedding is postponed. That causes more suspicion by Barry and considerable hurt to Andrea. Gerald is just not at all the same man he was before he went away, and she begins to wonder if she ever really loved him at all. Meanwhile Barry and her are becoming close, all in their efforts to help Gerald, of course.

When Peabody turns up one day things really begin to get out of hand. Peabody knows the truth and has evidence of Harold's game and the murder of his brother, but he won't talk if he's paid 12,000 pounds. With his knowledge and evidence he intends to bleed Harold dry of funds. Harold realizes:

He knew what he was in for — an unscrupulous bleeding, by a monster of iniquity almost as ruthless as was he himself. (p60)

So Harold knows what he must do and does it. He murders Peabody, then dumps the body, but he is discovered sneaking back into the house through a window by Andrea and Barry. They were supposed to have been out to the theatre together but have come home early. They feel something is not right.

Next day the murder of Peabody — as yet unidentified — is in all the newspapers and Barry recognizes the photo of the murdered man as the person who had visited Gerald at the house just the day before. Barry is immediately suspicious. Barry confronts Gerald/Harold and gets him to admit he murdered Peabody because the man was blackmailing him. Harold asks for Barry's support and silence. Barry, reluctantly gives it.

"Look here, Jerry." Barry replied. "It's bad enough you having committed a murder — don't try to justify yourself into the bargain."
"Shocked?" said Mills, the faint sneer returning.
"Did you expect me to take the news that my best friend had taken a human life, calmly?"
"He wasn't human, none of his kind are."
He was alive anyway — until last night!" said Barry. (p76)

Barry keeps a close watch on Gerold/Harold, following him to a pub where Harold gets soused on cheap booze with an even cheaper slatternly street woman. Barry is utterly shocked by this behavior and acts to take care of his friend by carrying the unconscious man back to his apartment. There he notices something even more shocking than his friend's unconscious drunken state — Barry notices Harold has no gold teeth in his mouth. So now he knows for sure that this man can not be Jerry!

Barry immediately leaves Harold in the care of his very proper butler Percival with orders to watch him and keep him there any way he can until he gets back. Percival is an amusing minor character, the most proper of all English Gentleman's gentlemen. One wishes there was more of him in the story.

"But sir — we are not very adequate when it comes to the art of fisticuffs." (p-86)

Meanwhile, Barry picks up Andrea, then goes to Gerald/Harold's dentist and discovers the truth. He convinces the dentist to take Jerry's dental records and then accompany Barry and Andrea to his apartment. Percival meets the trio at the door.

> The door opened, and Percival, the valet, looked out at her. But not the usually immaculate Percival she knew. This one sported a multi-colored, swollen eye, and a burst nose. His dressing gown was smeared with blood, and his hands dithered as they wiped industriously at his bloodstained chin.
> "Percival! What...?"
> "I told the master I was unused to fisticuffs, Miss," said Percival mournfully. "Mr. Mills woke up whilst we were in the kitchen preparing a cup of coffee — he appeared to be in a very bad temper, and insisted on leaving to return home. When we told him we considered he was in no condition to return anywhere, Miss, he became extremely vulgar in his language. He —-" continued Percival plaintively: "Hurt our feelings! Yes, indeed." (p-90)

Harold has split, but Barry and Andrea, with the dentist in tow, track him down back to the family home. There Harold confronts them with a gun but he admits everything; the murder of his brother Gerald; the murder of Peabody — he even mentions the little grey man who he insists has been following him. Of course, no one can see this grey man.

Harold next orders the dentist to tie up Barry and Andrea as he makes his escape, taking the 12,000 pounds he was to pay Peabody, planning to leave the country for America. He takes Andrea's roadster and drives off, all the time he sees the little grey man standing in front of him, the odor of Death about him, as the road ahead winds and turns dangerously, his attention fixates on the apparition. It will not go away!

> The little man in grey was there, even though Mills had covered his eyes — and now, at the last, his waiting was done. He was smiling — (p-96).

The book ends with a short epilogue set during the honeymoon of Barry and Andrea. Barry has reformed his wild ways, and the two live happily ever after. So in a way I guess this could be termed a darn romance! Somewhat. But it's a lot more — a well-written and intriguing noir thriller as well. The characters are well drawn, the writing is short and sweet, the story is rough and the end is satisfying. This is a most enjoyable noir murder mystery and quite underrated. I could not put it down, and I was compelled to find out how it ended. You can't ask for more than that from a short 96-page pulp fiction paperback novel. This one might just surprise you, just as it did me!

Update: This fine novel was reprinted in a British hardcover book in

2014 by the Linford Library under the title *The Little Grey Man* by Norman Firth. It is worth searching for.

Bruno Fischer:
A Writer We Should Remember

He was a class act all the way, the consummate gentleman and professional writer, and a very decent, sweet and warm person. He was also a very underrated writer, who wrote thrilling crime fiction and marvelous mystery novels.

That's the Bruno Fischer I knew, late in his life before his sudden death in 1992. He'd graciously been a guest at my New York City book show a year earlier and I did an interview with him in my book collector magazine, *Paperback Parade*. That led to my reprinting one of his classic crime stories, "Five O'Clock Menace" in my crime fiction magazine, *Hardboiled*. All that just naturally led to *A Mate For Murder*, an original trade paperback collection of his unpublished pulp thrillers written for the shudder pulp magazines of 1940. All these stories had sold, and he had been paid for them, but then with the advent of World War II, the magazines suddenly all folded and the stories were never published. They languished in his files for decades until he took them out and sent them to me. Once I read them, I knew that they had to be published in a new collection and they were. Thus was born, *A Mate For Murder and Other Tales From The Pulps*, a trade paperback published under my Gryphon Books imprint.

Sadly, Bruno did not live to see a copy of that book which came out only weeks after he passed away in 1992. It was his last book. He would have enjoyed it. I know that seeing those old pulp thriller stories finally collected in book form would have brought a twinkle to his eyes and a smile to his face.

That twinkle in his eyes was something I'll always remember

about Bruno. That twinkle in his eyes fit his personality so well because you could plainly see that behind his old eyes, was a mind that was as agile and sharp as it ever was. He was a master writer, a man of true intellect, but a weary warrior then grown in age.

Bruno was also a hero for progressive causes. When they really meant something. He had been the editor of *The Socialist Call*, and even ran as a Socialist candidate for the New York State Senate. He was later a founder of an independent community in upstate New York in the late 1950s for progressive and creatve people to live the kind of life they wanted to live. He was a non-communist democratic socialist, a man dedicated to making the world a better and fairer place. He was also one of the original founders of the Mystery Writers of America, an organization created to support and promote writers who wrote in that genre.

Bruno Fischer actually had three careers as a writer. His first career was as a writer of sensationalist shudder pulp thrillers for the pulp magazines of the 1930s. These stories had outrageous titles — usually creatively devised by overly imaginative editors — but the magazines were a good training ground for young writers. Bruno learned well. Today, almost a hundred years later, his early stories still stand up well. They are also fun to read.

Bruno began his second writing career in the mid-1940s on a much more serious note, with a host of popular hardcover traditional mystery novels such as *Quoth The Raven* (Crime Club, 1944); *The Dead Men Grin* (McKay, 1945); *The Pigskin Bag* (Ziff-Davis, 1956) and *The Restless Hands* (Dodd, Meade, 1949). These mystery novels were all later reprinted in paperback in the 1940s and 1950s by major paperback publishers such as Dell, Signet, and Pyramid, and were kept continually in print during his lifetime.

The third part of Bruno's writing career began in 1950 when he wrote original crime novels in paperback for Gold Medal Books. Gold Medal began by publishing paperback original novels — it was the first time ever for that book to appear in print — and they naturally turned to Bruno as one of the writers to supply them with quality original novels. Beginning with *House of Flesh* (Gold Medal #123, 1950); *The Lady Kills* (GM #148); *Fools Walk In* (GM #209) and many more. Bruno eventually produced a total of ten excellent original noir crime novels for Gold Medal Books. With all these original novels and reprints appearing, Bruno became one of the quintessential paperback writers of the 1950s. His work was very popular and widely reprinted in this country and around the world throughout the 1950s to 1970s.

It's a damn shame that so few of those fine novels and short story collections are in print today. Bruno Fischer is one of the neglected masters of classic crime fiction and his work is very underrated.

Bruno was also a hell of a nice guy and I felt privileged to know him, even though it was only for a few years. I still think of Bruno today, so many years after his death, and I miss him. He'd made that much of a lasting impression upon me.

Bruno Fischer was one of the true greats in the crime and mystery field: a classic pulp magazine writer in the 1930s; the author of many fine traditional mystery novels in the 1940s; and an excellent hard crime and noir storyteller with his Gold Medal original paperbacks of the 1950s.

Bruno Fischer is a writer we should all remember, and a writer we should enjoy and continue to read. I hope this brief article will help to keep his memory alive and help to bring his fine works into print once again for a new generation of readers to enjoy.

Update: In 2015, Stark House Press reprinted *The Bleeding Scissors & The Evil Days*, two of Fischer's most famous crime novels in an omnibus trade paperback edition.

Rediscovering Bruno Fischer

Bruno Fischer wrote 25 mystery novels that have sold over 10 million copies and have been translated into 12 languages. That's the cold hard facts of his writing career but it tells you nothing about the real man. The real man was neither cold nor hard, but a wonderful writer and the most decent of gentleman. I met Bruno and got to know him during the last years of his life and was privileged to have him as a guest at my annual book show in New York City. He was a joy to be around, with a winning smile and a mischievous twinkle to his eyes - even though he was almost blind from a life of writing and editing. He was very kind and generous and we became good friends — a friendship I treasure to this day. Bruno was a special person I will never forget. He generously allowed me to reprint some of his short crime stories in my magazine *Hardboiled*, and eventually I published a collection of his horror/terror pulp tales, *A Mate For Murder And Other Tales From The Pulps* under my Gryphon Books imprint in 1992. Sadly, before that book appeared Bruno passed away from a stroke on March 16, 1992 while vacationing in Mexico with his wife, Ruth. It was a terrible time and as the years passed Bruno's books went out of print and were only available in old rare hardcover editions,

or yellowing vintage paperbacks from the 1940s and 50s. Bruno Fischer was becoming a forgotten author, but he was never forgotten by serious crime noir fans who knew the 'good stuff' and savored it.

Bruno's work is the good stuff! It is time to rediscover Bruno Fischer and his classic crime fiction, and the perfect place to begin is with the two outstanding suspense thrillers that make up the 2015 edition from Stark House Press: *The Bleeding Scissors & The Evil Days*.

Bruno Fischer was a master storyteller who conjured his magic with words as he learned his craft in the pulp magazines of the 1930s. Under his own name, and a plethora of pseudonyms, most notably Russell Gray and Adam Train, he wrote pulp suspense noir tales that were dark stories of tension, thrills and train-wreck intensity. In each tale he piled on the tension and suspense until it grew to a pulse-pounding crescendo. These stories became hits with the reading public of the era and were beloved by editors of the pulps who always asked him for more. These stories are still great fun to read today. In some cases Bruno wrote most (if not all) the stories in some issues of those old pulp magazines. This training ground in the pulps enabled him to hone his talent to a sharp precision, and as that talent grew it transformed him into one of the best crime suspense authors in the pulp magazine field.

Later, through a series of hardcover crime novels published in the 1940s (all of which were reprinted in paperback by Dell and Pocket Books in the 1940s and 1950s), as well as some outstanding crime noir paperback originals done for Gold Medal Books throughout the 1950s, Bruno Fischer eventually became one of the best and most popular crime authors of the era.

The two novels that make up the special Stark House Press edition of *The Bleeding Scissors* (1948), and *The Evil Days* (1973) are examples of Bruno's best work. They highlight his wonderful plotting and creativity, mixed with his trademark suspense and tension, all building with every page you read. Reading these novels is a pulse-pounding experience as each scene piles on the stress and tension to dizzying heights.

In *The Bleeding Scissors*, Leo Aikens is caught up in a seemingly humdrum normal domestic life, until his wife, Judith, turns up missing. Has she run off? Or is it something worse? Evidence points to conflicting answers — of which the police have none — but the tension and plot twists come fast and furious. Leo soon realizes that he must seek out the truth himself so he begins his own investigation to find out exactly what happened to his wife — and his wife's sister — who is also missing. The two women have simply disappeared and there seem to be no clues. No reason. However, the young women have a local reputation among some in town as the 'wild' Runyon Sisters. Leo grows concerned over those rumors, but he knows Judith, and is sure she is in danger and that she has not just run off with some 'mysterious young man' as the cops and neighbors tell him.

Leo's investigation leads him into a complex case full of sinister characters, back-stabbing motives, blind greed, and heart-pounding excitement. The reader follows Leo with nail-biting tension as he gets closer to the truth and discovers answers he does not want to face. This novel is a fine noir, full of memorable characters such as Leo's enigmatic wife, Judith, and a charming fellow known as Singleton — both of whose motives are suspect. Bruno Fischer keeps the twists and turns racing right up to the end as he piles on grand doses of tension and suspense. This is a most memorable noir crime thriller, an enjoyable read of the type they just don't write anymore. It is a classic!

Then in the 1960s Bruno took on a job as editor of Macmillan's Collier Books, a paperback outfit, as well as education editor of the Arco Publishing Company. He had been an editor in his younger days, editing *The Socialist Call* in the 1930s, but then left to write crime stories full-time for the pulps. In his ten years as editor at Collier Books he was responsible for publishing many fine books. However his editing work cut severely into his writing output so it was not until ten years later, in 1973, that he published his 25th and last novel, *The Evil Days*. This one is simply outstanding!

In *The Evil Days*, we are introduced to Caleb Dawson, solid citizen, along with his very nice wife Sally. They are contemporary suburbanites on a tight budget, trying to eke out their life with two young kids. He is an editor at a big New York publishing house — much as Bruno was himself at the time. And here Bruno includes much fascinating and rather cynical but pinpoint truth about the publishing business and the writing game.

In one cynical scene that most likely came from Bruno's own experience in the business, he has his hero Caleb talking with another editor about the publication process in their office:

"Caleb, are you there?" he called over the partition.
"Yes."
"Last night I spent a little time on that Carlton novel you asked me to look over. By all means take it on."
"Don't tell me you liked it!"
"What's that got to do with it? It's up to his usual standard — incredibly bad. What's to the point is that he sells."
"I know. That's why I hesitate to turn it down. If only he knew a bit

about writing."
"If he learned how to write, he'd rise to mediocrity and lose his public."

That's some biting satire right there — but most probably very accurate!

Caleb and his wife are soon thrust into a whirlwind of dire circumstances when she finds a treasure trove of priceless jewelry in a strip mall parking lot. Instantly their life changes as they see this windfall as the answer to all their financial woes. The jewelry is said to be worth more than a quarter of a million bucks. Caleb and Sally's plan is to keep the jewels and sell them for cash — instead of return them to the rightful owner. That decision leads them into dark deception and danger as their moral standards collapse in the lust for riches. Of course in any good noir, these things never work out very well and the plot piles on the stress and tension, while including devious twists and turns that make this story an experience you will never forget. The book takes place in just one week, one chapter per day, it begins on a Wednesday and the pace roars like an out of control locomotive.

By day seven, a Tuesday, Caleb puts together the many pieces of this convoluted puzzle and it is a real shocker. You are in for a terrific mind-blasting conclusion where all the known — and some surprising, but fair to the reader, unknown — knots of this complex noir puzzle are revealed.

The Evil Days is Bruno Fischer's masterpiece. It is a little known sleeper of a noir that has until now escaped detection by more astute critics — other than Ed Gorman, who has praised it highly. Now you can experience this fine novel yourself. Greg Shepard and Stark House Press have done a great service for all crime and noir fans by bringing out this attractive new edition of *The Bleeding Scissors* & *The Evil Days* for a whole new generation of fans and readers — all of whom can now rediscover the outstanding noir crime fiction of Bruno Fischer. I'd like to say now *relax* and enjoy these two stories, but I've read them and I know better! *You won't be able to relax!*

Hard-boiled Paradise: Al Fray

They tell you Paradise can be a wonderful place, unless it's the tough noir world of hard-boiled crime fiction. That's a world that can be hard on the writers and often brutal for the readers to experience. Which most of us kinda like, actually.

We all know the greats in the genre who have gone onto their rewards: Chandler, Hammett, and lots more. One that went onto his reward but never made it to Hard-boiled Paradise was Al Fray.

Al, who?

Actually, his real name was Ralph Salaway (1913-1991), who for a brief five-year period from 1956 to 1960 wrote five outstanding and underrated hard-boiled paperback original crime novels as Al Fray. Fray had his first novel published in 1956, another in 1957, two in 1958, and his last in 1960, by three different paperback publishers. Then he seemed to have disappeared forever. Or did he?

Fray's work had themes. Two of the main themes or motifs in all his books that keep coming up again and again are trucking, or driving for a living, and gambling, especially a detailed and intimate knowledge of craps/dice and scams, cons, and bust-outs associated with crooked dice games.

Unfortunately, I don't know a heck of a lot about Fray (Salaway's) real life background, but it seems a lead-pipe cinch that from his books and protagonists he had an intimate knowledge of gambling since his early years. His characters take book (bets) and shoot dice, sometimes even running the dice games, sometimes crooked games in High School, in the Navy, in Korea, and they sometimes even get caught. And when they do they never forget it!

A crooked diceman getting caught cheating in a game full of angry losing swabs aboard a Navy ship at war can land a fellow in a terrible jam. This happened to Fray's lead character in the novel, *The Dice Spelled Murder*. Fray knows and uses the term "gobs" (slang for sailors) and mentions the important Navy town of Norfolk, Virginia in this novel – he wouldn't know these details unless he had seen some Navy time himself, probably in Korea as the hero of his novel did. Fray's other characters also are often truckers, and he seems to have intimate and personal knowledge of this trade as well. And somewhere along the line, Fray could have been a pro lifeguard in Los Angeles in the 1950s because that background comes through in two of his books as well. But this biography of Fray (Salaway) is all supposition on my part based only on information within his books.

These five books offer some outstanding hard-boiled crime stories and some interesting characters. This is not classic work, Fray is not Chandler or Hammett, but he is very, very good and his books are a sheer pleasure to read. Very enjoyable. And you can't ask for more than that from any author.

Al Fray debuted with *And Kill Once More* (Graphic Book #118, PBO 1956, with cover art by Saul Levine). In this first book a pro lifeguard in Los Angeles, Marty Bowman, also becomes a bodyguard to lovely Kate Weston and ends up involved in murder.

Marty's a lifeguard, and his dream is to buy a commercial swimming pool and set up classes, parties, and live the good life (probably a 1950s southern California dream) – or continue the easy life of a lifeguard and beach bum. However, his private eye brother goes out of town and sets up Marty as a bodyguard for a doll that seems like easy money, and the curves come free.

Again, as in most Fray novels, nothing is as it seems at first, and there are possible ulterior motives by the dame. Marty is paid to protect Kate from some sinister danger she'll not talk about, and one she will – her friend Sandra is being held prisoner by a cruel husband in a secluded desert estate. Or so it seems. So Kate and Marty go along on a holiday that starts off looking like fun. But when the host is murdered, Marty appears to be a likely suspect in a frame with a great cast of wacky characters who are guests at the estate that weekend. It's a hard-boiled twist on the traditional murder mystery and Fray pulls it off well. It reminds me of Raoul Whitfield's *The Virgin Kills*, which has its setting on a rich man's yacht. Fray's book is a fun read and his apparent personal knowledge of the life and business aspects of swimming, lifeguarding, and the pool biz, add to the rounded character of Marty. I like Fray's writing too, it's no nonesense, sparse but it gives you all you need to know to move the story along, and there are good twisty plots where unexpected things happen. I also like his characters, especially his hard-boiled guy heroes who ring so true, and the femme fatale dames mix sex with danger in a way James M. Cain would have been proud. Fray was definitely onto something. Unfortunately, *And Kill Once More* probably got little notice, no reviews, and too few readers. Graphic didn't do another book by Fray, but Fray didn't let that stop him. He moved up to better pastures, because his second book next year came out from a better publisher, and to me this book is one of his best.

The Dice Spelled Murder (Dell Books First Edition #A146, PBO 1957), is the first book where Fray will delve into his main theme, gambling, craps, and especially and most interestingly, various ways to cheat at dice.

Danny Hogan is thrown out of high school for cheating with shaved dice at craps, and he's given the choice of jail or the Navy. Jail is not an option so he takes the Navy. It was the Korean War era and we were at war. In the Navy, Danny continues his cheating ways aboard ship and gets caught. He receives a terrible beating, something that stays with him for the rest of his life. Now years later in civilian life, Danny tries to turn away from dice and cheating, which is all he knows how to do, when he meets up with wicked Velda, a red-hot, red-headed dame who snares him into a crime team-up. The scam is to take conventioneers at ritzy hotels in a crooked floating crap game. Dangerous, but the payoff could be large.

Danny's a nice guy, he doesn't want to do the scam but a sudden trucking accident where he almost lost his life in an unsafe vehicle makes him change his mind. However, he's scared to do the con, he still smarts from being found out on that ship years back and knows the beating he'll get if he gets caught this time could be fatal.

Nevertheless, Velda and Danny team-up. All Danny wants to do is get enough cash for his dream – to own his own trucking company – all Velda wants is to own her own motel.

From page 22, Fray writes about Hollywood dreams:

"*...by the very nature of things the great majority were destined to* *travel down the same rut they toiled in today, the dreams getting more vague with the passing years, the rut wearing deeper, until at last the rut attained a final depth of six feet..."*

They do well at first, raise a lot of cash, rip-off a small-time syndicate. Danny ends up seeing some jail time, and eventually is sprung by Velda and a friend. But things are not right.

Danny's narration also reeks with craps and gambling lore and cheater's pointers by one who apparently knew – great scam artist and confidence man info. Fray knows his stuff. The games are described perfectly, every action, every player, maneuver, victory, defeat, is written with fascinating detail and hard-learned insight.

Fray's writing is excellent in this book and really captures the hard-boiled feel of the hardball trucker and ex-GI back from Korea looking for a break – or a dream. The book compares favorably with Jim Thompson's *The Grifters*. It's not as nasty in tone, but it gives a lot of detail on various scams and the players in the game. I think it is an unacknowledged classic of its type, the grifter/scam novel.

Fray seemed to get better and better with each book. In 1958 I think he hit his stride with two books out that year. Both were paperback originals from Dell Books. The first was the trucker saga, *Come Back For More*, the second was the noir mystery with a lifeguard protagonist, *Built For Trouble*.

Come Back For More (Dell Books First Edition #A161, PBO 1958), is a revenge book, and a damned good one. Fray's hero is a former overweight bank clerk named Swede Anderson who becomes a tough guy grifter and trucker and now goes under the name of Warner McCarthy. McCarthy joins forces with feisty Gail Tyler who has just inherited a trucking business from her murdered husband and is struggling to make a go of it for herself and her young daughter. Shades of *Shane* without horses but with trucks in the roughneck trucking business.

Syndicate guys want to buy Gail out but she won't sell. Then they start to put on the pressure. Along comes McCarthy to work for her and he starts to turn things around in the failing outfit. The mob takes this rather badly and what we end up with is a well-fought, hard-boiled novel that screams toughness and attitude with every word. This is the book that got me searching for and reading the other four Al Fray titles – and I've never been disappointed. It's a good book and a minor classic.

Built For Trouble a Dell Books First Edition #A167, PBO 1958, cover price 25-cents. It includes probably what is one of the worst-ever covers done by Robert McGinnis, it's pretty bad. It shows the delicious and evil

Nola but must have been done by McGinnis on an off day, or it was a rush job. Also, collector's note, there is a variant edition on this one, with a 35-cents cover price and a line under "Dell" on the spine being the only differences. All this aside, *Built For Trouble* is a fine noir crime story with a sexy and devious femme fatale.

Eddie Baker is an easy-going Los Angeles beach lifeguard who goes out to save a woman from drowning one day but he ends up being saved from drowning by *her!* It's the usual Fray twist in plot with a lifeguard setting he's used before. The woman who saves Eddie is Nola Norton, petite sex-pot bombshell actress, who incredible enough ends up saving the life of the big male lifeguard! To be sure it becomes a major media story. Eddie becomes a laughing stock, the papers play it up big and his bosses angry at the ridicule he's brought to them and their profession force him out of his job. It was a job Eddie loved, a real sweet gig, and he is crushed.

That's the first time Nola screwed up Eddie's life, but not the last.

Eddie's life goes in the toilet after that, he not only has lost his job but he looses his girl too. He ends up leaving town, drinking, and his downward spiral continues as he tries to understand how this could have happened to him. Then he hears the news another lifeguard named Sawyer, a shadowy character, has died from bad booze. Eddie smells a rat and thinks it could be murder. He checks out Sawyer and discovers that he also had some business with Nola, and in checking his place finds a can of air. He realizes Nola and Sawyer faked her drowning and planted the air canister for her to use when she *saved* him. Now he knows he was set up!

Eddie does more investigating and finds evidence of the scam and then digs into Nola's past. She's a wannabe actress who because of the publicity from the incident with Eddie has landed a big money part in a new film. Now Eddie decides to get his revenge and begins a shakedown plan to get $75,000 from Nola and her crud agent.

At first all goes well, Eddie gets the first installment of $10,000. Then Nola proposes a counter plan, and in effect makes Eddie's plan a part of her own publicity scheme to make her film a hit. Eddie sees the promise of more cash and goes along, now a partner with Nola — not a good idea — as he awaits his $65,000 payoff. But Nola's not only a beauty, she's got a brain-and-a-half and it's all wicked and treacherous. Eddie knows he has to watch her, he knows all her words are an act, but he begins to fall for her.

Eddie is also interested in Carol, the business partner of Nola's crooked agent, Joe Lamb, who planned the original scam with Nola. When Joe is killed, Eddie ditches the body and he and Carol try to cover it up. It's a sweet job. Eddie's waiting for his money from Nola. Meanwhile, Nola is wondering what happened to Joe.

Soon, Nola finds yet another guy to help her, and they get Eddie out on a boat to make more plans — but the real plan is to drown Eddie at sea. All accidental like. There's a climatic battle, Eddie escapes, the boat blows up with Nola on board and Eddie's thrown clear into the ocean and swims for shore – and life.

Al Fray's last hard-boiled opus was *The Dame's The Game* (Popular Library #G-431, PBO 1960, with a cool private eye and dame cover by Harry Schaare). Barney Conroy is the hero in this one. He's a Las Vegas private eye who specializes in catching cheaters for the big casinos. Fray's hero is working the other side of the fence for once in this book, he's legit, though he has a shady past of using shaved dice and gambling scams. It takes one to know one.

On page five, Barney describes himself and the dame in his next case:

"I'm Barney Conroy, a private investigator with a highly specialized field. My practice is limited to games of chance... and what she had in mind was right up my alley, but I turned it down. There's plenty to do right here in Nevada where the game is legit. I headed toward my car which was back in a corner of the parking lot, figuring to be in my own place in just a few minutes, a small new motel at the edge of town. Kate O'Malley would still be up. Kate was a red-head, divorced, 28, and owns the motel. She also owns a number of other things, including a set of curves showy enough for any chorus line, an agreeable personality, and if things worked out according to plan, I wasn't going to have to count the rest of the night as time wasted. I walked a little faster toward the parking lot."

In the lot Barney meets some pro hoods who brace him hard and throw him a beating. They want him to stay away from LA and not to take the crooked dice case Mrs. Tanner has offered him. Now Barney had already turned down Mrs. Tanner, but this beating makes him mad, and more — it makes him real suspicious. A beating by out of town dicemen doesn't make sense, it's not their style, so he knows there has to be more to this than meets the eye. There is, and Barney decides to find out what it is.

It seems old rich guy Tanner has gotten mixed up with a crooked crap game and lost over $200,000. Now, he's a millionaire, so he doesn't feel the pain that much, but his doll of a young wife Shelly does. She hires Barney to help find out what the con is and to convince her compulsive gambler husband that he's being taken.

Once again, Fray, through Barney, gives us an intimate and detailed run-down on all the aspects of a crap game con, including the various ways to cheat suckers. This time, unlike Danny Hogan in *The Dice Spelled Murder*, Fray has Barney on the legit side of the dice game.

In *The Dame's The Game*, the plot starts out simple enough but soon dovetails into murder, a Korean War traitor, the FBI, and communist agents who want access to the secret research done at Tanner's electronics company labs. The crap game was a con – but the real scam was to take over Tanner's business – one way or another – and sell the government secrets to Moscow, a la Cold War intrigue.

This is a rousing tale with a sure-fire action climax as Barney meets an old boyhood enemy and the FBI gets involved in the action. Here the Fray hero goes full circle, from beginnings as an outsider and grifter to working *with* the FBI on a case that in effect, has to do with national security. It's a good story and shows Fray's growth as a writer.

Then in 1960, Ralph Salaway, writing as Al Fray, stopped writing fiction. Salaway died in 1991 at the age of 78. But he lived another 31 years after he finished that last book. So what did he do those last 31 years of his life? I don't believe he wrote another word of published crime fiction. And that is a true shame. He was good. Not great, but real, damn good! And he was getting better and better and definitely had the magic.

So what happened to Ralph Salaway after 1960? Well, I began to wonder. I also wondered why Salaway used a pseudonym. When I did a Google search under "Fray" nothing came up. However, when I did it under "Salaway" I discovered some interesting information. Now, what I'm about to write here is all surmise, but it seems to fit so it may be possible.

"Ralph Salaway" came up only twice under my Google search and both listings had to do with the Los Angeles Unified School District (LAUSD), in their Visually Impaired Program. Now Fray's books all take place in the Los Angles area so it makes sense that Salaway could have lived or worked there. It also makes sense that the kind of hard-boiled crime fiction he wrote would have been better off published under a pseudonym during that era, especially since he was associated with the public school system. My friend Walter Wager wrote his I Spy and Mission Impossible TV tie-in paperbacks as "John Tiger" because at the time he was working at the United Nations in NYC. Writing spy fiction during the Cold War might have caused him difficulties he didn't need on the job. That could have been a reason why Salaway used the Al Fray pen name.

Regarding the question of what happened to Al Fray and why no more books appeared after 1960? Well, according to information on the LAUSD web site; in 1960, *their* Ralph Salaway was appointed Supervisor of the Blind and Partially Seeing Program (The Blend School) in the Los Angeles School System. There is a photo of him on their web site. The second mention is that in 1972 Salaway retired and established a Visually Impaired scholarship for kids with a $20,000 gift.

Is the LAUSD Salaway the same Salaway who wrote hard-boiled crime novels in the late 1950s as Al Fray? It seems possible. The coincidences make it seem very possible. Also, the name Al Fray, sounds very close to Salaway.

In any case, their Salaway was obviously very involved in helping visually impaired children in the LAUSD, and he considered it important work. Their Salaway put his money where his mouth was with a generous gift of cash to create a scholarship for these children upon his retirement. He and his memory are lauded on the LAUSD web site.

Unfortunatley, when I emailed them for information I did not get any reply.

However, I still believe that it is very possible that *my* Ralph Salaway could be *their* Ralph Salaway. If so, that could explain what happened to Al Fray and why he stopped writing. As Al Fray, Salaway had reaped only modest success as an author, after all. After five years and five books Fray might have read the writing on the wall about his writing career. Was it a dead-end with no one noticing? Or, he may have realized that helping visually impaired children in need was a much higher calling than being just one more crime fiction writer.

Whatever the truth is, *my* Ralphy Salaway wrote 5 damn good books as Al Fray and they should not be forgotten, and *their* Ralph Salaway was a decent and generous man who helped children as a mentor and educator and should not be forgotten either. If they are the same man, so much the better. If they are not, the contributions of both were substantial and important. Maybe both are in their own paradise now? They should be. They deserve it.

Al Fray's five books were published as paperback originals in the USA. They are available today on out-of-print web sites and are well worth reading.

Eve Drum: That Lady from L.U.S.T.

Her name is Eve Drum and she is The Lady from L.U.S.T. — League of Undercover Spies and Terrorists — and she was a real handful! She described herself in her first adventure *The Lady From L.U.S.T.* thus:

> *The sexiest spy in the world. Anything you can do I can do better. I'm good at kung-fu, safe-cracking, knife-throwing, sky-diving — you name it! Don't tangle with me because I'm a killer and I don't care if I use my body or a Beretta. Swing along with me as I go into action against a super bad guy who wants to get America and Russia in a fight that will destroy half the world. You better believe it, good buddy, I always finish what I start.*

Eve Drum uses sex and violence with deadly precision and to outstanding effect in a series of 18 paperback spy adventure novels in the Lady From L.U.S.T. series, and in 7 more paperback spy adventure novels in the New Lady From L.U.S.T. series. All books in the series were credited to Rod Gray.

Eve Drum, is also nicknamed agent Oh-Oh-Sex, a definite tip of the hat to James Bond. In fact, these books have a lot in common with Fleming's 007, but in a more sexualized, sexy and fun manner. Eve is the narrator of each book and tells her own story in her own way. The wacky writing and wild spy adventures are worthy of a talented pulp writer like Michael Avallone who did a lot of this kind of thing (the Coxeman series and others) — but the man behind the Rod Gray pseudonym is actually Gardner F. Fox.

Gardner F. Fox (1911-1986) was the consummate professional pulpster. He wrote science fiction, historical novels, sleaze, everything. He began writing in the pulp magazines of the 1940s and 50s, and in the paperbacks of the 1950s to 1970s. He wrote comic book stories for D.C. Comics from 1937 to 1968, and many other comic book outfits throughout his long career. He wrote a host of fine Conan pastiche heroic fantasy novels in his Kothar and Kyrik series, and with many fine historical novels. Fox also wrote the sexy spy Cherry Delight series as Glen Chase, along with almost every type of novel for almost every vintage paperback publisher. He wrote many novels for Ace Books. He also wrote at least ten paperback originals for Gold Medal Books beginning in 1953. Gardner Fox wrote under many pseudonyms in the paperbacks and he wrote hundreds of paperback books.

With Eve Drum in The Lady From L.U.S.T. series, Fox did some of his most amazing and fun sexy spy-spoof writing. The novels are interesting wild romps, well-written and fun to read. The books themselves all feature lovely sexy gga covers, some with art and some with photos. The great campy titles are a lot of fun, they always mix sexual innuendo, or a play on words with a popular book title or some other aspect of popular culture. Thus we have the science fiction adventure where Eve takes an erotic trip to the year 3693, a teaser page for, *Laid In The Future*:

I grabbed up my black nylon brassiere and panties. I was reaching for a garter belt when David said, "No garter belt, no stockings. No time. Besides, you don't get to wear clothes, going into the future."
I did a doubletake. "How's that again?"
"No clothes. Transmitter won't take them,"
I go naked?" I howled.
Stepping forward, I let my hips swing. I might as well give the boys a show while I was at it. My breasts jounced, my buttocks shook.
I walked into the year 3693.

David is her "tall gorgeous blonde hunk" of a C.I.A. caseworker, David Alexander, who works with Eve, but does not control her. Other fun book titles include the kiss my ass teaser, *Kiss My Assassin*; the obvious James Bond spoof of *From Russia With Love — To Russia With L.U.S.T.*; and even Frank Sinatra's *Luck Be A Lady Tonight* song title spoof, which becomes *L.U.S.T. Be A Lady Tonight*.

In the second novel *Lay Me Odds*, on the back cover blurb Eve tells us some more about herself in her own special way:

LAY ME ODDS — if you have the guts. My name is Eve Drum. I'm THE LADY FROM L.U.S.T. — the wildest, nuttiest secret agent who ever drove the Kremlin Out of its Vodka-guzzling skull. They aren't kidding when they call me the sexiest spy in the world. As Agent Oh Oh Sex I take on the kind of assignments Jimmy Bond can't handle. All hell breaks loose when I go into action against the sinister forces of H.A.T.E. don't tangle with me because I'll love you to death. I have a license to kill and I don't care whether I use my body — or a bullet. Sex is my deadliest weapon, but I'm just as good with a knife. Don't tell me about Judo or fast cars or brainwashing because I know it all. I'm good and you know it. Watch me use exotic Eastern sex techniques to turn H.A.T.E.'s villainous spy-masters into helpless blobs of desire. Swing along with me as I bump and grind through London strip clubs in pursuit of missing microfilm. Join the fun as I mix business with pleasure, martinis and Molotov cocktails. With a Beretta in my bra I'm an up-dated Fanny Hill, a tastier brand of Candy, a lethal Lolita. My crazy life is just filled with bloodshed, bedrooms and belly laughs.

That'll give you a good taste of the style of these books, they're wild and unabashed fun. Eve, as an agent for L.U.S.T. fights all kind of evil enemy organizations known by incredible ominous acronyms. There seemed to be a plethora of them in the 1960s. This all began, of course, with James Bond, who fought a secret war with SMERSH and SPECTOR. (On an interesting aside, the first US paperback of James Bond in the US, *You Asked For It* [Popular Library re-title of *Casino Royale*] featured a blurb referring to the hero as "Jimmy Bond" so Eve's description of Bond above is actually accurate). Nevertheless, back to the acronyms, initials for super secret spy organizations abounded in 1960s popular TV spy shows. Remember Maxwell Smart of CONTROL who fought against KAOS? Then there were the men from UNCLE who fought THRUSH? Well, Eve, as the lady from LUST works for a super secret part of the secret CIA with her case officer David Alexander. She fights against various acronym villainous organizations like HATE (The Humanitarian Alliance for Total Espionage) in book #2, *Lay Me Odds*, a group of Russian Kremlin bad guys. She also fights the minions of ALLAH (Arab League of Loyal Agents of Hate), a group of Middle East fanatics in book #4, *5 Beds To Mecca*; and the monstrous oriental crime cartel called DRAGON (Dedicated Red Army Guards of Nanking) in book #3, *The 69 Pleasures*. In book #12, *Blow My Mind*, the world is threatened by a new form of ESP — extra sensory perception — but Eve counteracts it with her own ESB — extra sensuous body! In the New series, in book #1, *Go For Broke* and in book #6, *The Lady Killer,* Eve once again takes on the agents of HATE. It's all in good fun.

For collectable paperback fans a lot of the fun of collecting these books are the great sexy cover art, and cover photos. Fabulous collectible cover artist Paul Rader did the cover art on the first 9 Tower paperbacks, which was also re-used on the two British reprints. Rader was a terrific artist, his women are lovely and luscious and he makes Eve Drum a truly delectable dish. Rader used his tell-tale initial "R" on the cover of the first Tower book in the series, and in the second his signature "Rader" is visible under Eve below the dice. His signature or initial do not appear on any of the other covers as far as I can tell, but Rader collector and scholar Lynn Munroe assures me Rader did all of the first 9 Tower editions. The cover art is lovely, hot, sexy and bold, quintessential Rader at his best. The later books in the series feature cover art by other artists in the Rader style, and in some later books and reprints we have cover photos. The 7 books in the New Lady From L.U.S.T. series feature all gga photo covers. They're nice, but I prefer cover art rather than photos generally. The books are not all that common to find, especially in nice condition, and they present some confusion to collectors. Some of the books were reprinted under different titles, and the numbering on some of the books was incorrect, see list below — but they are a nice series of fun paperbacks with great sexy gga cover art. Eve Drum is just fine with me!

The following lists are not conclusive, but they will give you a good idea of the books available in these two series.

THE LADY FROM L.U.S.T. ORIGINAL SERIES
#1: **The Lady From L.U.S.T.**, Tower Books #43-804, 1967 c-Paul Rader
Belmont Tower #51102, 1967
Belmont Tower #50516, 1973, as *Lust, Be A Lady Tonight*.
K & G Publications, UK, 1968, c-Paul Rader
#2: **Lay Me Odds**, Tower Books, #43-860, 1967, c-Paul Rader
K & G publications, UK, 1968, c-Paul Rader
Belmont Tower Books #50542, 1973
#3: **The 69 Pleasures**, Tower Books #43-912, 1967, c-Paul Rader
Belmont Books #2043, 1973
Belmont Tower Books #50559, 1973
#4: **5 Beds To Mecca**, Tower Books #43-944, 1968, c-Paul Rader
#5: **South of The Bordello**, Tower Book #44-171, 1969, c-Paul Rader, listed as #8 on cover.
#6: **Kiss My Assassin**, Tower Books #44-160, 1968, c-Paul Rader, listed as #7 on cover.

#7: **Sock It To Me**, Tower Books #45-212, 1969, c-Paul Rader.
Belmont Tower Book #50604, 1973, as *The Poisoned Pussy*.
#8: **The Hot Mahatma**, Tower Books #44-989, 1968, c-Paul Rader, listed as #5 on cover.
Belmont Tower Books #50628, 1973
#9: **To Russia With L.U.S.T.**, Tower Book #44-126, 1968, c-Paul Rader, listed as #6 on cover.
Belmont Tower Books #50628, 1973
#10: **The Lady Takes It All Off**, Tower Books #45-276, 1969
Belmont Tower Books #50536, 1974
#11: **Lady In Heat**, Tower Books #45-299, 1969
Belmont Tower Books #59649, 1974, photo cover.
#12: **Blow My Mind**, Tower Books #T-095-3, 1970
Belmont Tower Books #50660, 1974, photo cover.
#13: **Laid In The Future**, Tower Book #T-095-1, 1969, cover art.
Belmont Tower Book #50667, 1974, photo cover
#14: **The Copulation Explosion**, Belmont Book #2008, 1970, photo cover Belmont Tower Books #50678, 1974.
#15: **Turned On To L.U.S.T.**, Belmont Books #2170, 1971, photo cover. Belmont Tower Book #50692, 1974
#16: **The Big Snatch**, Tower Book #42-276, 1969, listed as #10 on cover, cover art looks to be Rader?
Belmont Tower Book #50710, 1974, photo cover.
#17: **Easy Ride**, Tower Books, #?, 1970
Belmont Tower Books #50727, 1974
#18: **Skin Game Dame**, Belmont Books #50214, 1972
Belmont Tower Books #50742, 1974, photo cover.

THE NEW LADY FROM L.U.S.T. SERIES
#1: **Go For Broke!**, Belmont Tower Book #50777, Feb, 1975, photo cover.
#2: **Have A Snort!**, Belmont Tower Book #50794, 1975, photo cover.
#3: **Target For Tonight**, Belmont Tower Book #50805, 1975, photo cover.
#4: **The Maracaibo Affair**, Belmont Tower Book #50814, 1975, photo cover.
#5: **Voodoo Kill**, Belmont Tower Book #50829, 1975, photo cover.
#6: **The Lady Killer**, Belmont Tower Book #50838, 1975, photo cover.
#7: **Kill Her With Love**, Belmont Tower Book #50858, 1975, photo cover.

NOTES: Information for this article came from my own collection of books, as well as "Gardner F. Fox in Paperback" by Roy G. James in

Paperback Parade #27, 1992; from bibliographic information supplied to me from Daniel Charleston; and from cover art information supplied by Lynn Munroe.

Negative of A Nude & **Murder**

The cool thing about actually reading some of the vintage era crime paperbacks from the 1950s and 1960s is that every so often you come upon one that's a real keeper. It is a book that it seems no one may have read in 30 or 40 years — but it should be read. So here's my chance to clue you onto a terrific private eye novel, but before I do that I have to let you know that it has two titles — two titles but it is the same book.

The book was originally published as *Negative of A Nude* and it is by Charles Fritch (Ace Books #D-367, paperback original, 1959, with terrific cover art by Robert Maguire). The book was later reprinted as a rare Australian digest under the title of *Negative of A Murder* (Phantom Classics #37, 1961). They changed the word 'nude' for 'murder'. In either edition, it is a compelling read and follows the adventures of former heroin addict and ex-cop — now private eye, Mark Wonder. It takes place in the dark underbelly of Los Angeles in the 1950s.

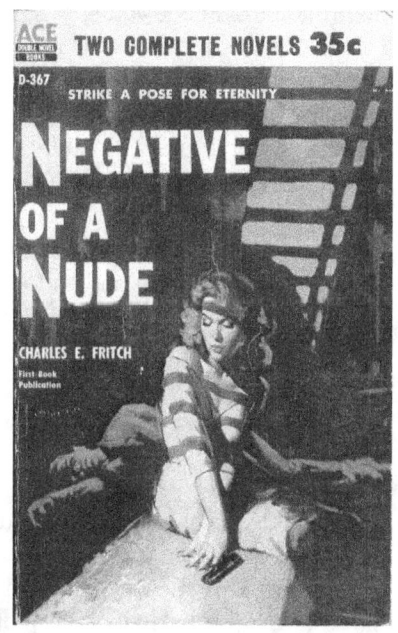

Fritch was a California writer who wrote for the digest magazines of the 1950s, and was even editor of *Mike Shayne Mystery Magazine*, as well as some other crime and science fiction digest-size magazines of the era. He was also a pretty good writer in his own right. He wrote a pile of pulp crime and science fiction stories and some novels. He was more than a competent writer and in this book he does an excellent job telling Mark Wonder's tale of loss and danger with a fine-edged hard-boiled attitude. I think the book may be a lost minor classic of the private eye genre.

Fritch here is redoing Raymond Chandler and he does him pretty damn well. His private eye is a spin-off of Philip Marlowe, a cynical and skeptical guy at best, and he is placed in so many interesting situations it keeps him busy and the reader fully interested.

Fritch's writing is taut and lean but juicy, full of fine tid-bits that flesh out the story and his hero really well. Fritch is good at it too, he obviously enjoys what he is doing with Mark Wonder in this book, having fun pasticheing Chandler, and it's fun for the reader to read his Chandlerisms.

Another interesting aspect of the story is the background description of the world surrounding the early photographic studios of the 1930s and 1940s — when the camera was coming into it's own with smaller, cheaper and more portable models that allowed the picture-taking hobby to develop among regular males. Mostly males interested in taking nude photos of nubile young gals. Fritch calls these "glamour studios" and talks about the photographer's clubs (or 'camera clubs') prevalent in California at the time. Notable model Betty Page posed for such photos early in her career. These studios and 'clubs' allowed amateur photogs to do 'art shots' and nudes of young women who were models on their staff. It was very popular at the time among many males — who obviously had more of an interest in sex than photography.

Negative of a Nude is a very well-written book that will keep you reading until the end. Fritch has his private eye do the right thing, solve a brutal murder, and tie up all the lose ends by the conclusion of the novel — and he adds in a few interesting surprises! In fact, the plot here is masterfully done and the last few pages move with the power and force of an express train. If your sort of thing is to read a taut story about a hard-boiled private eye up to his neck in dames and danger then this is one you should definitely not miss.

The Search For Otis

Every once in a while you come across a writer whose work you really enjoy. Sometimes it's a new author, but often the discovery of a neglected writer from the past can offer just as much pleasure — if not more. There's that thrill of discovery that always brings wonderful dividends when you come upon such an author. In this case it is a relatively unknown 1950s paperback author — G.H. Otis.

Back in 1996, I began a search for information on G.H. Otis. As far as I could tell he wrote only two excellent hard-boiled crime noir novels: *Bourbon Street* and *Hot Cargo*. Both novels appeared as paperback originals in 1953 from a long-defunct, often-forgotten, certainly obscure, lower-end, small paperback publisher of the era: Lion Books. Lion was influential in it's day though, specializing in hard-boiled crime and noir fiction, publishing fine original works by Jim Thompson, David Goodis, Robert Bloch, David Karp, Richard Matheson and others. G.H. Otis sits comfortably with these masters, though unlike them, he is hardly known at all.

The two books by Otis are good solid work, well ahead of their time and in many respects, hard, crisp, lean, clear and fascinating. Two fine classic noir novels. Then that was it! As far as I knew, he wrote those two books and nothing else! Why? There was not a peep from him afterwards, not another word, no more books at all. What happened? Did he write any other books? I began to wonder about G.H. Otis, and the more I thought about him, the more I was sure that the name had to be a pseudonym. If that was so, then who was G.H. Otis? So I extended my search.

Walking Down Bourbon Street

Bourbon Street (Lion Book #131) is the better of the two books, in my opinion. The cover blurb — that on many paperbacks of the era often exaggerated, if not outright lied about what the book was about — this time it tells it right and true:

A loot-mad thug takes New Orleans apart!', 'Savagery prowls the back alleys of New Orleans while a gunpunk tries to pull the deal of his life'; 'A novel of America's rulers — and of the people they own and crush.

For once, the blurbs got it right.

The inside teaser page goes a bit further and proclaims the hero as a noir villain who finds himself:

Trapped by a gutter...he looked at the street. Dark and dirty and twisted. Bums in the alleys, sleeping off the no-food days and rotgut nights. Cockroaches crawling over their faces. Yellow-skinned girls waiting under the yellow lights, waiting for the New Orleans spenders to come down to the Quarter for a night of slumming. This was what he had run from. He had broken in a man's face, made a blood-deal with the syndicate, sold out a woman who loved him and ruined another he loved. All this, just to get off the street. And now he was back. And the shadows were waiting for him. And there was no place to run.

And let me tell you, the blurbs do not exaggerate. *Bourbon Street* lives up to everything they say and more! The 'hero' (actually an early anti-hero), is a tough guy, a former alky bum named Digger Mulcahy. His hard-boiled narration offers a fascinating insight into his life, world, and thoughts.

Handling Hot Cargo

A few months later, Lion Books published the second Otis novel, *Hot Cargo* (Lion #171, with cover art by Robert Maguire). The blurbs tell it best:

They carried 129,000 tons of explosive oil — and an TNT woman.

And on the teaser page, the blurbs add:

A shipload of hungry men — and one man-starved woman. The tropic nights were still and sticky. The engine room was a steam bath, airless and smelly. The drums of oil were tinderboxes, ready to blow star-high.

But, nothing was as hot as the bare-legged woman named Sheba who strutted the decks and turned 19 love starved men into a shipload of fevered animals.

But still — Brody thought — he could get the ship through, get it to its port, even though one engine was gone and the crew was drunk. He'd get her to port.

Except there was no port... The only place they were going was to a midnight rendezvous in the middle of the ocean — where a five-inch gun was set to smash Brody and his ship straight to hell!

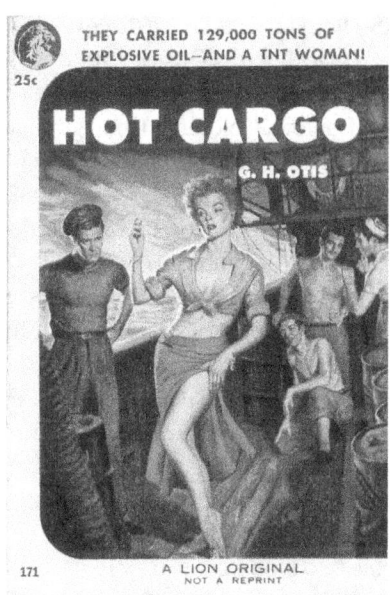

Once again, as with *Bourbon Street*, the blurbs for *Hot Cargo* do not lie. They don't even exaggerate! The cover art by Robert Maguire shows Sheba dancing provocatively for the horny male crew on a hot tropic night, enticing them to fight over her, to spill each other's blood for her, as Brody looks on — wanting her more than all the others but knowing she's deadly poison.

The hero here is Ed Brody, a character similar to Digger, but not the twisted and vicious anti-hero that Digger is. Brody is a more cynical loner, tough and sharp, more decent. Brody is on the run, Otis never tells us from what.

Hot Cargo, like *Bourbon Street*, is an incredible tour-de-force, a hard-boiled, realistic, often brutal story about a brutal world and the people who make it that way. It is quintessential noir at it's best.

Reading Otis

So what about my search for Otis? Who was G.H. Otis? Thanks to the kind assistance of veteran scholars Victor Berch and Bob Briney, with an assist from Jeff Vorzimmer, I was able to piece together the following story. Even today with the publication of an edition of these two books by Stark House Press in 2020 — and even though the Internet makes it possible to find a lot of data on authors that was not available in 1996 when I first wrote the original article — the irony is that it is still near impossible to find much on this author today. My search for Otis led me to this incomplete conclusion — but I present what I know here in the hope that some day someone will be able to fill in those unknown areas.

So here is what I have discovered about the author known as G.H. Otis.

G.H. Otis was Otis Hemingway Gaylord, Jr. He was born September 8, 1924 in Boulder, Colorado, and died February 26, 1992 at 68 years of age, in Boulder, Colorado. Upon graduating from high school in 1942, he joined the Navy where he served for the duration of World War II. He attended the University of Colorado and worked his whole life as an ad rep for newspapers. He was married, with one child, and he never made a living as an author.

Aside from his two Lion Books as Otis, Gaylord ghost-wrote eight western paperback novels under the name of Peter Dawson, which was itself a pseudonym of Jonathan Glidden. These eight Bantam western paperback original novels as by Peter Dawson were: *The Savages*, 1959, #1984; *Yancey*, 1960; *The Texas Slicks*, 1961, #A2275; *The Half-Breed*, 1962, #A2371; *Bloody Gold*, 1963; *Showdown*, 1964, #J2835; *A Pride of Men*, 1966, #J3130, and *The Blizzard*,1968. While I have not had the pleasure of reading any of these eight Bantam western novels, judging by his two Lion books, they're probably terrific too.

It is also asserted by some that in the 1960s Gaylord wrote some softcore adult paperbacks (commonly known these days as "sleaze"), however I could find no evidence of his having written any of these type of books, no information has ever shown up.

Through the Copyright Office in Washington D.C., I received reports that offer the following additional information on this author who has become an enigma to me.

The copyright application for *Bourbon Street* (actual publication date by Lion Books was March 27, 1953) was received by the Copyright Office July, 1953. At that time Gaylord gave his home as Aspen, Colorado, but it is shown in one of the other forms that in June of 1953 he was actually living in Mexico City, Mexico. Gaylord's agent at the time was Marguerite Harper, located at 50 East 42nd Street, New York, New York.

Five months later, the application for *Hot Cargo* (Lion Books publication date was November 13, 1953), received on December 28, 1953, shows things a bit different. Gaylord's address in December, 1953 was 703 11th Street, Boulder, Colorado and his agent had been changed to DA Magazine Management Inc.

However, Gaylord did write one book under his real name — only one — *The Rise and Fall of Legs Diamond* (Bantam Book #A2079, paperback original, 1960). This movie tie-in novel is based on a screenplay by Joseph Landon and has cover art by Stanley Zuckerberg. The film featured dapper Ray Danton in the title role of the crack shot gangster, and was directed by Budd Boetticher, famous for his Randolph Scott westerns.

Gaylord turns up next in, of all places, Walt Disney Studios in California. Their Employee Records Department gave me what little info they had on file for him after so many years: a short note that Gaylord was an advertising manager for nine months, from July 4, 1965 to April 30, 1966. I have not discovered any more data about his life from this time, to his death in 1992.

My search took me online, and I also asked knowledgeable scholars and collectors I know for any further information, but there was nothing more on Otis, or Gaylord. One almost wonders, did he want to be found? He did write with some authority about New Orleans of the era, and about working on an oil tanker, so he may have had some of this experience early in his life that he put into his two books for Lion. Perhaps.

Otis Hemingway Gaylord, writing as G.H. Otis, wrote two damn fine hard-boiled crime noir novels that should not be forgotten. He was a hell of a fine writer. That is why I am so elated that Stark House Press decided to publish their edition collecting these two terrific Lion Books into an omnibus trade paperback — books that have now become noir cult classics. Once you read the novels that make up this book you will take a deep dive into the grim wild world of hard crime and noir.

I envy you reading these books for the first time, or re-reading them in this new edition. I know you will enjoy them and will never forget them! Although I haven't ended my search for Otis, at least you can enjoy these two spectacular reads, and maybe you will even begin your own search? Enjoy!

C.J. Henderson, Jack Hagee, and Me

A long time ago, in a world very far away, Wayne Dundee created and edited a little fanzine-type magazine called *Hardboiled*. That magazine contained the hardest damn crime fiction you'd ever want to read. I savored each long-awaited issue as it appeared, reading them religiously, little realizing at the time that the contributors and letter writers whose names appeared in those pages would become a who's who of hard crime and noir fiction for the later era of the 20th Century.

Hardboiled (HB) contained hard pulp crime the way it should be written — with a relentless hard-ass attitude that had not been seen since *Manhunt* or *Black Mask* — and there was one guy who wrote stories that I thought were the best of the best in those pages. His stories were gripping, searing, brutally honest and damn good. I'd never heard of him before, he was just some guy with the byline C.J. Henderson.  In stories like "What You Pay For" (HB #4, 1986); "Nothing Comes Cheap" (HB #6, 1986); and especially "Toothpick" (HB #8, 1987) Henderson chronicled the tough but brutally honest adventures of his maverick private eye and overall troublemaker, Jack Hagee. From then on the world changed.

Henderson's Hagee was a tough Brooklyn private eye, and since I was a guy who lived in Brooklyn, both character and author were of interest to me — but I'd never heard of this guy Henderson at all. He seemed to be as much of a writing maverick as Hagee was a maverick character — and soon I would learn how right I was about that.

So I wrote *Hardboiled* editor Big Wayne asking him about this Henderson fellow, mentioning how much I liked his stories, and he gave me Henderson's address. It turned out the guy not only lived right here in Brooklyn where I live — he lived only a little ways from me! So I wrote Henderson. We met. Over the years we became good friends and had some great times chewing the fat about crime fiction, Jack Hagee, my own hard crime guy Vic Powers; also topics like science fiction, films, politics, any damn thing at all — but the subject always came back to hard-boiled crime fiction. And Jack Hagee.

In those days everything we read and wrote was hard-boiled in some way, certainly everything written by Chris - as I called him — had a hard-boiled edge to it. Everything, even fantasy stories. He was a very versatile writer and could write anything about anything. The words just flowed out of him, like they'd been bottled up inside him since he was born — and they were beautiful, searing, honest words. I realized a great truth about this guy, my friend Chris, this C.J. Henderson guy was a natural... a natural writer! He had the talent. He had *it!*

As our friendship grew, Chris continued writing Jack Hagee stories, among others (such as his popular Teddy London tales), and I began writing my Vic Powers stories, and publishing my magazines: *Paperback Parade* for book collectors, and *Detective Story Magazine* (which would morph years down the line into *Hardboiled* when I took it over from Big Wayne in 1991). But that was yet to come. In the meantime in the 1980s Chris and I continued our friendship — writing our stories, dreaming our dreams. He wrote a *lot*. I published a lot, and wrote a lot too.

I loved his Jack Hagee stories. Hagee was Chris as he was and as he wanted to be, he was Chris's alter ego and Hagee said the things in print Chris spoke in real life. Hagee, like Chris, was an outspoken, overly opinionated, very real, fascinating raconteur. I was happy when I published "A Game To Be Played" in the second issue of my *Detective Story Magazine* in 1988. The next year I published "You Can't Take it With You" in *DMS* #5. From then on C.J. Henderson wrote at a rapid pace and Jack Hagee stories flew out of his typewriter — and eventually word processor — to appear like magic in a burst of manic creativity. Each story was a wonderful, hard crime gem, worthy of *Manhunt* or *Black Mask* — *damnit*, even worthy of being written by Raymond Chandler and Dashiell Hammett. Or Spillane himself! Crime writing legends of the caliber of Richard S. Prather, Mike Avallone, Richard A. Lupoff, William Campbell Gault all lauded his Jack Hagee stories. As fast as Chris wrote-em, Big Wayne and I published 'em.

Eventually Chris and I realized he had written enough stories to fill out what would make a nice size book. A Jack Hagee collection was something we both dreamed about — he as a writer — I as a fan and a small press publisher. We made it happen in 1990 with the first Jack Hagee book, *What you Pay For* (Gryphon Books). It was a 500 copy limited trade paperback that collected all 11 Jack Hagee stories up to that time in one volume, including a never-before-published tale "Bread Ahead", all wrapped in stunning cover art by the great James Warhola. The image of Jack Hagee on the book cover is the image of Chris from back in the day.

From then on the legend of Jack Hagee and C.J. Hendeson only grew. While *What You Pay For* never became a best-seller, not even selling out its original print run, it was read and enjoyed by true hard-boiled fans and readers. Reviews were very positive, and the book and Hagee began to build a following and buzz among those who make crime books successful. Jack Hagee and C.J. Henderson were on the move. My friend was making it in the writing game and I was happy because his talent deserved it. Within a couple of years Jack Hagee had attracted the attention of major publishers and soon Berkley Books published three new Jack Hagee novels: *No Free Lunch* (#1, 1992); *Something For Nothing* (#2, 1993) and *Nothing Lasts Forever* (#3, 1994). Hagee was off and running.

I was proud when I was asked to contribute a blurb for that first book and I said, "Henderson knows the mean streets around us today and makes them sing with the blood and sweat of life." And I meant every word of it. The three Hagee novels were very good — not as great, nor as strong having the visceral power shown in his short stories — but really good hard crime novels. They are underrated books and are real sleepers for hard-boiled aficionados. Today they have become cult classics.

Then, just as things seemed to be going full tilt for Jack Hagee the rug was pulled out from under the tough Brooklyn PI and Berkley decided to move their publishing program in another direction. The publisher (who also published Chris's Teddy London occult detective novels, under the pseudonym Robert Morgan) wanted him to concentrate in that new direction — and Jack Hagee was left aside. Chris also wrote comic books, and other novels with new characters in the fantasy and horror genres for Tor and other major publishers that were also popular. Though Chris wrote an occasional Hagee short story from time to time, the Jack Hagee novels were quietly allowed to go out of print. And that's where things stood for many years. Along the way, *What You Pay For* was reprinted by another publisher, so the Hagee *stories* stayed in print, while the Berkley *novels* languished in the land of out of print books where collectors and fans kept them alive. The story of Jack Hagee appeared to be over and done.

Then I heard the terrible news that Chris was ill with cancer. It was a big blow to everyone who knew him. He was a large guy, seemingly bigger than life and seemingly impregnable. He wasn't, he was just a man, a good guy who tried his best, who did what he loved doing, who wrote great books and now was fighting the greatest fight in his life — trying to beat cancer. He fought well. If anyone could win and beat the beast we thought it would be Chris. He kept up a good front, something Jack Hagee would have done, showing his hard-boiled toughness with his usual attitude. I thought Chris was going to make it. When I spoke to him he sounded positive, even hopeful. Then one day I got the dread call from his good friend Bob Smith. Chris was dead. Hagee was dead. There is nothing left to say.

There is some comfort though in the thought that he died doing exactly what he loved to do, for I heard later that Chris had been at his desk writing a new story — I like to think that it was a new Hagee story — when he felt very ill. He had to be rushed to the hospital and he passed away soon after. My good friend was gone. We'd had some bumps in that friendship over the years — decades really — but we always remained good friends. It's hard to keep a dry eye as I write this.

Chris's passing on July 4, 2014 was a massive blow to his family and all of us who knew him. A lovely gathering was attended by legions of family, friends and fans in his honor in August, a veritable convention — C.J Con. It was just as Chris would have wanted it, a gathering of good people, great food and lots of strong drink. And that, I thought, was that. Chris was gone now, but he was never out of our thoughts.

It was months later in November at Rich Harvey's Bordentown pulp show when I saw friend and crime author John French. Well, we just naturally got to talking about Chris and then Hagee. When he let me know about a long lost Jack Hagee novel, I immediately stopped in my tracks. I blurted out, *"What long lost Jack Hagee novel?"*

Then John told me that Chris had written a fourth book in his Hagee series for Berkley that had never been published. The manuscript had been lost for 20 years and he had only recently found a copy that Chris had sent him years ago. To say I was shocked and amazed didn't quite make it. John and I got to talking about the book. He told me he was then in the process of editing the novel and Rich Harvey was going to publish it. I asked if I could write the introduction and John and Rich agreed.

No Torrent Like Greed is that fourth and long-lost Jack Hagee hardest-boiled crime novel. It is hard-boiled pulp the way it should be. It's a wonderful book. It is Chris back in fine form and full voice, and Hagee and he spout off about their many foibles in their hard-boiled opinionated best. This is attitude plus! The book was obviously written sometimes after the third novel, I would put it circa 1994, and there are some minor dated aspects to it. Hagee mentions floppy disks and mobile phones, but like reading vintage Chandler, Hammett or Spillane, we don't read them for the outmoded technology either. We read them for the great characters like Sam Spade and Mike Hammer — and Jack Hagee — and the terrific hard crime stories. The relentless hard-boiled attitude. *No Torrent Like Greed* has that in spades.

No Torrent Like Greed takes place a mere five weeks after the events in the third Hagee novel, *Nothing Lasts Forever* — which in light of events turned out to be an amazingly ironic title. In this new novel, Chris has Hagee skewer New York City in his own special way as only a person who lives here can really know it — a working person talking truth, not some uptown spoiled yuppie Wall Street trust-fund fool riding their bleeding heart sanctimonious high-horse. In other words, a novel written circa 1994 during the height of the rot and riot brought on by the Mayor Dinkins administration. However Chris and Hagee are not at all out of touch with the present in this novel, ironically the citizens of New York voted in Mayor Bill DiBlasi who brings with him all the old pols and broken baggage of the Dinkins administration. So for Hagee, the more things change, the more they remain the same. Henderson and Hagee spew forth a variety of sharp opinions and comments in this book. You don't have to agree with all of them — or even any of them — but they do give pause for thought, and to me they ring true as the day they were written. The more things change, the more they do remain the same. The novel also continues Hagee's relationship with his friends and associates. Returning are his info specialist, Hubert; newspaper reporter Rich Violano; street people and sometime agents, Popeye and Grampy; and Hagee's gal Sally Brenner, *New York Post* editor.

No Torrent Like Greed presents Jack Hagee at his best and toughest yet. Henderson puts Hagee neck deep into the most dangerous and convoluted case of his career — but it all begins so innocently. Then things get down and dirty and the game being played gets worse, becoming a rollercoaster of violence and terror. This is a hard crime growler of a book, a loud voice from C. J. Henderson roaring at us from beyond the grave. He would have loved that. Here he is making his point and telling his story, even after his death. Nothing would please Chris better and nothing could be better for a reader than having Jack Hagee back again in a new lost crime novel by C.J. Henderson — the quintessential pulp writer of the modern era. Now get to reading! You are in for a real treat my friends.

Update: *No Torrent Like Greed* and many of the Hagee books by C.J.Henderson are still available in attractive trade paperbacks from Bold Venture Press.

The Steve Bentley Thrillers

Being a guy who loves to read a good hard-boiled crime or noir, the only thing better than discovering a crime novel that really grabs me and is a pleasure to read, is learning that particular book is one of a series about the same character. Such a series is comprised of the nine Steve Bentley thrillers by Robert Dietrich (aka E. Howard Hunt).

Aside from being a former O.S.S. operative during World War II and an ex-C.I.A. guy who was one of our most effective undercover spooks during the Cold War; involved in the Bay of Pigs fiasco and later in the Watergate Break-in that brought down the Nixon Presidency — E. Howard Hunt was also a hell of a fine writer.

In a 1979 interview in *Paperback Quarterly*, Hunt said writers that influenced him were, "Ernest Hemingway, for the sparceness of his description, the 'male' oriented themes. Raymond Chandler, for precision of dialog and colorful, memorable descriptions. John Dos Passos for imaginative structure." He also added that he didn't really like any of the covers of the 23 paperback originals he wrote. He felt the cover art "cheapened" the contents. I couldn't disagree more, but it was his call as the author.

Hunt wrote more than 50 fast-moving political thrillers, spy novels and hard-boiled crime mini-masterpieces that have too long been overshadowed by the political scandals during the Nixon years. Hunt wrote under his own name, but also as Robert Dietrich, Gordon Davis, David St. John and John Baxter. He also wrote some very significant non-fiction about the spy game. Politics aside, it is time that E. Howard Hunt's fiction deserve a detailed and unbiased look. My aim here is to tackle that job in one small part by delving into his Steve Bentley thrillers.

Hunt, writing as Dietrich, has Bentley introduce himself on the back cover of *The House on Q Street* thus:

The Name's Steve Bentley... I'm no private eye with a snap-brim hat and a .45 in my armpit. In Korea I was a C.I.D. agent, but I never heard a shot fired in anger. The rough stuff had to wait until I settled in my Washington digs as a tax consultant. I guess maybe the man had something when he said money was the root of all evil.

Yes, he's a tax consultant, and he is a C.P.A. (certified public accountant). It is not exactly what you'd think of as the standard hard-boiled dick — but Steve Bentley is not at all like he seems. Maybe he's a bit like his creator — who was not what he seemed either? Bentley is not a cop. He's not a private eye. Truth is, Bentley is far better! Bentley has experience with U.S. Army C.I.D. (Criminal Investigation Division) in Korea, and he helps cops in an unofficial capacity, so he has private eye and investigation experience. Bentley is smart and cool, he knows his way around Washington and politics, the power and the powerful — and he gets involved in all kinds of fascinating cases. The nine books in this series will keep you entwined with plot and characters as Bentley moves each chess piece to solve the case.

Bentley is a mixture of sophistication and of a 'regular guy'. Maybe like Hunt himself? While Bentley has a ketch harbored on the Potomac, he's not some Travis McGee clone, he has an apartment and works out of his tax office. He drinks rather more than he should and often smokes a pipe. Bentley also has a small support cast that round out the series and most of them appear in each book. They get Bentley cases, offer support, and bring in needed information. His office gatekeeper is his secretary, Mrs. Bross, a tough bird who regulates his comings and goings with military precision while she is doing all she can to land herself a Marine husband. Then there is top-flight D.C. lawyer, Hod Gurney, who got him the case at the Q Street house; D.C. homicide detective, Lieutenant Kellaway, a canny cop and good friend; and private eye Artie Von Amond from the District Detective Agency, a tireless investigator. This small

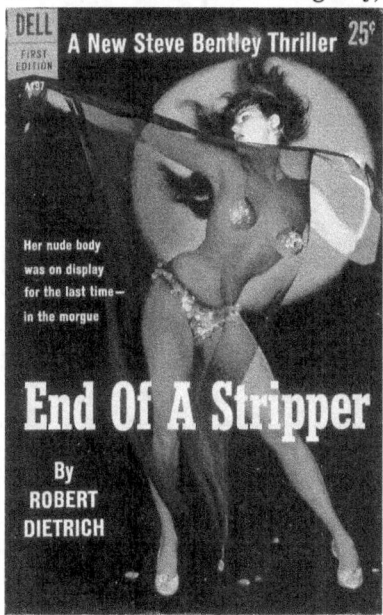

group enable Bentley to operate through the tangled web of Washington, D.C., the most complicated and dangerous political city in the world. In the background is the tough, smart, gangster Maury Renzo, based in Baltimore but with tentacles all throughout D.C., who also figures in some of the books. Bentley and Renzo have an 'interesting' relationship — sometimes adversaries, sometimes allies, but always with respect for the other's talents.

Best of all, the books themselves are all short to-the-point, searing pile drivers of pulp-crime stories that are impossible to put down. Seven of the nine books saw original publication as Dell First Editions, slim staccato paperback volumes of just 160 to 190 pages beginning in 1957. These are fast crime dramas the way they used to be — the way they still should be, before publishers had authors endlessly pad out books to get excess verbiage and exposition which added extra length and pages to too many books. The bottom line for the author and publisher — a higher cover price. However the Bentley books don't skimp on plot or characterization, and the exposition is first-rate — some of it reminiscent, and maybe even rivaling, Raymond Chandler himself. Hunt is that good. The later two Lancer editions are the same short but concise length. All 9 books are paperback originals and all are out of print today. Reading them all in order was a wonderful experience.

The first Steve Bentley crime novel is *Murder on the Rocks* (Dell First Edition #A141) from 1957. This begins the series. The cover blurb of *Murder on the Rocks* proclaims, "A cool corpse…a hot jewel…a torrid woman."

This fast-paced thriller has it all, action as well as thoughtfulness, all in a good mixture. Bentley is a sophisticated man about town, a cool character, a decent guy, a man who knows the ropes and the movers and shakers, and a man who knows all too well what the score is. He's a smart cookie. He's also tough when he needs to be.

The theft of a priceless jewel could cause embarrassment to an important South American country embroiled in civil war. Politics and the mob figure in this drama set in Bentley's home base of Washington, D.C. The players include two wily and oversexed sisters, both playing Bentley for their own reasons, and he's playing back of course; then there's a couple of corpses, politicians, cops and mobsters. It's a good mix, the characters feel real, not pulp stereotypes but concisely depicted individuals who ring true to form.

The hunt for the Madagascar Green, an enormous 29-carat priceless emerald, leads Bentley on a wonderfully plotted case that leads through old time Georgetown and the District of Columbia as it used to be. The

'District' plays a role in the stories as a living place and Hunt/Dietrich really make it and the people come alive. It's a wonderful look back at things the way they used to be — and the way things used to be done in the old days — in all it's best and worst aspects.

The House on Q Street (Dell First Edition, 1959) is the second book in the series. In this one Bentley takes a financial case for heroic General Ballou, who is being blackmailed. He realizes he's taken on more than he bargained for when he gets involved with the general's daughter. Bentley tells it best when he says:

Take Miss Francie Ballou, for instance. Her address — a magnificent old Colonial house on Georgetown's Q Street, where every breath costs half a dollar. But at 17, she was — in order — an ex-addict, a mother, and one-third of a murder triangle. She was also one hell of a woman. Which explains, I suppose, why I stayed around too long after the shooting started.

Dietrich/Hunt also shows a narrative drive in these tales and a feel for character and description that Chandler himself might envy. Right off on the first page, he opens the book with this little gem:

It was a gray spring afternoon, sunless and smoky with fog. The

kind of day that frays tempers, when cars lock bumpers and taxi drivers brawl with cops. The kind of weather when you can walk into a bar, order a glass of beer and get your throat cut.

Or this tasty bit from page 33 about a special club for the idle rich:

It was a sprawling Victorian castle with scrolled eaves and Charles Addams gables. No light escaped louvered windows that would be curtained inside. It stood just inside the District line, acres of swampy land around it, low taxes and no neighbors near enough to be nosy. The parking lot extortionist wore a flamed ice-cream uniform and a peaked cap like Peron in his heyday. I nosed the Olds inside the steel-mesh fence and let him get behind the wheel. "Easy on the fenders," I told him. "I only carry hundred-dollar deductible."

Or this example of the D.C. mean streets circa 1959 from page 64:

While elsewhere in the city there were crap games in smoky back rooms, knifings, muggings, stick-ups, rapes. And poisoned alky. On F Street the legless man stares up from the sidewalk, his monkey rattling pencils in a cup. Beloto runners dart furtively down alleys, into restaurant kitchens. Mark the bet, collect and out to the alleys again: spidery sunless labyrinths better known to rats and starving dogs. At Union Station a man is getting off the train from Miami, briefcase filled with bindles of granulated narcotics grown in Iran and refined in Berne. Out of Marseilles by way of Havana. The fast boat across the Florida Straits to a mangrove rendezvous. Later tonight the alcohol lamp in a hundred rooms, the needle, the jolt of long-craved tincture spreading sweet fire through dry grateful flesh.

The thing is Dietrich/Hunt uses this Chandleresque language sparingly, but he uses it well; it is done thoughtfully so that it melds with the story and action, offering a depth not seen in most pulp crime fiction from this era. It never becomes pastiche. He also only uses the best examples, short and concise, to the point, placed in the text only to make a point. The language is never used for fluff, never to show us how clever or Chandleresque the author can be. This language is not done as pastiche or parody, but only appears when it works within the framework of the story he is trying to tell. It works extremely well.

One more interesting little thing, on page 97 is an early use of the term "car-jacker" — and that in a paperback published in 1959! I thought that crime and the term for it began as a 1980s phenomenon. I noticed many more items such as that in these books. These are very interesting books just as sociological histories.

Once again Bentley becomes embroiled in a murder mystery that begins as a blackmail case with a hot babe, the General's spoiled daughter. There is a murder, then it is discovered that a murder of a doctor eight years previously was done with the same gun and the cases are connected. The case gets hot when the mob gets involved, the General's daughter and Bentley get a 'thing' for each other, and the gal's kooky brother causes problems with an obvious phony confession. The question for Bentley is, who is the brother trying to protect? And where is the gun that was used in both murders? That turns out to be the key.

Bentley puts it all together in a fine bit of traditional detective work. There's even a nod of the head to Dashiell Hammett in his construction of a plan with mob boss Turk Almieda to sell out one of his own hoods, McQuarry. They set him up as the fall guy for the two murders, to neatly tie up the case reminiscent of Sam Spade and Gutman's plan to have Wilmer the gunsel be the fall guy for the murders in *The Maltese Falcon*. From page 131:

"Wrap up McQuarry for the cops. Write him off. Be a good citizen helping the ends of justice." I dropped ashes on his carpet. "What the hell else can you do?"

Almeida's shoulders moved as though he were sighing inwardly. "He's scum," he said bitterly. "I don't expect you to believe it but I had nothing to do with where he went tonight. Much less killing the old lady. He dreamed up the whole thing or he got it somewhere else. Maybe you know which."

I said nothing.

Almeida's head turned and his eyes gazed at the closed door. "He was playing his own game," he said in a remote voice. "For his own stupid reasons. He took the chances. It's time to cancel the bets."

By the end of the book Bentley ties it all up very nicely, a well plotted story and a case where he brings together all the various strands of a complicated web of crime. It's a good book and a hell of a read.

The third Bentley novel is *End of A Stripper* (Dell First Edition #A197, 1960). The blurbs proudly proclaim, "Her nude body was on display for the last time — in the morgue."

The sexy stripper cover art by Freeman Elliott is simply incredible! Very hot! This seems to be the toughest book in the series to find — when I looked there was only one copy on ABE and I got it!

In this one a little man takes a candid photo of Linda Lee, a high-priced stripper doing her act. He's beaten up for doing it by two thugs, while the camera with the incriminating photo winds up in Steve Bentley's pocket. The little man winds up dead the next day. He turned out to be a private eye doing some work and the two thugs visit Bentley, take the camera and then throw him a nice beating. Steve is not happy about that, but while they took the camera, he has the film!

Linda Lee the stripper seems to be the key to the mystery. Seems she had a thing with a Congressman, also with a gangster, and now Bentley has a thing for her.

Throughout the novel, Bentley refers back to his earlier two cases — from the two earlier books. His group of support characters continues to show up or be mentioned which fills out the books giving them more depth, and makes them into a coherent series.

In the end, Bentley gets the killer of Linda Lee. On the last page of the book, page 160, Dietrich/Hunt has Steve Bentley tie it all up with this sad moody noir passage:

Behind the Municipal Building the sky was the color of smoke in a room after everyone has gone. The coldness of dawn made me feel old and empty and alone. The gray sky held a single star, as distant and lonely as memory, and I thought of the job I had finished for a girl with golden hair who was probably all that they said she was. Except to me.

The fourth Bentley novel is *Mistress To Murder* (Dell First Edition #B163, 1960) with another gorgeous semi-dressed dame on the cover by artist Robert McGinnis.

Steve Bentley is at it again, this time he's driving along a rural highway when he finds a young beautiful and unconscious woman — don't we all! Anyway, she has been thrown from a horse. He stops to help but another driver arrives, slugs him, and drives off with the gal. Well, Steve isn't happy about what the guy did or the sucker punch he was given. He wants to know what happened to the girl so he makes it his business to find out. That gets him involved with a wealthy family, an evil baron, and two beautiful women as different as night and day.

Bentley inserts himself into the problems of a 19 year-old half sister of a baroness who is being kept a virtual prisoner by her sister and the baron, for reasons unknown. It makes for an interesting and sexy mystery novel.

One of the many fine descriptions in these books that stood out for me was a simple paragraph, just a short look at a hotel on page 77:

> *It was a hotel not old but no longer new, built when beige brick was all the rage. Sofas and chair backs stained with hair oil, a couple of tired window boxes and a seedy-looking pansy behind the desk. I stuck a nickel in the self-service newspaper rack and pulled out a morning paper. Then I strolled over to one of the chairs and sat down. The bell captain was an inch over five feet tall, with a face like a John Bull beer mug and eyes as shiny as the casques of scarab beetles. He was perched on a bench, drumming his nails on his knees and waiting for the ceiling to cave in. After a while his eyes roved around and settled on me. I crooked a finger. He glanced at the desk clerk, got up slowly and idled over. The clerk kept on sorting room keys.*

Priceless pearls and a murdered baron complicate things for Bentley and the two sisters. Then he is set up for a particularly nasty murder that changes everything and the true nature of the case. Now the killers and the betrayers finally become clear. The ending is an amazing but sad revelation. This is a hell of a crime novel!

The fifth Bentley novel is, *Murder On Her Mind* (Dell First Edition #B163, 1960), with still more stunning cover art by Robert McGinnis of a lovely but sophisticated bad girl. The cover blurb proclaims, "She was a lush-bodied Latin chanteuse with a song on her lips, passion in her heart, and murder on her mind."

Private Eye Artie Von Amond refers a lush Latina singer — Chula Marques — to Steve Bentley. She needs a CPA to fix her finances but she proves to be a woman of many faces and some of them are the faces of murder.

On page 5 Bentley amply describes his first meeting with the glorious Chula:

> *I heard a cough behind me, turned and saw a girl standing just inside my office door. She was about twenty-five, and was wearing a coral linen suit, white gloves and white shoes. Her gloved hands held a white leather purse. Her long black hair parted at the middle and was gathered behind her head in a tight bun that glinted like onyx. Full eyebrows arched above large liquid eyes, and coral lipstick accented smoothly curving lips. Below them an uncompromising chin. Her skin was the delicate tan of golden meringue, her features were perfectly proportioned, her expression calmly self-possessed. Except for higher than average cheekbones, she was typical of Spanish or Central American beauty. Her lips moved and a low voice said, "Mr. Bentley?"*

Bentley's cop friend Kelleway is out of town, so Bentley gets mixed up in a Maryland murder with big D.C connections that lead to revolutionaries, gun runners and gangsters. With Kelleway gone, Bentley has to deal with Sergeant Wolcott who is not one of his fans. On page 65 we get a good description of Wolcott, and what cops have to go through in the District:

Another frustrated, bitter cop, pushed around by influence and taking it out on those who hadn't any. Possibly a good detective, though, in a town tough for any law enforcer. Washington, Capital of the Union. With more rape, perversion and crimes of violence per capita than any city in the nation. A city that pays married policemen so little they hire out as cabbies to eke out a slender budget. A city where one chief of police on a ten-thousand-dollar salary bought eight cars and four houses in two years and killed himself while under investigation. A town with as much dope and prostitution as Havana. A town where Fat Boy Brown, the policy king, owns three pink Cadillacs, half a dozen hotels and some of the choicest real estate in the District. Our fair city.

The book concerns gun running to a South American revolution that takes place in 1959 — when the book was written. I wonder if the story presages what Hunt was involved with then in secret activity in Batista's Cuba, perhaps such would lead to the Bay of Pigs invasion and fiasco in 1961?

Regardless, Bentley discovers a tough mobster is running guns to these revolutionaries and gets involved with the daughter of the revolution, Chula, and her father who is leading the coup. In the end Bentley solves the case on all fronts but Chula and her father get what they want too. The revolution goes through, they go home, Bentley is left alone and missing her at the end. This is a good hard crime novel with plenty of intrigue and twists in plot, but not one of the best books in the series — but it's a fine murder caper novel and darn good enough!

Steve Bentley's Calypso Caper (Dell First Edition #B182, 1961) is the sixth Bentley thriller. It features another outstanding sexy female pin-up style cover by Robert McGinnis.

This one takes Bentley to the U.S. Virgin Islands, in Charlotte Amalie on the island of Saint Thomas, where an unsavory character named Victor Polo has just been murdered. Bentley knows of him only peripherally and is there to do some tax work for friends. The change of locale works well in this book and adds a calypso beat to the narration and dialog. Bentley hears one song sung by the locals about the Polo murder:

Mistah Victor Polo was a Big Time Mon,
He gamble for money wherevah he con.
Win lotta money, then lose it fast, too.
Mistah Victor Polo — he all through.

The song gets Bentley interested in knowing what really happened. The Virgin Island locale makes for a nice change from Washington, D.C., with it's own particular characters with their own customs and ways of doing things. That includes murder. After the murder of Polo things start to get out of control on the island.

Then the knifing of lovely *mulata* dancer Reba Royce causes Bentley to look deeper into the case, and he finds out quite a bit. Such as the fact that many of the powerful men on the island were involved with Reba, including his friend, Sonny. Then when his friend Sonny is accused of the murder, Bentley investigates to prove him innocent. That's when things really start to get hairy.

Polo turns out to be the key to many of these events. Years ago he was partners in a casino on the island, went bust, then escaped to the mainland. In the States he robbed a bank and went to prison. Now years later he came back to Saint Thomas and Bentley wants to know why. Rumor has it Polo got cheated by his casino partner. When he ran away instead of getting out with a briefcase full of cash — half of the casino dough which was the deal — when he got to Miami he discovered all he had was a briefcase full of old newspapers. His partner had cheated him. Now he was back to collect his share. Now he was dead and Bentley wants to find out why, in what is an intricate but fascinating case. It's a very good crime novel with a surprise killer and a memorable ending.

The seventh Bentley thriller, and his last book for Dell, is *Angel Eyes* (Dell First Edition #B203, 1961). Once again, Robert McGinnis supplies some absolutely stunning cover art, showing us a sexy black-haired minx in black negligee playing a bongo drum. The back cover blurbs tell us:

I'm Bentley, Steve Bentley. You might ask what a C.P.A. is doing assisting the D.A. and chasing a murderer and racketeers. Well, it all had to do with the "Good Neighbor Policy." I happened to become involved when my oh-so-friendly neighbor in a black negligee invited me over for a nightcap. Only before I could change into something a little more comfortable, some other Romeo stole the scene — and some incriminating evidence. He left my neighbor with a stocking around her neck. He left me with a hunch who did it.

Steve meets a new neighbor in his apartment building — she seems to have moved in while he was away in his last adventure in the Virgin Islands as told in the previous book.

She nodded thoughtfully. Then she titled her head provocatively and purred. "I'm Peachy."
"What I can see from here is sensational."
Her nose wrinkled. "I mean my name, you. Peachy. Peachy Bolac."
"Steve Bentley."
"I know. I read your name card. Want a drink, Steve?"
"That's real neighborly," I mused. "I might just accept a dram of chuckleberry cordial."
"Whatever that is."
"Or anything else you might have handy. Tell you what, I'll change my shirt and slide over. Say ten minutes."
"The door'll be open." She drifted back inside and I went into my apartment.

Peachy Bolac is a lovely and sexy little minx, a 25-year old charmer, whom Steve calls Angel Eyes. He's quite smitten with her, but Peachy is the gal pal of 64-year old Senator Tom Quimby. That poses a bit of a problem for him, but far worse is when Steve finds Peachy dead, raped and strangled in her bed with a nylon stocking. A photo of the senator is also missing. Steve is involved now and he calls his cop friend Kellaway as the case begins. *Angel Eyes* is a very fast-paced thriller and one of the best books in the series.

The last two Steve Bentley thrillers were not done for Dell Books but published by Lancer Books in 1962 as paperback originals. By this time Lancer Books, the new publisher, touts that over 2 million Steve Bentley books have been sold.

The eighth book is *Curtains For A Loser* (Lancer Books #71-311, PBO 1962, with great gga cover art by Ron Lesser). The gorgeous Ron Lesser cover art is in the McGinnis style — and it is even signed by Lesser in the McGinnis style, imitating McGinnis' signature. When I asked McGinnis about this he was not upset at all, but just gracefully smiled and said that he was happy at the sincere imitation and flattery shown him and his work by Ron Lesser in that cover art.

The book is a bit less graceful. Steve ends up with a coked up nympho doll of an actress who falls for him — even as her daughter and Steve fall for each other and murder stalks them all.

Beautiful nymphomaniac actress Morgan Vernay cheating on her businessman millionaire husband with a famous playwright — shades on Marilyn Monroe and Arthur Miller perhaps — runs into trouble and needs Steve's help. When she's accused of writing some big checks she never said she signed — not a big deal because they have tons of money but it may indicate old family help may be crooked — her jealous husband suspects her of paying blackmail, or worse, a lover!

Complications also arise as Steve meets Morgan's 19 year old daughter Monique, in this from page 18:

When I reached the entrance I peered in and saw no one. Then I saw her at the edge of the pool near the ladder. A girl of nineteen or so, in a brief Bikini, sitting with her legs under her tanned thighs, long wet hair slicked back from her forehead and parting over her shoulders. Her tawny body had the taut curves of a swimmer and her face wore an alert, gamin look. Her curving eyebrows were dark and full and her fingers on the tiles were long and flat at the ends. As her head tilted slightly she said, "I wondered how long it would take you to come over."

Steve's getting into trouble now. Two murders later, he is up to his neck in a case he'd rather leave alone — but for the nubile young and lovely Monique! The book ends with a shocking murder and a solution you'd never guess — and an emotional bittersweet romance for Steve Bentley that is rather touching. A terrific tour de force, a great read!

The ninth and last Steve Bentley thriller is *My Body* (Lancer Books, #70-010, 1962), with another lovely woman on the cover, art by Ron Lesser, this time still in the McGinnis style but not signed in imitation of McGinniss's signature. The art is sexy and exciting. In an interesting twist on cover art, when Lancer Books reprinted this book (#75525, 1973) they not only re-used the Lesser cover art from the 1962 first printing — they put a copy of the actual earlier book on the cover of this book! The book was reprinted in 1973 by Lancer to tie-in with the then infamous Watergate scandal then in the news and Hunt's place in it. The cover proclaims the following quote in large type:

E. HOWARD HUNT *IS* ROBERT DIETRICH
(from the *Chicago Daily News*).

In the meantime Steve's last adventure takes him to Nassau, in the Bahamas, on what is supposed to be an easy and quick 2-3 day inheritance accounting case — but it ends up a lot more complicated.

When an old Washington Grand Dame dies, she leaves 37 million dollars and Steve Bentley goes to Nassau to audit the books of Eaum Resources in a job given to him by his lawyer friend, Hod Gurney. Once in Nassau, Steve gets involved with two luscious young women and the very brutal murder of the man who runs the company he is to audit, via a booby-trapped shotgun.

"Leslie could offer a man everything but love," the cover blurb tells us. Soon Steve meets 19 year old Leslie and her 28 year old step mom Rita, and the two involve him in a whirlwind of desire, intrigue, and murder. A lot happens as Steve investigates, such as 19 year old Leslie is almost drowned in a Scuba diving accident that Steve discovers was no accident. Between the young wife Rita, and the daughter, Leslie, Steve has his hands full in a neat little story of embezzlement and murder. Hunt gives Steve's narration a wry, cynical style reminiscent of his hero Raymond Chandler and *his* heroes' hard-boiled detective Philip Marlowe. In the end Steve deals with both women, sorts through the fraud and murder and solves it all very nicely, just as well as Hammett did in *The Thin Man*!

Sadly this is Steve Bentley's last crime thriller and Dietrich/Hunt leaves readers wanting more — but while Steve's adventures were ending Hunt's were just beginning and his earlier out-of-print paperback originals were soon being reprinted. He was also writing new thrillers that all became bestsellers.

You can't talk about the Steve Bentley books without mentioning the cover art, and the author behind the pseudonym — E. Howard Hunt. We'll look at the cover art first:

The paperback editions showcase some of the best sexy-gal pin-up cover art of the vintage era. While the first Bentley book suffers from minimalist cover art by Art Sussman which is not much to look at, cover art vastly improves on all subsequent books with the lovely and sophisticated female images done by classic illustrator and paperback cover legend, Robert McGinnis. That McGinnis cover art has also made these books very collectable, irrespective of their contents, and while the content of these books is what this article is all about, the cover art must be mentioned. However, the Freeman Elliott cover art for *Death of A Stripper* has to be seen to be believed. It's incredible! The cover for *Curtains For a Loser* is by Ron Lesser who is imitating the gals done by Robert McGinnis.

Now we will look at E. Howard Hunt. Hunt wrote crime, spy, suspense thriller paperback original fiction for a variety of publishers, *Stranger In Town* (Signet Book #729, 1949) was an early paperback reprint but his paperback originals began soon afterwards, probably with Gold Medal Books in 1950. His first book was *East of Farewell* (Knopf, 1942), written during his service in World War II under his own name. His last fiction novel was *Sonora* published under his own name in 2000. In between Hunt wrote at least 41 crime thriller novels. He was a *Life* magazine correspondent on Guadalcanal. Hunt won a Guggenheim Fellowship for his writing in 1946.

E. Howard Hunt was a fascinating and mysterious figure in American history because while on the surface he was just a pulp crime paperback writer — in reality he was an undercover C.I.A. spook involved in all kinds of top secret U.S. Government missions from the 1940s into the 1970s.

Everette Howard Hunt, aka Robert Dietrich, was born October 9, 1918 and died on January 23, 2007 in Miami, Florida of pneumonia. He served in World War II aboard the destroyer USS *Mayo* and the Army Air Force, and eventually the Office of Strategic Services (O.S.S.), the precursor of the C.I.A. Hunt joined the Central Intelligence Agency (C.I.A.) in 1949 as a political action specialist in what came to be called their Special Activities Division. Some of his work included anti-Castro and many Cold War actions such as The Bay of Pigs. His spook career culminated with his involvement in the Nixon White House. With G. Gordon Liddy, he was one of the secret team of ops in the Nixon White House known as 'the plumbers' — who fixed "leaks" and did political dirty tricks. His first covert White House operation was the break-in at the office of Daniel Ellsberg's psychiatrist in 1971, resulting in *The Pentagon Papers*. He was later involved in the Watergate scandal that resulted in the resignation of President Richard Nixon. Along with Liddy, Hunt engineered the first Watergate break-in and was convicted of burglary, conspiracy and wiretapping, eventually serving 33 months in prison.

Politics aside, Hunt left a lasting legacy of fine hard crime and spy novels that can be enjoyed by all fans of the genre regardless of their political belief. Hunt was a C.I.A. spook, a covert op, an undercover investigator — so he knew what he was writing about and it comes through in his books with many keen observations and insights. Hunt was also a master writer and a natural storyteller, and his work should be reprinted and remembered by new generations of crime readers and fans.

By the way, for the sake of completion, Hunt did write three previous books as Robert Dietrich, but these early attempts under that *nom de plume* are *not* Steve Bentley thrillers. However, they are very capable crime novels. The earliest of these books is *One For The Road* (Pyramid Book #128, 1954, cover artist unknown), about Larry Roberts, a drifter who "worked the rich widow racket..." Next, is *The Cheat* (Pyramid Book #135, 1954, cover art may be by Robert Maguire). This one tells the story of Robert Webster who discovers the truth about a woman he loves. For the third Dietrich book Hunt moved to a more upscale, and better paying market at Dell Books. Here he would stay for the next seven Bentley books until he moved onto Lancer Books in 1962. This third non-Bentley Dietrich book, *Be My Victim* (Dell First Edition #106, 1956, cover art by Art Sussman) is a thriller about a Florida mobster who sets up the hero by bringing in a dangerous woman to bring him down. These three early Dietrich non-Bentley titles are all paperback originals. They are worth seeking out, and while not Steve Bentley books, each contains aspects that make the Bentley books such outstanding reads.

The nine Steve Bentley books are slim mini-classics of crime noir excellence. They're influenced by the Raymond Chandler style but work well on their own with fast-paced plotting and concise characterization. Bentley is a very cool, capable and likeable hero and gets involved in some fascinating cases. These are great reads and you can't ask for much better than that in pulp paperback fiction. So pick up a Steve Bentley paperback today and get ready to enjoy some pleasurable hours of crime and capers in the long-lost world of 1960s Washington, D.C. — when things were more innocent and so much more simpler — *or so we thought!*

Hero's Lust
A Top Crime Noir Sleeper!

Lion Books in the 1950s was a mini-powerhouse of hard-boiled and noir paperback original crime fiction. They published just over 200 books in their main series, mostly crime and westerns — but even their western novels were brutal, hard-boiled, violent noir. Their crime novels were something much more — even better — with stories that went far beyond anything anyone else was publishing at the time. The Lion series is loaded with unrelenting noir crime masterpieces, and some real sleepers for readers and collectors.

Lion Books originally published 10 of the intense crime noirs of Jim Thompson, who has become a legend today — including his most famous crime novel, *The Killer Inside Me*. They published hard-hitting original crime noirs that have become modern classics by such greats as Robert Bloch, Day Keene, David Goodis, Richard Matheson, David Karp, Richard S. Prather and Don Tracy.

Arnold Hano was responsible for obtaining most of the books. He became editor of Lion Books in 1950. It was said he furnished outlines of exactly what he wanted to see from some writers (such as Thompson), and they followed his directions, but in their own way. He also published crime novels written by prisoners and also new Black writers, with work from the slush pile. He had a very good eye for quality.

However, Lion also published a lot of books by writers most people never heard of even back then — writers whose names have been sadly forgotten today. While the author's names may have been forgotten, their books and stories have not, and many of these books have taken on a life of their own in the hearts of collectors, readers and crime noir aficionados the world over. These are the kind of books knowing readers rave about to each other in their most private moments when talking obscure great crime noir favorites.

Three of these novels make up a Stark House volume offering some of the best examples of that unique fiction Lion Books was so famous for. Greg Shepard, editor of Stark House, has chosen three winners — all mini masterpieces. These are obscure novels — real sleepers in the parlance of true aficionados who love nothing more than to discover a great lost work and share it with others. In these books you will embark upon a new and mysterious excursion into the darkest pit of noir desperation, crime and corruption, three novels you will not soon forget.

In these three novels: *Hero's Lust* by Kermit Jaediker (1953) — followed by two equally hard-hitting novels — *The Man I Killed* by Shel Walker (1952, pseudonym of crime writer Walt Sheldon); and *House of Evil* by Clayre and Michel Lipman, (their only novel, 1954), you will make some very pleasant discoveries.

I don't know much about Kermit Jaediker, who wrote the lead novel in this book, but he is said to have been an early Golden Age comics writer and cartoonist. *Hero's Lust* is his only paperback original. While he only wrote two novels, he sure knew a lot about the inner workings of corruption and politics and he takes the reader on a full-face nose-dive into the charnel pit of these evil influences. I believe Jaediker even invented a medical scam in this novel I'd never heard of before — ghost doctors! I won't go into the details here, I'll let the hero of this novel explain it to you. You will be amazed!

Red Norton is the hero of Jaediker's novel, a two-bit reporter for the *Courier* of Crescent City who plays ball with the crooked mayor and his criminal gang. Mayor Gowan pulls all the strings and controls everyone and everything, but he has a soft spot for Red, and takes him under his wing. From this privileged position, Red sees just what the mayor's corrupt tentacles have done to his city, the people, and himself, but he is ensnared deeply in the trap and he doesn't care so long as he gets his pile — and he does. A more accurate title for this book might have been *Heel's Lust*, because Red is certainly a full-fledged heel, but just when things seem to be going great for Red, a dame is thrown into the mix to complicate his life.

Ann Porter is a sweet gal, young and cute and Red can't help but be interested, but she's got TB. Ann has been carefully chosen by the mayor to be the focus of a newspaper story by Red promoting the mayor's new Medical Center — and the mayor and his administration, of course. Ann is sent there to get the lung operation that will cure her. The Medical Center is the gleaming gem in all the mayor's dirty rotten schemes, it is the one thing in his life he has created that is not touched by graft and corruption — as far as he knows. It has one of the best surgeons in the city, Dr. Winston, who will perform the operation to save Ann's life. Red falls hard for Ann.

Things start going downhill when Red is approached by a friend who is an honest newspaperman from a rival paper. Bernstein believes Red still has some principles left, and seeks to recruit him into a scheme to get the goods on Mayor Gowan and bring down his administration, and the corruption it fosters. Meanwhile, Red is falling in love with Ann, so he considers working for Bernie, but he is no sucker. Red knows that Mayor Gowan has all the answers and he has Red firmly under his thumb.

Mayor Gowan rules by fear and intimidation and with bribes, but when that doesn't work he has a select group of men willing to do what needs to be done. Hartung, his police captain bodyguard, is a vicious thug who likes to catch rats, douse them with gasoline, and then set them ablaze for fun. He does the violent work and likes it. Murphy, is a brutal louse whose advice for any problem is to get rid of the problem. Then there's Frankie, a weasel set-up man who Red mistakenly trusts. The mayor also has actual gangsters on the payroll like Mike Calitorcio, which means he has eyes everywhere and on everyone. Red feels trapped and he knows it.

The battle between the Mayor and Bernstein causes Red to fall smack in the middle of their dangerous war. This sample from page 39 will give you an idea of just how trapped Red feels:

The Mayor and Bernie. It's their fight. It's their fight, but you're in the middle, a nut caught in the jaws of the biggest nutcracker ever made. When those big shining jaws come together, they could crack your shoulder blades and the bones of your arms and the bones of your hands, until you couldn't wash them of anything, and the bones of your thighs and legs and ribs, and then the jaws would slide up to your skull and slowly, surely, with a loud crunching sound, they would crack the bony white walls of your skull and suddenly the walls would cave in, crunching into sharp white splinters...

Well, you can see Red Norton is in deep trouble, with a dame he loves, and the strangling noose of corruption breathing hard down his neck. This is political noir on the local level, the personal level, a hard-fought, hard-scrabble novel of the way life really was back then — and still is today. It's a timeless story. The names have been changed, but the same type of corruption goes on and on.

I'm not going to get deeper into the plot of this novel, as that would spoil the story for you, but let me just say that there are a lot of twists and turns in this story and what happens in the end will be totally unexpected. You're in for a fine ride — and that's just the first novel in this exciting three novel package of classic Lion Books noir masterpieces. You're in for a real treat!

A Cop Called Wolf

Wolf Cop by Richard Jessup, Gold Medal Book #s1172, a paperback original from 1961, is one of those classic Gold Medal noir cop thrillers that really delivers. You won't be able to put it down. As far as I know it has never been reprinted — but it sure should! I read the book for the first time in 2009 and afterwards felt compelled to write this article for my book collector magazine *Paperback Parade*. It was slated to appear in issue #74, but because of publishing complications, it did not appear until 25 issues later — so the spotlight on this book has been waiting in the wings for quite a while. Now it is overdue for this appreciation.

Wolf Cop concerns Sergeant Tony Serella, a tough cop — what other cops call a 'wolf cop'. He's an obsessive copper who's a hell-bent over-achiever. That causes jealous cops to go up against him, crooked pols to betray him, and he gets a bum rap of police brutality. The cover art for this Gold Medal paperback edition is by Bill Johnson and shows Serella kicking in the door of a woman's apartment as she looks on in terror. Wolf cop! Eh, well not really, for the scene is not a part of the book. In fact, Serella and his partner Trace, seek to solve the apparently unrelated vicious murders of two innocent older women.

The cover blurb tells us:

"*Serella was too good to be bought, to big to be bent. He was an honest cop — a loner who wouldn't run with the pack. That's why they called him wolf cop.*"

In the course of his investigation, Serella goes up against the crooked politics in the cop house, from bosses like the Chief of Detectives, various inspectors, the Commissioner and even the city mayor. He bends the rules to help a young prostitute find a new life as she struggles to get her friend off heroin.

Serella also tracks down the rumor of a gang war as mobsters from back East are coming to town to take over the rackets and the drug dealing business. Amongst all this, Serella tries to live as a loner whose life is spiraling out of control, called a wolf cop by other cops who are fearful of his ambition and hard temper.

Things soon come to a breaking point for Serella. He's even got a girl on the hook who he is interested in, name of Ida Ballantine, and he's struggling to form a life with her — but before he does he has to settle all the old business. That means finding the killer of the two old ladies, help his hooker friend, catch the hoods in the act before the mob war starts, and finally sidestep a political battle to win a court case where a two-bit teen hoodlum has cried police brutality that has put Serella and the entire city police department on trial. The action and intensity move along to a brilliantly done climax of a trial where Jessup ties all the loose ends together in a most satisfying conclusion.

Sergeant Tony Serella is a complex character, not as tough or as lone wolf as he's initially made out to be, but he's trapped in a tight noir mess he can not see any way out of. The solution to his problems could get him kicked off the force, or even get him prison time. This book packs a superior story about a terrific and fascinating lead character, and that takes it above and beyond a lot of the stuff being written today. It also shows how so much has not changed in many decades since this book was written. It is a fine noir classic. Give this one a read and you will love it too!

The Elusive Joe Barry

He wrote in the tradition and style of Dashiell Hammett, but he was no Hammett. Hammett was *great!* But Joe Barry was still *real good*, so to me, that's pretty close to the master. It means he was good enough, and he certainly deserves to be read. And if you read him, you'll like him — especially his hard-boiled heroes Rush Henry and Donn O'Mara. He's one of the forgotten masters from the old days who does not deserve to be forgotten.

So who was Joe Barry?

What books did he write?

I first met Barry when I read his novel *Homicide Hotel*, and promptly began searching for all his other work in paperback. It wasn't all that easy. His books were published, it seems, by every obscure paperback outfit of the era. *The Payoff*, was a Prize Books digest, his other books were published by Handi-Books, and in Canada by Harlequin Books, all tough to get. There was one Ace Book, a vintage Double. *Homicide Hotel* was Phantom Book #500 and is a scarce rare digest. Almost every hard-boiled fan who collects vintage paperbacks probably has a Joe Barry book in his collection — *that he has probably never read!*

Joe Barry was an old-style fictioneer. He wrote hardcovers, and was reprinted in the early paperbacks. He wrote in the Dashiell Hammett mould, with three hard crime hero series that are quite a shade better than most imitators of Hammett's Sam Spade or Chandler's Marlowe. It's pulp fiction at it's best, with real heroes and slam-bang action.

Barry's three detective heroes are hard-charging, hard-boiled Rush Henry; sophisticated Bill August; and an almost kinder and gentler private eye hero, Donn O'Mara. Barry's characters are more human and humane than the usual type of hard-boiled PI characters. They're average kinds of guys trying to do the right thing. And against all types of odds they eventually succeed, to the reader's delight. These are good books. The enjoyment for the reader is following the story of these heroes' success. Barry is an entertaining and eminently readable writer whose work could be called simple — but only because he is so good. I think it is actually fairly subtle, but he sticks to basics in telling a damn good story. Literal. Straight-ahead. No nonsense.

Today, Barry's works are virtually unknown outside of a small group of detective story fans and vintage paperback collectors. The reason for this is that in most cases his novels appeared only in paperback, and then by small and obscure publishers whose books are almost impossible to obtain today. They were probably as hard to obtain when they first appeared in the 1940s and 50s, when you think about the distribution system back then. Small, obscure, marginal publishers, now long out of business. Handi Books, Phantom Books, Famous Mystery, Prize Mystery — they're not even memories today in the publishing field outside of a few collectors. They were not exactly household names in the publishing field even when they were active.

In the only instance where a major U.S. paperback publisher released one of his books (Ace Books did *Kiss and Kill*; while Harlequin Books in Canada did four reprints of his earlier Rush Henry titles which originally appeared from Handi Books), these editions are even more expensive and harder to find today than the books published by some of the smaller marginal publishers. In addition, the four Harlequin Barry titles can be especially scarce and expensive in nice condition — all are within the scarce first 100 Harlequin Books — way before Harlequin Books began to publish romances — and they were not sold in the U.S. Copies of these might be a bit on the pricey side. The Ace Book of *Kiss and Kill* seems uncommon but is available if you look. It's is an early Ace Double, #D-47, a paperback original from 1954.

However, don't get me wrong, no Joe Barry book, except *Homicide Hotel* is really rare, but all are not easy to find, you'll really have to search for them — but they are around. The one good thing the readers and collectors of Joe Barry have going for them is that hardly anyone knows about his books. You occasionally see them available for sale and a sharp collector or discerning private eye reader can pick them up for a decent price. There may be a time in the future when this will not be so. Barry's books are good reads. All of them are out of print today and have been for about 50 years. His three hardcover firsts are scarce. None of these books, as far as I know, have never been reprinted.

Many of his paperbacks were often packaged terribly, with lousy cover art, or in the case of *Homidice Hotel*, a prime example of a cheap and sleazy digest paperback with brutal bondage cover art. While that may be popular today with *collectors*, the cover art *on* that book had absolutely nothing to do with the story *inside* the book. A cover like that must have been a death knell to Barry's writing career as a serious crime novelist back then, putting off many potential readers. Especially many women readers!

Hardly the kind of thing Anthony Boucher would ever review!

In fact, many of Barry's books feature good but rather misleading covers and incorrect blurbs about the story. Nevertheless, the story here is important and it is the story *inside* these books that is good and deserving of attention from detective and hard-boiled crime fans. You'll not be disappointed if you come across any of these and give them a read. They're quick and flow along well, quality fast fiction, and Barry is good at telling his story and keeping the reader interested. Though it may sound a bit trite, his books have a specialness to them that once begun are hard to put down. I really like his characters, especially Rush Henry. And while Barry is not great — he certainly had his moments in books like *Homicide Hotel*, *The Pay-Off* and *Kiss and Kill*. He aimed for that ideal Hammett and Chandler often achieved, and on his best days, Joe Barry hit that mark, or at least got very close.

Not much is known about Barry. What I've been able to discover was because of famed mystery collector and scholar Bob Samoian in a 1986 letter: "Joe Barry was born in 1909. From 1933 to 1946 he was a radio announcer, producer and script writer at radio station WHO in Des Moines, Iowa. On the radio he was known as Barry Lake, and one of his books was also reprinted under that name. Barry's radio work specialized in broadcasting football games, sports events, inspirational poetry readings on Sunday nights, and lectures to vocational classes. He was married and the father of two children. He had a B.A. degree in Interpretive Speech. He once worked at the Chicago World's Fair pulling a rickshaw!"

I began my own fascination with the work of Joe Barry after reading his novel *Homicide Hotel*, and was amazed at how much I liked it. Forget about the outrageous cover art for the moment — I am talking about the written story inside the book. This book was *not* at all what I thought it was going to be! The sleazy digest packaging held a hidden gem between it's wild and lurid cover, resulting in one of my earliest articles about vintage paperbacks, "I Read Homicide Hotel" originally published in Jon White's *Paperback Forum* #2 in 1985 — an early paperback collectors magazine.

Joe Barry had three private eye series. The books were all novels. The first and best to my mind was the Rush Henry series of five books published from 1943 to 1950. Next, in 1950, Barry had a one-book PI, Bill August. In 1951 to 1954 there are two Don O'Mara novels. All in all, Barry wrote and had published eight private eye crime novels, though there are many paperback reprints during the vintage era — including a surprising number of books in Canada, Australia and even Sweden!

Rush Henry was Barry's most successful character (though I think his two O'Mara books were his best — he was definitely getting better as a writer as he got older). Rush Henry was introduced to the reading public in 1943 at the height of World War II in *The Pay-Off*. Henry begins as a crime reporter who goes to a corrupt hell-town named Weston to clean it up. Shades of Hammett's 'Poisonville' in the Op novel *Red Harvest* here — and well-done shades. While Hammett's novel is the more original and ground-breaking work, Barry's has a better character and is more *fun* to read. There, I said it!

Rush Henry began in 1943 as a hard-hitting ace crime reporter for 'Pappy Daley's Chicago newspaper *The Express*. He'd worked for the paper since 1936. Years later Henry graduated into a full-scale private eye but still maintains his ties to 'Pappy' and the paper. In his first case, after basic training and on furlough from the Marines, Henry decides to visit his home town of Weston to take care of some unfinished business before he ships out to go to war. Namely to find the murderer of his father — the legendary reporter Nick Henry. But Weston is now a town owned and run by an organized criminal gang and for Rush to go back there after 16 years causes all kinds of people, all kinds of serious concerns.

Pappy councils Rush against going back and going up against the gang:

"Are you sure you want a lead? I'm never very fond of setting a new match to an old flame. The wrong people always get burned. You will be up against something you've never hit before, Rush. An organized gang that owns the law, the courts, everything in the town. That's a big head start for any battle."

After the novel — it's 1943 and there's a war on — Henry joins the Marines. He becomes a Marine lieutenant working for Army Intelligence against the Nazis in America which brings us to the plot of the next novel, *The Third Degree* (1944). This is one of the best Henry books, full of spys, intrigue and action, and is even better than the previous book. In this one Henry discovers that the enemy plans to use a new form of sabotage — which Henry calls 'Saturation Sabotage' — but in today's terms would be called plain terrorism. Henry says to Pappy:

"…only a fool would believe that these boys Hoover caught are the only saboteurs in America. There are probably thousands, some of them citizens who've lived here for years. Now, take a central plan embracing the use of all these potential saboteurs on one operation. Say one day. Hell, they wouldn't even have to torch the war Plants. They could bomb a couple of hundred theatres, busses, trains and hotels and panic the whole damn country. They could start a bunch of riots. I'm damn sure they were just perfecting technique in that Detroit riot."

Interesting premise and way ahead of its time for 1943! Also interesting, I think, is that this article appeared in *Paperback Parade* #53 in 1999 — two years before the terrorism attacks upon our country of September 11, 2001!

After the war, and that book, Henry comes back to civilian life and becomes a detective, chronicled in *Fall Guy* (1945), and one of his earliest cases as a PI is *The Triple Cross* (1946).

"He wondered what kind of detective he had been The picture of a private operative that he dredged up from his mind was a cross between Philo Vance and Nick Charles. They always seemed able to take a series of unrelated facts and build them into a neat answer to any

question that needed answering. He decided that he wasn't that kind of detective. He wasn't any kind he had ever heard of before. He'd have to dream up a new kind of detective and be it. The only thing he could think of to do right now was to move around and stir people up. Let them think he knew something while he was trying to learn something else. He'd get everybody as close together as possible and then light a fire under them. He'd catch what boiled over, maybe it'd be the answer."

Henry also has a loyal group of aides and friends who help him in this novel. Gertrude, his office secretary; and Merwin, his not-too-bright but loyal goffer — as well as his good friend and the man who taught Rush everything he knows 'Pappy' Daley. There's also Marion Dorr, Pappy's secretary and Henry's gal — who becomes a partner on the case when as a domestic couple they go undercover together.

The Triple Cross begins in Joe Barry's (Barry Lake's) own home town, Des Moines, Iowa. Rush gets a bullet and amnesia. Later:

"...he knew he was after a murderer, but who the murderer was he still couldn't remember. Nor could he remember who the murderer had murdered. But one thing was obvious — the murderer hadn't forgotten him!"

The Rush Henry Stats: He's 32 years of age, 175 pounds, 6 feet even, dark hair with a slight wave, blue eyes, unmarried. Police reporter with the Chicago *Express*, until Spring, 1942; Marines 1942; Military Intelligence, March 1943, medical discharge with silver plate in shoulder April, 1944. Since 1944 runs a detective agency in Chicago.

The last Rush Henry adventure (forming a kind of circle in that it is similar in some ways to *The Pay-Off* which began the series) is *The Clean-Up* (1950). In it Henry has to clean up a wide-open town called Forest City. However, in this one, instead of being a reporter, he is now a hard-boiled private eye. While the books are similar in many ways, there are also stark differences and a much harder edge in *The Clean-Up*.

The next Barry hero is Bill August, a more suave and sophisticated character who only appeared in one book, *Three For The Money* (1950). This one is a sharp blackmail case that has more than it's share of murder!

My own favorite Barry hero is Donn O'Mara, who appears in two excellent novels, *Homicide Hotel* (1951) and *Kiss and Kill* (1954). O'Mara is like Rush Henry but older and more grown up. O'Mara even drinks the same booze that Henry drinks, Old Overholt. Did Barry drink the same? I wonder? *Homicide Hotel* is a hard-boiled murder mystery with O'Mara tracking down the girl-friend of a rubbed-out mobster whose stash of millions of dollars also disappeared with the girl. Aside from O'Mara getting a beating, punching out a gangster who deserved it, and pushing a gangster's moll, he seems a remarkably well-behaved fellow. In fact, in this book O'Mara even meets a nice girl, falls in love, and though tempted by at least two other women, stays loyal to his gal. In the end he finds happiness with her in a truly happy ending. It's a good murder mystery, don't let the brutal bondage cover or the sleazy digest packaging put you off. You will miss one of the neglected little classics of private eye fiction that has never been reprinted.

In *Kiss and Kill*, O'Mara almost seems to be the brother or mirror-image of Bill Gault's Joe Puma, they're kind of similar types, hard-boiled but with real heart. In this novel, we have O'Mara getting involved with international dope smuggling into New York City and a gang war between dope pushers. O'Mara's partner Lon Hoge is murdered — the only clue being a smear of lipstick on the dead man's kisser. It's a good story. If you have a copy, read it — if not, search it out!

For a while I though Joe Barry might have been a pseudonym of Jack Woodford, but that is not so. In *The Pay-Off* Barry writes the cryptic dedication: "To dad who introduced me to Jack Woodford, who practically wrote this book for me." Still, I wonder just what the connection was, if any.

Today, the eight private eye novels by Joe Barry are all but forgotten, but they shouldn't be. They're good books, great pulp crime adventure reading at it's best. Search them out. *I know you'll enjoy them!*

I Read
'Homicide Hotel'

Yes, I admit it, I did read it. Every word! From the sleazy exploitation bondage and torture cover, right on down to the very end of the story. Let me tell you it was quite an experience and a bit unexpected. It's one of those things every vintage paperback collector can't help to do at times — and therein lies a tale.

It all began during one of the Sunday book shows that were held at the New York Statler Hilton way back in the day. I was looking through some nice old books when I was attracted by a loud *"Pssst!"* A disreputable character intent upon separating me from my money? Perhaps? Well, let us investigate. Slung over his shoulder was a large green army bag, which he opened with a provocative tease, whispering in a conspiratorial tone, *"You interested in any of these?"*

The bag was filled with crime, murder and mystery vintage paperback goodies. Well, that did it, and I went to it like a fish to bait. With deft fingers, I looked through the lot (the loot!) and picked out a few cool items. Then he told me, *"Got something real special here."*

That's when he pulled out one of the 'holy grails' of crime digest paperbacks, *Homicide Hotel*. Well, I couldn't have been more surprised if he had produced a copy of *Zip Gun Angels* — but that's another story. Regardless, I knew that book was for me.

Homicide Hotel is a first edition (it has never been reprinted and likely never will be) published in 1951 by Phantom Books (#500, the first book in this short series), by Joe Barry. Joe Barry was actually Barry Lake. The book has what I would say is the most brutal torture/bondage cover art I have ever seen on any vintage era digest. It shows a young and beautiful woman made up with hot red lipstick, tied to a chair, menaced by two nasty thugs. One holds a bottle of chloroform, while the other brutally pulls her head up by the hair! The terror is clearly seen in her face and eyes as the men advance to do their worst. Talk about violence towards women! This cover really takes the cake. It is quite disgusting in those terms. The fact that anyone, anywhere, would issue a book with so offensive a cover — even by the standards of old-time paperback publishers who were notorious for doing anything to make a sale — strained my credulity about the value of the writing and story between the covers. Nevertheless, I had to find out. Well, the price was right, so I took it home and looked it over. The more I looked, the more intrigued I became, until I took the plunge. I knew I had to read *Homicide Hotel*.

It was not what I thought it was at all.

Basically, the book is a murder mystery novel with a hard-boiled detective a la Raymond Chandler's Philip Marlowe, or Dashiell Hammett's Sam Spade, who tracks down the girlfriend of a rubbed out mobster whose stash of millions of dollars also disappeared when the girl did. Detective Donn O'Mara is just as hard-boiled as Spade and Marlowe, and while he is as tough as Mickey Spillane's Mike Hammer, he is nowhere as brutal and perhaps a bit smarter. O'Mara is actually thoughtful and intelligent and the story is a tightly plotted novel of interesting characters whose motives kept me guessing until the very end.

And you know what? Surprise! I liked it and it's a damn good book!

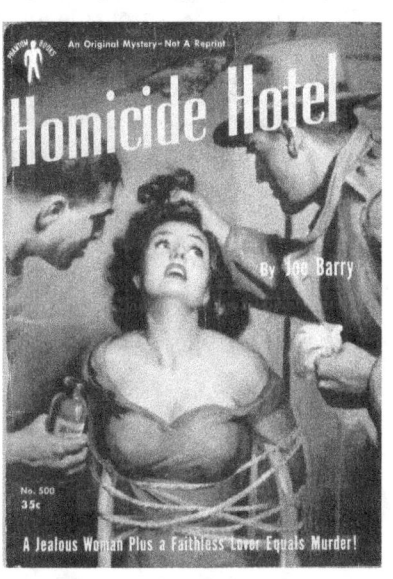

Of course the package is something else altogether. Friends who saw me reading it at work were wondering just what kind of weird stuff I was getting into. Not too worry I told them, just research for an article on old paperback books I was writing. Sure, they replied, and they looked at me a bit funny.

Aside from O'Mara finding the body of a murdered man in a hotel (and this takes up about one page of the book) the story doesn't even take place in a hotel at all! Then why the title? And as for that example of unbelievably brutal bondage/torture art on the cover — no scene or event even remotely close to this occurs in the book at all. The cover doesn't even excerpt a minor scene from the novel and expand upon it, which many paperback publishers used to do in their cover art, to exploit a sale. Back then they would have the artist illustrate only the most 'juicy part'. Of course there is some violence in this novel — this is, after all, a murder mystery — but there are very few killings and all of them take place off stage. There is no lingering on violence, such as in modern slasher movies. No sadism here in the story at all. Except for that cover art!

Aside from O'Mara getting beaten up, and punching a gangster, and a gangster's moll, he is a remarkably good and well-behaved fellow. In fact, he meets a nice girl, falls in love, and though tempted by at least two other women, stays loyal to his gal. In the end he finds love and happiness with her in a truly happy ending.

But this is still a tough, hard crime novel that fans of the genre will want to read and they will enjoy it. Unfortunately, I do not know who the artist was who did the cover art. The book is just one of 14 in the rare US Phantom Books digest series of crime novels published in 1951 to 1952. It is a key digest series, with some important and expensive books among those 14 titles, including original digest-size novels by Day Keene and Harry Whittington. The books are numbered from #500 to #513, with *Homicide Hotel* being the first book in the series. Phantom Books would also become a series of digest crime pulp novels published in Australia with redrawn covers from the American paperback editions — but that Aussie series would run to over 300 books!

However, it all began with *Homicide Hotel* and Joe Barry, who has written a book full of action and suspense that keeps you reading. It is a classic crime novel noir not to be missed by any fan of the genre. Hard to believe it when you look at that cover.

But, then, you know what they say about judging a book by the cover...

Taffin:
and a short interview with his creator,
Lyndon Mallet

Prepare to meet Taffin!

There is no one quite like him in hard-boiled crime fiction.

Mark Twill Taffin is a big English bloke created by British author, Lyndon Mallet. Taffin stands over six feet tall and is solid, shrouded in dark clothing, wearing his ever-present dark glasses so people never see his eyes and never know what he is thinking. So he is most enigmatic. However, his appearance seems incongruous when juxtaposed with his public behavior. For Taffin is soft spoken, a man of few words, always polite — he never curses and does not appreciate foul language — and while he totally understands the power of violence extremely well — he does not like to use it and in fact rarely needs to. For Taffin has 'other' methods to convince people to see his point of view. His methods are often just as effective as outright violence, but not as criminal as the use of outright violence. While if need be, Taffin can be as hard-hitting violent as the job may call for, his true talent and power is in being a master of 'the talk'. His personal interactions with people through close-spoken confidential words make for fascinating reading. Mallet's use of dialog and short concise phrases to move the story along briskly makes for a compelling read.

The Taffin books are a terrific series of hard crime novels. The reader thrills to the mesmerizing strategy used by Taffin as he weaves his web of masterful intimidation to get his jobs done. Taffin is a master of 'the talk' and intimidating ways that get people to see his side of things, and act accordingly. He also has bit of a local reputation that no one wants to go up against. Officially, Taffin is a small town 'debt collector', but he is a master at using 'pressure' in various forms, rather than gratuitous violence to get what he wants for himself, or his 'clients'.

Taffin originally appeared in three UK paperback originals that I think of as The Taffin Trilogy — for want of a better name — but there is more to the story than that. The three books in chronological order are: *Taffin* (NEL, paperback original, 1980); *Taffin's First Law* (NEL, paperback original, 1980), and *Ask Taffin Nicely* (Bonnington Books, trade paperback original, 1989). From the perspective of a fan of vintage pulp crime paperback cover art, these covers are not much to look at, but with these books it is the words inside that really do count — though as one sharp observer noted on the cover of the first book Taffin is shown holding a broken bottle in a most aggressive manner! The photo is credited to Adrian Mott.

I discovered the first two New English Library (NEL) Taffin paperbacks many years ago and was bowled over by them. They were not just good reads — they were *great* reads for any hard crime and noir fan. In fact, I liked the books so much I wrote about them in my book column in *Hardboiled* #47, the last issue of my now defunct hard crime fiction magazine in 2014. As far as I know, there are no US editions of these books.

Here's what I wrote about the first two Taffin's in *Hardboiled* #47:

"I never heard of Mallet but these two books are masterpieces of hard crime. They follow the life of a guy named Taffin, a wise-guy thug for hire, but a smart guy too, who controls the village of Lasherham in the English countryside like an old-time Mafia don. He is a masterful intimidator, and eschews violence generally, though when violence is called for, he can deliver. He is not greedy and even sometimes helps people in the community — when the community people are too weak to act. Reading these books is sheer joy as you watch just how Taffin masterfully controls every situation — and he always wins! Just great fun and worth searching for!"

I wrote those words back in 2014 and my enthusiasm for this series had not diminished one bit. In fact, it has absolutely grown. I always wondered about who the author might be, and about information on him, but I never followed up on it.

Then in late 2016 while I was perusing the latest issue of Justin Mariott's *The Paperback Fanatic* (#35), a fine British magazine for paperback collectors — much like my own long-running US magazine, *Paperback Parade* — I read Justin's fine article on the British New English Library (NEL) paperbacks of the 1970s-80s. The article included covers of many of these now very collectable NEL vintage paperbacks, including *Taffin*. Along with showing the cover, Justin wrote an intriguing bit about the author, Lyndon Mallet. It turns out that Mallet was a copy-writer. Perhaps he worked in the publishing field, maybe even at NEL? I began to wonder about him. I did a search on Mallet because the article also mentioned the intriguing fact that there were *three* books in the Taffin series — not two as I originally thought! *Three*? So what was that third book? I had never heard of any *third* book! Then I found out there is even more to this story than I ever imagined!

In the first book, *Taffin*, we meet Mark Twill Taffin and get a good taste of the mood and feel of the small English village he unofficially rules. Property developers are moving into the area and causing all kinds of consternation among the locals — and things soon get out of hand. Taffin is called in, using is own inimitable style to solve the problem.

Taffin's First Law is the second book in the series. It takes place two years later when people thought Taffin was dead. Not true. In fact, he's back! But in his absence some of the younger bloods have taken over his 'patch', so he has to move back in and take back what is his. In the meantime he begins to build a small organization of sorts from the remains of the smarter of these young bloods. It's a masterful approach.

The third book, *Ask Taffin Nicely* came out in 1989 as a larger size trade paperback — but it came out after the film. *What film* you may

ask? Well, as it turns out, there was a Taffin film in the UK, but the film is about the first book, *not* the third book.

The MGM film, *Taffin*, based on the first novel in the trilogy, came out in 1987 and it stars James Bond actor Pierce Brosnan, *before* he had the James Bond role. This was Brosnan's first lead role in a feature film after his hit TV series *Remington Steele* (1982-1986). The film moves the location of the action to Ireland, but aside from that it contains much of the mood and style of the first book. Taffin's brother, Mo, and his gal, Charlotte also appear, along with some of his younger bloods. Brosnan does not wear Taffin's trademark dark glasses which I think was a mistake, it lessens his ominous character, but he seems to take on the role with relish — and you could see when watching this film where he would make a most credible James Bond. This is a good film, it kept my interest, has some fine action and story to it, but does not quite measure up to the subdued intensity of the books. Brosnan does not have the solid, stocky, dangerous look of the Taffin we see in the books. The books have a quiet but very understated menace to them that the film tries to capture, but only does so somewhat. However, the film is still a must for any Taffin fan, and it is a good crime movie worth watching in it's own right. It may even be considered an unacknowledged classic crime cult film.

Now to the novel. The third novel, *Ask Taffin Nicely* from 1989, was published two years *after* the film appeared, so it was obviously not written as a tie-in to the film — otherwise it would have been published before, or at the same time the film appeared in 1987. Mallet, it seems, just wanted to write another Taffin, and this is a good one. It's a bit more dark, as there is a child murderer lurking in the small village of Lasherham, and things like that do NOT happen in this quaint pastoral English countryside village. Taffin is also older and wiser now, and reluctantly gets involved, as he is personally insulted that such a thing can happen on what he considers his 'patch' — the area under his 'care'.

After a Google search I discovered that Lyndon Mallet had a website and was on Facebook, and I was amazed and overjoyed to find out there that he had written a *fourth* as yet unpublished Taffin novel, *Taffin on Balance*. I was really stoked now! I had to contact him. Through the aid of ace crime author, Paul Bishop — whose own earlier praise of the these books in 2008 helped to get the good word out on them — I was able to contact Mallet and cobble together the following short interview from various emails we exchanged in early 2017. I hope you enjoy it, and I know you will enjoy all *four* of the Taffin books.

GARY LOVISI: How did you come to write about Taffin and where did he spring from?

LYNDON MALLET: I am so glad to hear you enjoyed Taffin. The character (and supporting cast) have developed over time and revisiting their world has been like catching up with old friends. For me, Taffin was always the thinking person's heavy — more interested in mind-games than violence, though not averse when necessary. Taffin is a mixture of people I've known with a bit of my own background thrown in. I left art school broke and got involved in the used car trade to subsidize learning to fly. Later I ran a creative consultancy in Soho (London) and found that business has its challenges. We only ever had two bad players but on each occasion I found dark glasses and a overcoat worked wonders.

GL: Can you talk about Taffin's interesting way of dealing with trouble?

LM: Taffin has a genuine distaste for violence and prefers mind games and sleight of hand. What you imply — what people perceive — is what counts. Get it right and you don't need to say much. The character I tried to develop early on had more natural insight than he knew. By the time we get to *Taffin on Balance*, he has discovered *Aesop's Fables* and classic problem-solving techniques like The Gordian Knot and Ockham's Razor. Without realizing it he was always drawn to this way of thinking.

GL: Can you talk about what NEL Books was like back then in 1980 and your editor there?

LM: I was introduced to NEL by my agent Jonathan Zackon. My editor and guide through that journey was Carola Edmond. When *Taffin* was ready she immediately commissioned a sequel, *Taffin's First Law* which some people understandably read first: my mistake. Carola was tragically killed in a cycling accident just before the movie was commissioned. *Ask Taffin Nicely*, which she also edited, is dedicated to her.

GL: What did you think about the film? It was Brosnan before Bond.

LM: The film. The Taffin I write about is heavily built, slow-moving, monosyllabic and facially expressionless. Pierce Brosnan is one of the nicest men you'll ever meet. He was extremely kind to my son Jay (a special effects cameraman) when they met on the set of a Tony Scott movie some years later. But Pierce was Bond. Since then Taffin has lost weight and trimmed down a good deal. If *Taffin on Balance* was filmed now, Pierce Brosnan would be perfect.

GL: Can you give us a hint about the new Taffin book and when it will appear?

LM: I finished *Taffin on Balance* in November, 2016 and I hope it adds another dimension to the characters. They're all older and wiser (?) which can't be a bad thing. The new book is ready to go and I am waiting to hear what kind of a deal we have. The sleeve notes will read something like this: *Taffin on Balance*, once a heavy debt-collector, Taffin has settled down in his home town with his long-time girlfriend Charlotte to run Muscle Motors, restoring and selling classic American cars. Some locals still lionize him, insisting a film they've all seen was based on his resistance to a ruthless developer. Taffin never comments on this and lets it be known that, in spite of their confidence in him, he will not be drawn into local conflicts in the future. But the past is close behind. Someone is trying to put Muscle Motors out of business and Taffin is forced to dust off his old skills. The threat is personal, deadly, and puts him in touch with corruption reaching from his home territory into the Cabinet Office.

So, there you have it. If you love to read well-crafted, exciting, thoughtful hard crime fiction with a British flavor, start now making your acquaintance with Taffin. You are in for a real treat!

That 4th novel, *Taffin On Balance* came out in 2017 in a UK trade paperback.

A Ride Down
One Way Street

At first appearance, this is just the usual 1950s short-format Pyramid vintage paperback, but a second glance reveals this one has all the right stuff that made these hard crime noirs so effective and popular. This novel is full of hard-boiled attitude, with a tough hero on a dangerous case, as sexy gals do all kinds of shenanigans in a crooked town of dirt and decay to bring him down. Dashiell Hammett would have gotten a kick out of this book, and in some ways it is a homage to his own cult classic, *Red Harvest*.

The book in question is *One Way Street* by Nick Marino (a pseudonym, and more on him later), originally published in hardcover by Henry Holt in 1952. However, the popular versions of this mini crime classic are the two paperback reprints by Pyramid Books (#65, from 1952 and #158 from 1955). Both Pyramid paperbacks have excellent cover art depicting sexy femme fatales right out of noir hell, and tough guys in scenes directly from the story that drip hard boiled violence, tension and bad attitude.

Mike Maccauley is one of those tough guys, an assistant district attorney whose boss has tasked him with finding the killer of a low level

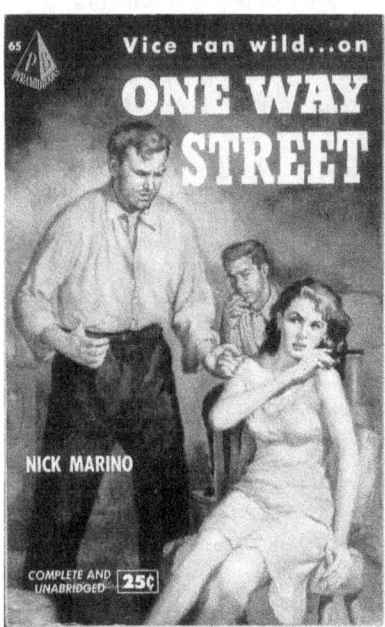
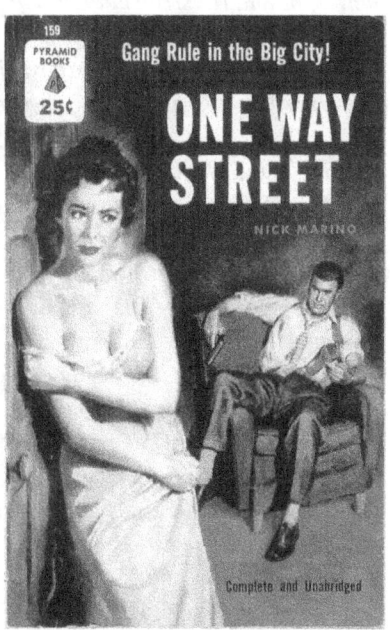

criminal. Mike uses his fists and his wits to investigate what has become of a guy named Sammy Castle, a loveable, half-pint bookie who got in over his head and has since disappeared. Sammy is presumed dead, but why would anyone want to kill him? He's a nothing guy.

Well, it seems that a lot of people were interested in Sammy, or more properly, in what Sammy knew. You see, Sammy had weaved an intricate web of deceit throughout the city for years among the various people and factions who run it. One of these is powerful Senator Fremont, who is beginning hearings to undo the local Mob rackets. Another is his lovely daughter, Babs, who is doing things for her own mysterious reasons. Then there's groups of ruthless racketeers who own gambling and sex clubs, a big-time mobster named Apollo who wants to run the town and all the people in it, and other people both powerful and powerless who don't want their apple cart upset by Mike's nosing around the rackets.

The action opens when Mike meets a sexy red-head named Della in a local bar. She chats him up, then drops the bomb that she was a friend of the late lamented Sammy with some inside info to spill. When she tells Mike that she's afraid the same thing that happened to Sammy will happen to her, so they head to her place for a more private talk. It would seem Mike and Della have a lot to talk about once at her place...but first...

She turned away from me and walked toward the sofa. She flung herself down, twisting her body temptingly. I stood for a moment looking at her half-covered, pink-white softness. Then I knelt down quickly and reached out, drawing her to me. Her arms were around my neck, her lips wet and urgent, searching for mine.

Hours later...we find Mike asleep in bed, but when he awakes Della is not there. He soon discovers Della sitting alone on the couch in the living room — with a bullet in her head!

Mike realizes he's in serious trouble now. Being a righteous ADA he calls the cops then goes to the office to tell his boss, DA Sunshine. What happens next freaks Mike out even more than Della's murder, because Della's body has up and disappeared. It seems that when the cops go into the apartment, they not only don't find her body, they don't find any sign of violence or any crime having occurred there at all. In fact, there is no record of a Della Lee even existing. It seems the gal didn't live in the apartment she took Mike to. So as far as the cops are concerned there was no murder, and there was no Della Lee! Mike smells set up...or something worse.

Of course this really has Mike freaked. He knows he's stumbled onto something deadly serious. But what does it all mean? Mike's more determined than ever to find out, and to find Della's killer. He realizes that her murder is somehow connected to the disappearance of Sammy Castle. So Mike goes on the hunt in what turns into a brutal, convoluted case with an interesting cast of characters who keep you guessing all along.

Blurbs from inside the book tell us:

Nick Marino is the pen name of a top-ranking author who has scored many outstanding successes in the field of literature. But it is in his latest novel, One Way Street, that he has created one of his most amazing characters, Mike Mccauley. The New York Herald Tribune ranks Maccauley right alongside the god of blood and guts, Mickey Spillane's Mike Hammer.

Well, Spillane's a tough act to follow, so while Maccauley isn't exactly a Mike Hammer bulls-eye, he gets pretty close. Mike Mccauley is as hard-boiled a tough guy as you're likely to meet in any vintage era paperback, and he plays a tough and dangerous game with deadly femme fatales and brutal gangsters. One thing for sure, if you like Mike Hammer, Mike Mccauley will not disappoint you and *One Way Street* is the tale of a Hammettesque hell-town that will keep you reading to find out how it all ends.

Marino has some nifty tricks up his sleeve to always keep the reader wondering what will happen next. Like when big-time gangster, George Apollo, bribes Mike with $20,000 cash to take his side against another mobster, up-and-coming Joe Friendly. Has Mike sold out, or not? We're actually not quite sure. Eventually we discover that he has sold out — but for his own reasons. Here's how the author describes it:

Apollo wasted no time about getting to the point. "Made up your mind, Mike?"
I said, "Why do you think I'm here?"
He didn't really need my answer. He knew it the moment I showed up at his office. He was just savoring the moment — watching another sucker come to heel.
He opened a drawer of the big desk, drew out a small metal box. They lived, these men, by little metal boxes. Ordinary banks weren't safe for their kind of money.
He took the bills out, hundred-dollar bills, new and crisp, and began counting.
"Here you are, Mike. Cabbage. Nice and clean. I hate dirty bills."

It turns out that both mobsters, and a lot of other people, such as Senator Fremont's daughter, Babs, and DA Sunshine want to know the secret that got little Sammy killed. Sammy, it seemed, had discovered the secret identity of fabled "Mr. Fix" — the top guy high up in politics and finance who is prime mover behind the mob and everything bad that happens in that city — and that is what got Sammy dead. Is it DA Sunshine? Is it big-time mobsters Apollo or Friendly? Perhaps Senator Fremont? Or even his daughter, Babs? Or maybe, can it actually be Mike Maccualey?

Nick Marino is a fine writer and is actually the pen-name of veteran pulpster Will Oursler (William Charles Oursler, 1913-1985) who wrote 45 books on a variety of subjects, including 12 fine mystery novels. He was adept at hard-boiled crime and noir.

One of Oursler's best mysteries under his own name was *Departure Delayed* (Ace Book #D-37, 1952) an early Ace Double; another was *N.Y., N.Y.* (Cardinal Book #C173, from 1955). Oursler also edited *As Tough As They Come* (Perma Book #P-118, 1951) a classic hard-boiled noir vintage paperback anthology.

There is one other book under the Nick Marino byline, *City Limits*, Pyramid Book #315, a paperback original from 1958. This one was reprinted as Pyramid Book #F-887 in 1963 and also in the UK by Digit Books as #R340 in 1958. However, *City Limits* was actually ghost-written by veteran mystery author and paperback hackster Richard Deming from an outline done by Oursler. So while *City Limits* has much of Oursler in it, it is not a *true* Oursler Nick Marino novel.

One Way Street is the *true* Oursler Nick Marino book. It has the tight plot, realistic characters and miles of mean street moodiness noir readers want in a hard-boiled crime vintage paperback. *One Way Street* keeps you guessing until the end and is a most satisfying read. Get a copy and enjoy the ride. You won't regret it!

Vin Packer: The Return

Marijane Meaker may not be that well known to most crime and mystery readers, but the name Vin Packer certainly is well-known. It is a name associated with some of the best-written and most collectable crime paperback originals of the 1950s and 60s. Meaker's books as Vin Packer, give us outstanding mystery, crime, as well as realistic and truthful juvenile delinquent novels. Later, as Ann Aldrich, she would write lesbian-theme novels that were far ahead of their time. Still later, as M.E. Kerr, she would write many fine Young Adult novels.

Beginning in the pulp paperbacks of the 1950s Marijane Meaker, under her Vin Packer and Ann Aldrich pseudonyms, dared what was almost impossible, writing about subjects that were never to be spoken of out loud, only veiled in whispers – especially for such a nice young lady. Crime, murder, matricide, juvenile delinquency, sex, including lesbianism. She wrote honestly about these topics and in doing so helped usher in the era of the paperback original with stories that grabbed readers as never before.

Meaker presented strong female characters in all of her books, women

much like herself, full of life and passion who were not afraid to stake their ground in a world that was often hard and unforgiving. Her original paperbacks were big sellers and very popular and they gave vent to feelings not often found back then for women in paperback fiction.

Marijane Meaker was born in Auburn, New York in 1927 and began her long and successful writing career at 23 years of age when in 1952 she began writing original crime novels as Vin Packer for Gold Medal Books.

Meaker worked for Gold Medal as a secretary and when the new publishing line was introduced – paperback originals – she wrote a book for it. That book was *Spring Fire* (GM #222) and it sold right away. As the cover blurb proclaims it's "a story once told in whispers now frankly, honestly written." It is a murder mystery about Leda and Mitch that takes place at a women's college which also involves their lesbian romance. The cover art by Bayre Phillips shows the two women in slips, sitting together upon a bed, but looking away from each other, as if highlighting the tension between them. It's an effective image and one that will often be used, in a variety of ways, on the covers of many books that deal with the subject.

Mystery critic Jon Breen said of Meaker's Packer books, "Her probing accounts of the roots of crime are richly detailed snapshots of their times, unconventional, intensely readable, and devoid of heroes, villains, or pat solutions."

When I asked her why so many of her characters seemed troubled, deluded or confused, Meaker told me, "I was following cases and fictionalizing them. I was young and perhaps cynical but I was trying to create interesting characters and they usually, to my mind, are not happy-go-lucky, upbeat personalities, particularly in the crime field. I wasn't trying to *say* anything – just tell a good story."

Ed Gorman puts it more simply, but to the point, "[Vin Packer] was one hell of a writer."

Some of her best Vin Packer crime novels are tense noirs that deal with people living secret lives or who are trapped in complicated relationships that often lead to murder. *Something in the Shadows* (GM#1146, 1961) is about Joseph Meaker (she sometimes used her own name for characters), Maggie and Hart find themselves in a brutal story of horror and crime. In *Intimate Victims* (GM #1241, 1962), we have an amazing novel of people who have literally changed identities and the good and evil that results. Then in *5:45 To Suburbia* (GM #731, 1958) she shows the two sides of Charlie Gibsons' life. Charlie rode the 5:45 to Westport every day, he was an important publishing executive, well liked, but also addicted to a powerful woman who had made him the success he'd become, and he could not break away from her. Thus begins his downfall.

With *The Girl on the Best Seller List* (GM #976, 1960) and *The Damnation of Adam Blessing* (GM #1074, 1961) we have stories that seem torn from today's headlines, but were written over 60 years ago! The former tells the story of a woman whose tempestuous book laid bare the secrets of the most influential people of a small town – and now they want revenge against her! The latter novel delves into the private and strange world created by a man, and the woman who dared enter it.

Meaker's books also included three tough but truthful juvenile delinquent novels, a once popular sub-genre of crime fiction. *The Thrill Kids* (1955) gives us kids on the prowl for kicks and murder. The cover art by James Meese captures the moment of lust and danger that runs through the book for one young woman. In *The Young and The Violent* (GM #581, 1956), the blurbs tell us, "expect to get hurt when you hit upper Park Avenue, where the asphalt battleground – and violence begin," it's a stunning crime novel of teenage armies and warrior gangs who rumble and murder each other to protect their concrete turf. A harrowing JD classic. Finally in *The Twisted Ones* (GM #861, 1959), we have another tense brutal novel of rape and murder among wild youth and gangs. These books were very popular and reprinted many times. And like all the books she wrote, as by Vin Packer, they were also based upon real cases that Meaker came upon in her research.

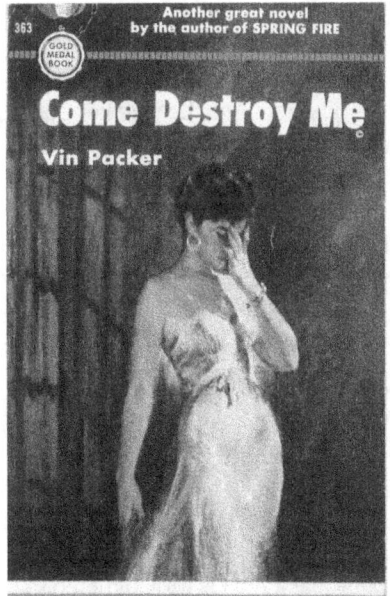

Perhaps her most intense and lauded crime novel is *The Evil Friendship* as by Vin Packer (GM #797). This brutal novel of murder and matricide is based on the famous 1954 Parker-Hulme murder case from New Zealand. Anthony Boucher characterized the story as "a lesbian Loeb-Leopold."

In fact, when I asked her about how she heard about the original case, Meaker said, "Boucher called the case to my attention. I sent for the trial transcripts. Juliet Hulme, it turned out, served only 5 ½ years and is writing best selling mysteries."

Marijane added in a further email: "The name Juliet Hulme took after she got out of prison and wrote murder mysteries is a famous one: Anne Perry. She's now the very celebrated author of all those Victorian mysteries. I knew a long time ago she had taken that pseudonym but I never mentioned it until the New York *Times* did a big write up on it when the movie *Heavenly Creatures*, (based on the case) came out…"

Meaker's other Vin Packer novels concern race relations and crime in the deep South of the 1950s. In *3-Day Terror* (GM #689, 1957) a small town is torn apart by a vicious killer. In *Dark Don't Catch Me* (GM #624, 1956), one of the major premises is the sexual tension between Blacks and Whites that boils over into racial anger and inevitably murder. Meaker said she based the first book on the famous Emmett Till murder case, and the other novel was based on various news stories she heard during the period.

In 1955, Meaker broke in a new pseudonym, and broke new ground, as Ann Aldrich. Under that name she published her first overtly lesbian-theme novel, *We Walk Alone* (GM #509). While some of her Packer books touched upon this subject mixing it with crime (such as with *Spring Fire*), the Aldrich books were expressly about lesbian lives and relationships and told their stories with an unapologetic honesty rarely seen in mainstream fiction dealing with this subject back then. The books were very popular with readers, male and female. Men bought and read books with lesbian subject matter for curiosity or titillation. However, women read them to discover a world they did not know existed, and for many women these books told them they were not alone, that the feelings they had for women, were felt by other women. It was a liberating feeling for many of these women back then.

"As a gay woman," Meaker said, "the themes were natural to me. I'm glad to see that after all these years, gay writing is viewed as a legitimate literature."

Marijane Meaker wrote 20 original paperback novels for Gold Medal Books from 1952 to 1965. She said, "I loved Dick Carroll!" – speaking of the legendary editor of the line and the originator of the paperback original – "I never knew the others. Those were great days!"

Shortly after Dick Carroll died, Meaker stopped writing as Vin Packer. Marijane Meaker has also written books for teens and young adults as M.E. Kerr. She adds, "I think it's easier to see the adult in the child – and easier to reach the adult through the child."

One of her most interesting books is non-fiction. This was *Highsmith: A Romance of the 50s* (Cleis Press, 2003) written under her own name. It is the story of how Meaker met the reclusive novelist Patricia Highsmith, who had penned noir masterpieces *The Talented Mr. Ripley* and *Strangers on a Train*. They met in a Greenwich Village lesbian bar, and began a two-year romance. Gore Vidal has called Highsmith "One of our greatest modernist writers." Meaker's book tells how these two popular mystery writers lived and loved during those long ago days of the 1950s.

When I asked her why she wrote the book after so many years, Meaker said, "There are two reasons I wrote the Highsmith memoir. First, I'm a writer, that's what I do. But I also knew Pat when she was young and not yet so jaded and bigoted. The Internet is filled with stories of her meanness, and prejudice, and also of her introversion, of her being a loner. I met that Pat many years after we broke up. She wrote me a letter c/o Author's Guild suggesting a visit. We hadn't seen each other in 32 years. All the while she was with me I remembered the old Pat who loved entertaining: cooking for people, laughing with them. She had become a self-pitying, hateful woman, only once seeming like her old self, and that was when she appeared before my writers' workshop and took questions and talked about writing. Then, as soon as we had left the building she described one eager questioner as "That Jew with the white hair," and asked not to eat dinner out because she didn't feel like sitting around and waiting for another drink. I wondered if my memory had tricked me, if there was any way I could recall her as I knew her, and what began as a small sideline exercise became a memoir. She came back to me vividly, and sadly – because that Pat had ceased to exist. The only explanation I have for the change in her was alcohol. She began drinking at breakfast and kept at it all day. Ever polite and "gentlemanly" she had brought both scotch and gin with her."

Stark House Press began a Vin Packer revival in 2007, reprinting her classic crime novels in attractive trade paperbacks that contain two Packer novels per book. Offerings include *Something in the Shadows* & *Intimate Victims*, and two matricide novels, *The Evil Friendship* & *Whisper His Sin*. These books are some of the best crime reading around and are real bargains.

Meaker fans will be happy to hear that Vin Packer has made a comeback! *Scott Free*, is an original mystery novel and the first in a new series starring a transgendered detective. Meaker said, "Scott, formerly Scotti, is a man from the waist down and a woman from waist up because she can't afford the surgery. But after solving a case and getting a reward she will be a full man in the next book."

Meaker told me recently, "I became interested in transsexuals in a negative way. I though it was a form of homophobia. I never realized how many very accomplished and formidable people had a different sexual orientation than what they were born as. The first book I read on the subject gave me a lot to think about, it was by a favorite British travel writer named James Morris. It was called *Conundrum* and it was about his yearning to be female. I began to read many novels, articles, biographical essays and research by specialists in the field.

"I had always wanted to do an adult detective series (I had done a 3-book Young Adult Series, by M.E. Kerr: *Fell, Fell Down* and *Fell Back*). I thought it would be fascinating to create a young man, married with a child (as they so often are before they finally surrender to their true selves), then beginning the long process to a sex change. I wrote the book at the beginning of 1990. Everyone thought I was crazy. My agent gave up on it… Finally, many years later, I updated it and Carroll & Graf bought it immediately. I decided my only adult name people might remember was Vin Packer. Also Stark House had begun reprinting old Packers, so I liked writing as her again, and anew."

Scott Free by Vin Packer came out in May, 2007 from Carroll & Graf.

Scott Jordan: The Hard-boiled Lawyer

One of the best of the hard-boiled detectives, and one of the most neglected, is the fast-living lawyer Scott Jordan. Jordan is the creation of Harold Q. Masur (aka Hal Masur), himself a practicing lawyer, born and educated in New York, who presented cases as fiction. Masur was a founder, with Bruno Fischer, of the prestigious writer's organization, The Mystery Writers of America. I knew Hal for many years. I interviewed him for my magazine, *Paperback Parade*, published some of his crime fiction under my Gryphon Books imprint, and he was a annual guest at my New York City book shows for about ten years. We were good friends, he was a class act, and he wrote some damn good books! I think his Scott Jordan novels are terrific.

Masur's lawyer-detective Scott Jordan is a smart guy and can be a tough guy when he has to be, but basically he's a decent guy trying to do his job and help his clients. He's definitely in that rugged Sam Spade mould, but he is a lot more human and humane. A truly good guy — much as was Hal himself.

Scott Jordan novels are full of action and entertaining hard-boiled dialog and description, but they also have interesting stories that make use of good plot elements and skilled detection. It's fun to follow Jordan on a case — he's no Perry Mason, and he's no Mike Hammer — but he gets the job done and he's the kind of guy you don't want to mess with. He's an intelligent guy, an educated man, and a fellow who won't stand still and let another person clean up a mess that's been dumped in his lap. I guess you might describe him as Sam Spade with a law degree. He's the type of lawyer that Perry Mason *should* have been, but wasn't. Perry Mason was watered down for more mass appeal. Scott Jordan is the real thing.

The first novel in the series is *Bury Me Deep*. It was originally written by Hal when he was serving in the U.S. Army in China during World War II. It is a great hard-boiled title that definitely sets the mood, and it is a fast-moving murder mystery. It begins when Jordan comes home early to find a beautiful but unknown blonde half-dressed and very drunk in his apartment. From then on things get ever more complicated when murder and intrigue rear their twin heads, with Jordan stuck in the middle trying to solve the crime, and clear himself of a murder charge.

Bury Me Deep was, like all of Masur's Jordan novesls, originally published in hardcover. The first paperback printing was published in 1948 (#558) from Pocket Books. It has seductively alluring good-girl cover art by William Wirts. It was reprinted in 1957 by Dell Books, and there is a 1984 Quill Books reprint that uses cover art based on the original William Wirts art from the 1948 Pocket Books paperback edition.

The second book, *Suddenly A Corpse*, was published by Pocket Books (#704) in 1950. It has great cover art by Bayre Phillips. One of the cover blurbs has Jordan tell us about the female villain of the novel:

"Don't push your luck, baby! A pretty gambler like you would make a prettier corpse."

The story begins with a phone call and a dead man, then escalates with fast action and some very good detection. It's a fun read.

You Can't Live Forever is the third Jordan novel, with a title right out of W.R. Burnett. The first paperback printing was from Pocket Books, (#860) in 1952, and has a wild Frank McCarthy cover featuring Jordan battling a pretty female murderess. The cover depicts the following fight scene from the novel:

"*I swarmed in and clamped a hand over her mouth. It muffled the outcry but turned her into a frenzied animal. She twisted and kicked and clawed. Fingernails raked my face. Spiked heels beat frantically against my shins. She got one of my fingers between her teeth and tried to amputate it.*"

Rough stuff, and this was way back in 1951!

So Rich So Lovely, And So Dead, is the fourth Jordan novel. Pocket Book reprinted it for the first time in 1953 (#988) with a lovely Stanley Zuckerberg cover. It was later reprinted by Dell Books in 1961 (#D383) with gorgeous Robert McGinnis cover art. McGinnis' cover was obviously influenced by the previous cover done by Zuckerberg, the pose of the woman is after all similar, yet McGinnis has refined the Zuckerberg image and updated it. It's much more vibrant and alive. Both of these covers are favorites of mine. They are great works of art from different decades, from two very individualistic artists, and they illustrate this hard crime novel extremely well.

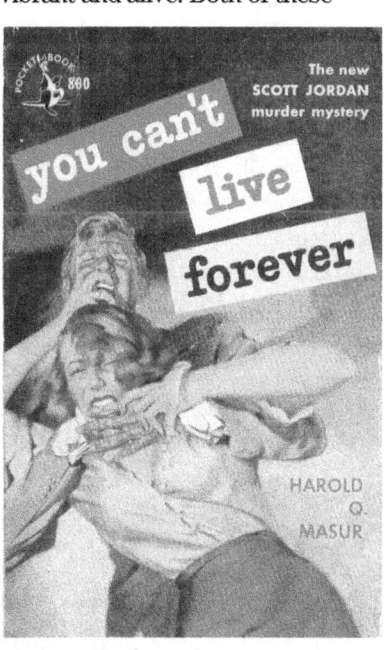

In this Scott Jordan novel we have a rich and beautiful countess, tagged by the newspapers as "the fabulous screw-ball" who seems to prove it to Jordan when she offers him $5,000 if he'll marry her. Jordan never gets a chance to accept her proposition, or to find out why it was offered, because in less than 24 hours she's murdered. Jordan finds himself in the soup again and has to find the real killer.

You get the idea. This is good stuff. The other books in the series — and there are more of them — I have only mentioned the first four paperback reprints here — are well worth seeking out. Masur was an under-rated author and his Scott Jordan books are just terrific reads. Most of them have not been reprinted for 40-50 years. So seek them out in vintage era editions and read them. You'll not be disappointed!

Falling Into The 'Sin Pit'

"She was dirt... and hungry and cheap and demanding. But it didn't matter. She was all these things, and I know it, but she was much more, too. She was fire and ice and fury, and when she came up to me – that first time – her mouth making little squirming noises, I knew she was all I ever wanted."

So says tough, and somewhat honest cop, Barney Black, about the girl of his dreams, Grace Trudo. He meets her on the investigation of her murdered 17yr. old friend, Randy Harding. Randy is shot with one .32 slug in the head and her body is found with whip marks. From that point on begins one of the toughest, most twisted, hard-boiled police procedural novels you'll ever read. You will not be able to put this book down.

Sin Pit by Paul S. Meskil (Lion Books #98, PBO March 1954) is 127 pages of gut-churning crime intensity. A fascinating and fun read, tough-cop Barney takes us on a journey through the sin pit – better known as "Sin City", AKA East St. Louis, Illinois. He starts off by telling us that "Sin City" is a hell hole town so corrupt that basically everyone is on the take, or for sale, or running some kind of scam. Even the cops – especially the cops. He also presents one of the ultimate femme fatales in the guise of Grace Trudo. The first time Barney sees Grace he describes her like this:

"She wasn't beautiful, like the movie dolls are beautiful, but she had more of what it takes to be a woman than anyone I had ever seen before. She was pure, raw sex. And I wanted her, just like that."

From then on life is all downhill for Barney as he pieces together what turns out to be a case more twisted than you'd think Lion Books or any 1954 crime paperback would dare publish. The case, (and I'm going to give away the plot here so if you want to just skip this part go to the next paragraph) concerns what twists into a lesbian S&M whipping case between Grace and the murdered girl Randy. See, it appears Grace's gambler 'husband' just liked to 'watch the special goings on in their basement S&M chamber between the two women'. But when Randy decided to get some cheating sex with Grace's husband, Grace kills Randy – but not because Randy is cheating with Grace's husband — but because Randy was cheating on Grace *with a man!*

So you can see Barney is stuck on this case and has to dig around, all the time a homicidal killer is murdering witnesses and then goes after Barney – even as his superiors on the police are watching him and getting increasingly suspicious that *he* may be the killer! In the meantime to solve this case, and to make the lovely Grace his, he has to find her and clear her. What he ends up doing is finding out that he is soon going way over the line, placing his career, his freedom, and even his life in dire jeopardy.

Sin Pit is a fine novel. This is the first novel by Paul Meskil, and his *only* book for Lion. I had heard that a few years back he was alive and living on Long Island. I saw him interviewed on some kind of police show back then. Meskil wrote a couple of other books that I know of, though at the time I first wrote this article I did not know the titles, one was a paperback original for Playboy Press in the 1970's, another was a Mob autobiography. Unfortunately at the time I had no information on these books but I have mentioned them elsewhere in this book, and if *Sin Pit* is any indication of his hard-hitting hard-boiled style they will be books you want to read. Meskil understands cops & crime, and the hard-boiled attitude that oozes through and rings true in a book like *Sin Pit*. It's a good read, one of those neglected Lion Classics that deserves reprinting. It would make one hell of a Film Noir.

UPDATE: When Meskil read my article, it led to him contacting me and eventually being a guest at my book show, an interview in *Paperback Parade*, and my reprinting *Sin Pit* as a Gryphon Books trade paperback edition using the original Lion cover art. *Sin Pit* has since been reprinted by Stark House in the 2022 omnibus *Lion Trio 3: Femmes Fatale*.

A Noir Unknown:
One By One

As any paperback reader or collector knows, vintage paperbacks have exploited every subject under the sun to make a sale — women, sex, drugs, race, prison, war, lust, gangs — whatever, so you know how it goes! However, a lot of really good books have been exploited themselves — some are about important or interesting subjects or relationships — such as the novel, *One By One* by Fan Nichols (Popular Library #409, from 1952).

The cover blurb announces some of the intent of the book and a bit about Dolly, the main character. It proudly tells us: "Dolly had less morals than an alley cat," Sounds like a cute kid! She's the type of gal who ran down and tamed her men, one by one, hence the title. And she's a real hellcat!

The blurbs on this book are some of the most outrageous I've ever seen on a mass-market vintage paperback, and they never fail to elicit a rowdy laugh when I show the book to friends. Books were certainly packaged differently in the early 1950s, and legitimate mainstream publishers got away with a lot — but collectors love this stuff today. Readers too!

On the back cover written in large red letters is proclaims, "She lived on Men!" That is then followed by a hard-hitting description of Dolly's interesting personality. It goes on to tell us:

Dolly was a blonde tramp with less morals than an alley cat — a cheap floozie who'd sell herself for peanuts to any man. Her world was a dark jungle of tawdry bars, rotgut whisky, and men with hot hands.

She seems like the perfect bad-gal, femme fatale. Even with all that, I had to admit this description must have went just a bit overboard. I mean...really? So with that in mind, I knew I just had to read the damn thing to see for myself.

Well, to begin with, Dolly's new boy friend, Jerry, picks her up (quite easily I can assure you) in a 'dime-a-dance joint'. Then he takes her across state lines to Las Vegas — violating the Mann Act — because it seems Dolly is underage and still 'jailbait'.

The story takes place during the Hoover years of the Depression, in the early 1930s. The book opens with Jerry stalking Dolly. He's going to kill her for destroying his life — the next chapter begins the story of that destruction as Jerry and a friend go to a cheap dance hall for a night's amusement, only to find themselves in the middle of a riot - started by Dolly. Dolly is rescued from the joint by Jerry and their relationship begins. Jerry should have stayed home that night, and he would have done so, had he known what was in store for him! Poor guy.

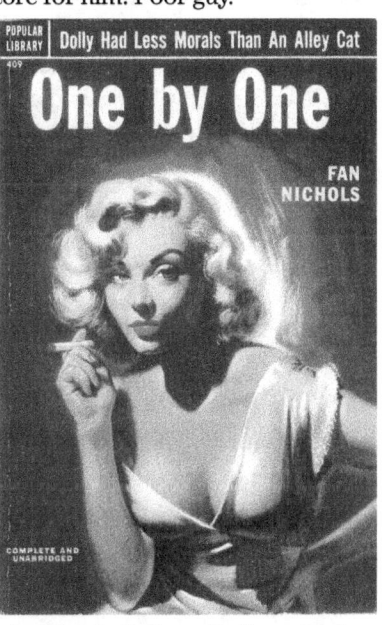

One By One is a surprisingly well-written noir novel by a veteran pulpster who wrote many fine crime novels. It features good characterization and descriptions, written with that cynical wit Dashiell Hammett and James M. Cain had popularized so well at the time. It has a down-to-earth, nitty-grittyness in dialog and description that makes it a fascinating read. You'd never know this though, because the way the blurbs advertise the book, they only concentrate on the tawdry exploitative angles and really miss the importance and interest of the overall story.

It is a compelling story as Jerry falls for blonde hell-cat Dolly and takes her to Las Vegas — though she's under 18 years of age and 'jailbait'. Perhaps *Jailbait* would have been a more accurate title for this book — but then again, Popular Library had already used *that* title a year earlier on their book #392. So they could not use that title. In fact, *One By One* even carries a house ad for *Jailbait* in the back of the book!

In *One By One*, Fan Nichols describes the terrible decent of Jerry's life into a year and a half of hell with Dolly. There is an eventual showdown where Dolly even tries to blackmail Jerry and his wife with a threat to send him to prison. In the end Jerry finally deals with Dolly and goes back home to his pregnant wife. In some ways this is a real soap opera of a novel, as it tells the tough story about a decent sort of guy who makes one bad mistake — and then all the other mistakes just naturally seem to follow him as if it is all automatic. Noir at high-speed!

Dolly is one of the nastiest women you'll ever meet in crime fiction. She is full of hate, spite, and greed, a person who uses everyone without care and destroys or corrupts everyone she comes into contact with.

Pure poison. Definitely not the type of gal a guy would bring home to mother — unless mom is a warden at a woman's correctional facility!

Given Dolly's personality, one wonders how Jerry put up with her. Something has got to be wrong with Jerry. Is he crazy, stupid, or just too damn horny? In one scene Dolly says (talking about Jerry to his wife): "He's wanted to kill me a long time but he never will. You know why? Because he wants to go to bed with me more than he wants to kill me."

One By One is a good read, that will grab you and not let go until you finish it. It is not a book you can put down — kinda like Dolly. It is about people with real problems and actual human feelings that surge out of control and cause even more problems. It's an interesting story about another world of long ago and a group of people who tried to survive in that world. Some succeed, other do not. It's noir to the core.

They Don't Dance Much:
James Ross' Fabulous One-Shot Wonder

A guy write's one book in his entire life.
One book, then no others.
No more is heard from him.
Maybe you figure, so what?

Except, if you're a reader and fan of hard-boiled crime fiction *They Don't Dance Much* by James Ross is an outstanding book you'll not want to miss and one you will not soon forget. If you don't have a copy, or have never read this book, you will want to search for it. It's kind of in the James M. Cain tradition, but with a title right out of Horace McCoy, characters out of Jim Thompson or David Goodis, and featuring mood and atmosphere by none other than Cornell Woolrich. All this from a hard-boiled crime novel written in 1940, before most of the hard boilers mentioned above had hit their stride. Pretty impressive. Especially for a one-shot wonder.

They Don't Dance Much was originally published by Houghton Mifflin in 1940, when Ross was just 29 years old, in a damn hard to find and very collectable hardcover first edition. It is a rare book, that in nice condition with dust jacket could cost you a few hundred dollars. Ross has said there were only 5,000 copies printed, and 1,200 were remaindered.

The book was reprinted as a mass-market paperback only once, by Signet Books (#913) in April, 1952, in a 'Abridged' version. However, there was also a 35-cent priced Canadian Signet edition, which was also a first printing from December, 1952, with the same book number and cover. This edition was also 'Abridged'.

There was later a British paperback edition that I have heard tell of, but I have never seen. However, in 1977, the Southern Illinois University Press issued an attractive and scarce reprint edition in Matthew Bruccoli's 'Lost American Fiction' series.

I have no idea what the abridgement was or how it affected the total work. I have only read the American Signet paperback and never seen the original 1940 hardcover, so I could not tell you if it was abridged for reasons of race, sex, violence, or length. Each a valid reason by itself, or all could be possibilities. Though one hunch might be length, as Signet may have cut the original book down to fit their paperback format page count. They had a requisite number of pages for their standard 25 cents mystery paperbacks back then. However, I can see it abridged because of racial reasons — and I will explain that further on.

Ross' main character and narrator, Jack MacDonald, tells a fascinating story (one that seems like it might be autobiographical, as it takes place in North Carolina where the author was born and lived). Jack tells of his friendship, partnership, and uneasy partner-in-crime relationship with a guy named Smut Milligan. Smut's a tough, savvy, big southern redneck out to make a go of it — by hook or by crook — with his high-class River Bend Roadhouse — a gambling den, honky-tonk, in the Carolina back roads in 1940.

With a name like Smut, you know the bad guy's gotta be really bad!

Smut Milligan's an interesting character. Early on in the book Jack gives us a brief intro to Smut:

"Smut Milligan was a couple of years older than I was, but I knew him pretty well. I don't know what his name really was. He didn't know either. He was adopted by Ches Milligan and his wife when he was a baby." (page 12)

And later on:

"After his wife died Ches Milligan had plenty of freedom. But he was sort of lost and took to drinking. He got to dinking so much that he lost his business. Then he put on a protracted drunk. He cashed in his insurance policies and stayed drunk till that was all gone. When he sobered up about all he had left was a shotgun and one shell. He cut the barrel of the shotgun and put he shell through his head." (page 12)

Of the young Smut, Jack tells us:

"When we were kids in high school I was a good catcher, but Smut was the regular catcher and I didn't get to play much. I lay out of school one year so he'd get on through and I could have the field to myself. He was a big, rough fellow and I was always afraid of him. But he seemed to like me." (page 13)

Jack's lucky Smut likes him, but Smut is a bully and proves to be so much worse.

They Don't Dance Much is a well-written, hard down-home type novel, with a regional style of writing popular at the time, similar in tone and feel to what Erskine Caldwell, William Faulkner, and Charles Williams were doing back then.

My only problem with this book was what I felt was a too liberal use of the 'N' word in the text. However, remembering this a novel from 1940, set in the deep South of that era, and it is a crime novel with nasty characters — people back then spoke like that. Not only were things different back then, this book lays it all bare and out there. Race hatred, crime, betrayal, lies, double-dealing, murder, and a gut full of rage and pain. Nevertheless, the 'N' word seems used by the author/narrator, (James/Jack?) without malice — if that can be said to be possible. Not in a blatantly racist or hateful way, it was just matter-of-fact back then, sadly the way people just spoke naturally, and nothing very special about it. All the more upsetting, actually — but Ross is telling it the way it truly was.

With all that, I think the book gives the reader a realistic look and feel for the language and its usage back then — the kind of deeply ingrained and matter-of-fact racism of the day. It is interesting how the word is often used and regarded by whites in the book, even well-meaning ones, who know better, who also use it liberally and matter-of-factly. What really bothers me about all this is that by having the author's first person narrator (Jack) sprinkling his speech with the 'N' word, it seems to lend a kind of tacit approval by the author of that type of speech. Yes, this was 1935 (in the deep south when the book took place) but even then the accepted term, the decent way to refer to blacks was to use 'negro'. Use of the 'N' word seems to me a dull spot in an otherwise brilliant book.

They Don't Dance Much is graced with a hard-boiled title right out of the classic Horace McCoy school, evoking thoughts of his books with titles like *They Shoot Horses, Don't They?*, or *I Should Have Stayed Home*. In the book Jack tells Smut Milligan's story (and his own), of how the two of them go into business together on a roadhouse.

Now in a bind for cash to pay the loan on the roadhouse, they discover that the local old coot and drunk, Bert Ford, has $30,000 cash squirreled away in his back yard. It's just itching to be taken. A lot of cash that will end their problems and give them both better days.

So Smut and Jack kidnap and torture Bert (in a truly horrendous scene) for the location of the money. In the end they make off with $12,000 in cash before they do away with poor Bert. The two killers take the money and run, leaving his body for disposal later. This will come back and haunt them. Real soon.

When things start to heat up on the murder of Bert Ford, Smut sets up Dick Pittman, a good-natured, easy-going black man who's a local bootlegger and friend. It's a lousy situation. Dick is put in jail, a stone's throw from a hanging for killing a well-liked white man. Jack knows Smut has set up Dick for the murder of Ford. He likes Dick and wants to clear him, but he's between a rock and a hard place. Jack doesn't like it but he doesn't know what to do about it.

In a way, Jack is relieved Smut didn't set *him* up for the murder — a definite possibility and concern, if you know Smut — but he's genuinely upset that an innocent and decent guy (even if he is black), is headed for a fall for this murder. And back then it was a hard fall — in 1940 Jim Crow North Carolina, a black man accused of killing a white man — life in prison for Dick Pittman — *if* he's lucky!

When Jack confronts Smut on this we have the following exchange:

"It's the rawest thing I ever heard of. You known Dick Pittman never hurt anybody in his life," I said.

"Don't be a damned fool," Smut said. "We got it pinned on him now, and that's the last of it. They'll convict him, but they won't kill him. Hell, everybody knows that Dick ain't got good sense. They'll just send him to the pen for life and in about ten or twelve years he'll be out again and on Relief."

"It's a damned dirty thing," I said.

"Well, I thought some about putting the gun in your locker," Smut said. "If I had, I reckon you'd of been happy now. I never in all my life seen such a sanctified man as you got to be since you helped me bump Bert off. But what the hell? Dick's just as well off in the pen as anywhere."

Smut got up then and began walking in a little circle in front of the cash register. He would fold his hands across his chest for a little while, then shift them behind him.

"In the pen he'll have just as good grub as what he gets out here. He'll have his clothes and his tobacco. He don't drink, so that won't bother him. He can't get any more mill women, but no doubt the prison

authorities' see to it and have enough saltpeter put in his coffee to keep his courage down. Hell, he's just as well off in the pen as he is out here. Better off, in a way."

"That's fine," I said. "You get me to help you do something that you won't tell me about. You just promise me some money, and when it turns out to be a murder you tell me not to worry. Then you chisel me out of the money. On top of that you try to poison me when I start looking for it. Now you get the murder pinned off on a half-wit. I got to hand it to you. You got everything."

Smut stopped his circling around. There was a sort of a baffled look on his face, like he wanted to explain to me why he had done it, but didn't know how to go about it.

"If you start out on the bottom you got to be tougher than all the folks that's between you and the top," Smut said. He was looking down at the floor.

It's interesting Smut was looking down at the floor when he said that last sentence.

Then add into the mix the hot and lovely Lola Fisher and there's more trouble brewing. You see, Smut's been having an affair with her behind her husband's back, and Jack sees this as a way he can get back at Smut.

Jack starts the trouble by writing anonymous letters to Charles Fisher:

Dear Mr. Fisher,
No doubt you remember a letter I wrote you some time back. I wrote you about how your wife was giving you the old double-cross now and then, when you were a good ways out of town.
She is still at it. She is making you look like a dope...

So hot, young, Lola is fooling around with Smut and Jack plans to get his revenge by setting up Smut and ratting him out to Fisher. And it works! But not exactly as Jack had planned. Nor as the reader figures, either. Things sort of get crazy, out-of-control, and the book ends on a wild and savage note — but strangely an almost flat note as well.

The book is not without it's flaws, but the virtures far outweight them. This book should have been a prime candidate for the old Black Lizard paperback imprint. The narrative drive, sexy atmosphere and seamly look at rural and small town Southern life and attitudes in 1935 Carolina, the interesting and well-fleshed characters, all make this book an interesting and fascinating read. The book is worth searching out if you like good hard-boiled crime fiction — it's not a private eye tale — but in a lot of ways it's a lot better. It is an excellent regional crime fiction story with a nice hard kick to it. You'll love it!

In an ironic statement right out of the darkest depths of noir, the jacket copy of the original 1940 Houghton Mifflin edition of *They Don't Dance Much* said about Ross:

"Here is no one-novel man... Before he is drafted he hopes to have completed his second novel."

That was printed in 1940 when Ross was just 29 years old. He never wrote another book.

While Ross never wrote another novel, he did write several aborted 100 page beginnings that were not finished. He did write and had published some short stories. He stayed a newspaper man and wrote in a 1977 letter about his writing:

"*I'm so far out of the mainstream of contemporary American fiction that neither magazines nor book publishers are interested in what I've been writing. But I plan to keep on writing anyway.*"

Update: After this article originally appeared in the UK magazine *Crime Time* in 1996, famed book editor and agent, Knox Burger sent me a letter with the following biographical data on James Ross that appeared in *Collier's* magazine circa 1951-52 for his story "Zone of Interior":

James Ross was born in 1911 on a farm near Norwood, North Carolina. "My early childhood was rather unhappy," he writes, "but when I was eight years old I started chewing tobacco. After that, I got along pretty well. After finishing high school, I was a sort of tramp athlete at various little-known southern colleges. During the Depression I played semi-pro baseball, farmed, and for a while taught night school in a CCC camp. From 1935 through 1941, I was a file clerk in the U.S. Collector of Internal Revenue for the district of N.C. I threw up this job at the beginning of 1942, and moved to Princeton, NJ., where I supported myself by free-lance writing and by marrying a girl who had a good job. I spent 1943-45 in the Army."

After the war, Mr. Ross was given a fellowship to work at Yaddo, a writer's colony in upstate New York. He is now back in Norwood.
He is the author of an excellent, if little-known, novel about a murder

in North Carolina, called, *They Don't Dance Much*, and has had stories published in a wide assortment of magazines, including *Collier's*, *Argosy*, *Partisan Review* and *Sewanee Review*. His other *Collier's* story was a gentle southern folk tale called "How to Swap Horses"; it was completely different from this one character, and we had a hard time deciding which of the two to include.

"Zone of Interior" is a pretty tough story.

As of this publication, I have not found any other James Ross short stories in any of the out-of-print magazines listed above.

Famed crime author George Higgins wrote of Ross:

"He advanced the craft of fiction as far as it could be advanced when he was writing, and no one was paying attention... Life's hard, life's very hard. It's harder without luck. But that, of course, was what he was telling us."

In a 1977 letter, James Ross mentions that he lent his only copy of his book to a Hollywood screenwriter who died shortly thereafter, and he never saw it again.

Don Tracy & *Deadly to Bed*

When you think about great underrated noir, and excellent hard crime writing and writers of the vintage era, a writer that does *not* usually come to mind is Don Tracy. That is a shame. He damn well should be remembered by any connoisseur of classic noir.

Don Tracy wrote at least four outstanding noir novels worthy of every fan's attention. He wrote one mini-masterpiece, *The Big Blackout!* (Pocket Book #6006, 1960, 1st paperback printing), which I wrote about a while back in *Paperback Parade* #88. He is also the author of two fine Lion Books. These were reprints of his previous 1930s hardcovers: *How Sleeps The Beast* (Lion Book #45, 1st paperback printing, 1950, originally a 1938 hardcover) a stunning interracial noir. Then there is the classic acknowledged masterpiece: *The Cheat* (aka *Criss Cross*, Lion Book #69, 1st paperback printing, 1951, originally a hardcover from 1934). This novel was made into the 1949 noir masterpiece film *Criss Cross* starring Burt Lancaster and Yvonne DeCarlo. So Tracy has some serious street cred with noir.

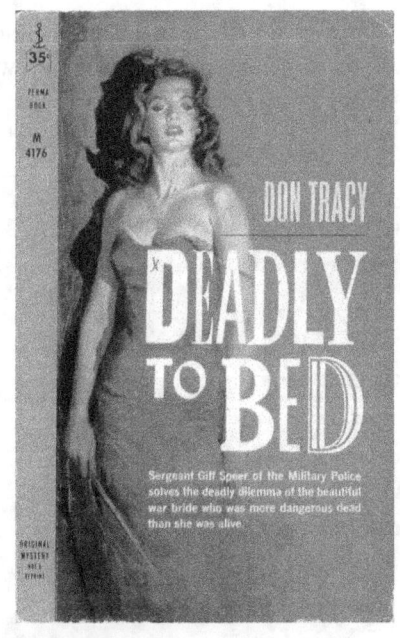

When I got a chance to come across another Don Tracy vintage paperback crime novel, I scarffed it up and read it right away. I was not disappointed. I savored it like all his others. *Deadly To Bed* (Perma Book #M4176, 1960, pbo, 184pp, with some nice gga cover art that is unaccredited, but it could be by James Meese), is another sure winner!

Tracy gives us a good twisty ride here. He seems to have served in the US military during World War II, in the Army, and offers some intimate knowledge of Military Police and G-2 Intelligence operations, which he puts to excellent use in this killer-diller of a murder thriller.

Undercover Military Policeman, Sergeant Giff Speer is our hero, a bright tough guy who loves the dames but does not trust them as far as he could throw one. He is sent to Fort Murray in US occupied Germany after the war to solve the mysterious murder of an Army captain's wife — a very lovely wife who seems to play a lot of bad games. She is also a beautiful war bride with a past. The fact that she has been murdered on a Army base where secret missile research is going on makes the murder all that more serious. In fact, she turns out to be one woman who proves more dangerous dead than alive, and the case twists and turns like a bucket full of agitated snakes as Speer works all the angles to find her killer. It is a tough and complex case. Speer goes undercover but has to keep what he learns close to the vest as he does not know who to trust. There are a lot of good suspects and all seem to have reasons to hate or kill the captain's wife — some of them are her husband, powerful officers, various lovers — both male and female — you get the point. It's a tricky mess for Giff Speer to figure out — but it is a super book to read!

During his investigation Speer is also ordered to stay away from the fort's golden boy — elderly Norwegian ballistic missile scientist, Doctor Karl Lundquist — and his lovely and luscious wife, Greta. It seems there is some possible Cold War espionage in the works regarding this case, so Speer must tread very lightly. It all makes the novel fast fun giving us an insider's view of the US Army post-War in occupied Germany, something not usually depicted these days but very serious so soon after the war ended, and in the light of the Nuremburg War Crimes Trials. This was an interesting part of post-war history, and of the workings of the US Army in Germany — and the results of the war.

Don Tracy weaves a hard-boiled noir tale that I feel Raymond Chandler or even Dashiell Hammett himself (who actually served in the US Army in WW2 in Alaska), would have been proud to write. Like all of Tracy's novels — he has also written some fine historical novels — however these four crime noirs, especially *Deadly To Bed*, are all masterpieces of the genre. Pick up this book and find out for yourself what I mean — you will not regret reading this very underrated author — and may even become a Don Tracy fan as I am.

Blackout is a Knockout!

The Big Blackout by Don Tracy (Pocket Books #6006, 1st paperback printing, 1960) is a fine hard crime and noir tale in the best Raymond Chandler tradition. Don Tracy's writing is fast-paced and lean, his characters well-crafted and he gives us a plot you could never figure out and that keeps you guessing. You can't ask for more than that in a slim 35-cents vintage paperback crime noir. The excellent 'fist in the face' cover art by an unknown artist really adds to the effect and gives you a none-too-subtle clue as to the impact of this novel. It is intense. It surely has impact!

Don Tracy is a name that will be known to some vintage paperback collectors but he has been forgotten by most readers today. Tracy was best known for a host of steamy historical novels in the 1950s and 60s, but before that he wrote hard crime noir thrillers. Two of these 1930s classic noirs, reprinted by Lion Books are *How Sleeps The Beast* (Lion #45, 1950) an inter-racial noir, "The Man — Negro, the Girl — White, The Payoff: LYNCH!"; and *The Cheat* (Lion #69, 1951), "Nothing stopped her, not even a husband" — which is better known under the hardcover title — also made into a noir cult film of the same name, *Criss-Cross*. So Tracy knew his stuff and had made his noir chops from the beginning. In the 1950s and 60s he wrote some fine historical novels, but in 1960 Pocket Books reprinted his 1959 Detective Book Club hardcover, *The Big Blackout* — and Tracy had lost none of his fine noir flare and style. It's a terrific story and a compelling read.

West Florida boatman Burt Lewis has a new life — a new wife and an infant son (named Bongo, of all things) — after a dark past lost to him in an alcoholic haze. Lewis has lost two years of his life in an alcoholic blackout and from what he can discern today, they were two very bad years where he did a lot of very bad things. Really bad things, but he can't remember any of them. It's a terrific noir premise and Tracy's description of the effects of alcohol abuse are truthful and even sympathetic to the illness — one wonders if he had personal knowledge on the subject. A lot of writers from that era did drink, and drink heavily.

However, this isn't the worse part for Lewis, because he's now got two tough guys who have come to the sleepy Florida town where he runs a fishing boat charter looking for him. He is also hot to find a guy named Bill Logan. Lewis, it seems used a lot of bogus names in his various scams during his drinking days, before he was sent away to Raiford Prison, joined AA and got himself clean. Now he's staying clean and trying to stay out of trouble, loving his new life and family. Then a tough guy named Adams comes looking for him. Adams is found drunk at his motel and Lewis, an AA advocate, is called in to help by the owner, hot sultry blonde, Ethel. Lewis discovers a letter in the man's wallet that says Burt Lewis *is* Bill Logan. That freaks out Lewis and sets his noir rollercoaster into high gear. Lewis sees to it that Adams is brought to a local rehab center to get sober, then later goes to question him about Logan — when he does, he finds out that Adams is dead. Shot in the head.

Lewis' problems are just beginning to multiply because he's got the local tough police detective Cliff Reitz after him in revenge for a beating he gave the cop when he was drunk — which Lewis also does not remember. Reitz's crooked partner, Bruton, is also after him, he's just a sadistic freak. Reitz wants to pin the murder of Adams on Lewis and see that he gets the chair so now the noir train is rolling along, picking up speed.

The story is told by Lewis in first person, and author Tracy tells it in a good approximation of Chandler's style. Here's a sample from page 5 about the relationship between Lewis and Reitz when the cop stops his car on a stormy night:

It was like I'd insulted his mother's memory. He lost the little grin and pushed his jaw out a bit further, so close I could see his chin in the dash light. There was a scar under the bristles that ran along his jaw from the deep cleft in his chin almost to his ear. I'd given Cliff Reitz that scar, or so they'd told me, and it was no wonder this guy hated me.

In another short passage from page 36, Tracy has Lewis give us a tiny but Chandleresque encapsulation about Tommy, who runs the dockyard gas station:

Tommy was inside, his chair tilted back beside the electric heater, reading the morning paper. He was a little squirt who'd been a jockey once and who, if he'd saved his dough, could have bought the oil company instead of just this station. The same horses that had earned it for him had taken it from him but he wasn't giving up that easy; the paper was turned to the entries and the wrinkles on his forehead showed he was trying to pick the big winner again.

Now Lewis is looking for Adams' murderer with Reitz breathing down his neck just waiting for a slipup so he can get him sent back to prison. Meanwhile, a second stranger named Paul Hawkins arrives and is also looking for Logan. Lewis realizes that whatever it was he did in that alcoholic two-year blackout as Bill Logan, he's in dire trouble for it now. He's not only terrified for his own life, but for the life of his new wife, and his infant son. Now he sees the good clean life he's built for himself slipping away since he got out of prison, and went straight and cleaned up on AA.

On page 54-55 the author has Lewis give us an accurate view of the damage alcohol abuse has given Lewis, which is far ahead of it's time for 1959:

Civilians, non-alcoholics, have no idea of what a blackout can be, not a two-year blackout, anyway. Everybody except a handful of understanding people would think I was lying, covering up, if I said I had a blank space in my memory for all that time. Everybody would think that I knew what Adams had wanted from me and that I'd killed him before he could get it.
So I threw all the fine ideas I'd had of telling the truth. I played it smart, the way I would have played it if I'd still been on the bottle.

Lewis is questioned by the cops, Reitz gives him a hard time but the other cops sort of believe his story — for now. So he is released. But not for long, Lewis knows. Then Lewis and his wife are attacked in their home by a vicious thug named Fisher and his partner — two cons from Raiford Prison who are also looking hard for this Bill Logan guy. They threaten Lewis's wife Midge and his infant son, telling her they'll make hamburger meat out of the baby. Lewis doesn't spill, and he's saved when the cops come by. It's Reitz with his partner Bruton, suspicious as always but their arrival sure saves the day as the two thugs split — but Lewis and his wife have taken a beating.

Lewis knows he has to be somewhat truthful with the cop now, so he tells Reitz the two thugs were looking for Bill Logan. He doesn't spill to the cop that he knows the thugs from prison, nor that he thinks *he* is Bill

Logan, but now he is getting some idea what this is all about. He realizes that things are worse than he thought. The noir train rolls faster when Reitz tells Lewis that the reason he came to the house in the first place was to show him a .32 revolver that he had found in connection with the Adams murder. He asks Lewis if he ever saw the gun before. Lewis says no. Reitz smugly says they'll run tests on the gun with the bullet that killed Adams and see what it tells him. Lewis is frozen in fear because he did recognize the old gun — it had once been his!

Now a new sick fear possesses Lewis. Is he being set up? Or, worse, was he still suffering blackouts that he did not know about? Even after all these years — had he really killed Adams in some blackout state? The horror of that almost makes Lewis go back to the booze bottle — but this time at least he stays sober as he resolves to get his wife and child out of town before the two thugs from Raiford come back for him.

By now the author has written Burt Lewis into as neat a tight little noir box of terror as one could get — and this is only the first half of the book! Then Lewis discovers that this Bill Logan stole $750,000 in dope that is missing from a New Orleans mob who are hot to get it back and kill him. Lewis wonders just what the hell kind of man he was, and on page 109 he gives us a hint:

As bad as the plain fear, maybe worse, was the thought that the Bill Logan who had used my body while I'd been on my record-breaking blackout had been a real, Grade-A, Number-One louse; a stinker who couldn't even shoot square with the mob he worked for. He'd been a dope runner, bringing in the damned stuff that ruined thousands of lives, the curse that was laid on mere kids by the pushers who got them hooked. Bill Logan — Burt Lewis, had been one of them.

Don Tracy's novel about the mystery of just who the heck Bill Logan is and where he is now, is as intricate and compelling as Eric Ambler's spy classic *A Coffin For Demetrious* — and it is almost as well done! This is a terrific novel. Don Tracy has Burt Lewis tie up all the loose ends as he tracks down the mystery of his missing life. It's a tight little noir package of just 166 pages. The book is a crime noir sleeper — find it — buy it — and read it. You will not be disappointed. You might even thank me!

Seven Hungry Killers on The Run

As far as I'm concerned, the only thing better than a well-done crime caper story, is a story about a well-done crime caper — that goes terribly wrong.

Such a book is *Run, Killer, Run* by Lionel White (Avon Book #T-361, 1959), a reprint of the rare digest-size paperback original *Seven Hungry Men*, Rainbow Book #121, from 1952. The cover artist for the digest edition is the great George Gross — and the female cover model is also known, she is Lila Lynn, famous for being shown on many paperbacks of the era.

Rand Coleman is the main character, described as "a three-time loser with a lifetime lease on the Big House". Mob shyster Mordaici Borgman comes to his rescue and gets him out of stir, but with the proviso that Rand do a job for him. There is always a catch, eh? It's an armored car heist amounting to two million dollars. A nice score that should go down easy, especially with an experienced man like Rand at the helm. Rand plans the deed and as leader forms a team of seven hoods set to do the job while lawyer Borgman smoothes the way with cash and contacts. But with such a fine plan and able crew nothing goes well from the start.

To begin with, Borgman has this live-in girlfriend, Pam, who just happens to be a troublesome nymphomaniac tramp, and that's putting it mildly. Pam finds out all about the big heist and even worse, she's dogging Rand with considerable sexual interest which is causing him difficulties. See, Rand doesn't want to piss off Borgman by boinking his over-sexed girlfriend. Rand owes Borgman for getting him out of prison, so while he's interested in what Pam has to offer, he decides to hold off on doing her. That causes no end of trouble for Rand, because when he refuses Pam, she makes up a story about *him* coming on to *her* to queer things between Rand and Borgman. Distrust between the two men grows and tension mounts as the day of the heist draws near.

The plan goes from bad to worse when one of Rand's thugs, a Mexican punk named Manny, discovered to be an unreliable junkie troublemaker, tells his flash broad all about the big caper. Now she is scheming and making demands to see her end from the job. Things start to unravel fast, with too many players knowing too much about the plan, while Rand tries to hold it all together. It's no surprise that once the heist goes into operation, the plan goes terribly wrong. Men get killed, as well as a cop — and everything goes to hell from there as the killers take it on the lam running for their lives.

This is just the kind of high-energy crime novel that Lionel White excelled at. Pulp paperback masters like Day Keene, Harry Whittington and certainly Lionel White knew how to tell a fine fast-moving story. The tension and action heats up when the two carloads of killers and their women race away from New York City, chased by cops in cars, speedboat, plane and finally on foot! From New York's garment district to the Florida Keys, this tasty little crime noir has it all.

It also has Kitty, the gal Rand really likes and really wants. As the hoods make their escape there is a developing relationship that grows between Rand and Kitty — two people from the wrong side of the tracks who find each other and true love in the chaos and brutality of this screwed-up crime. But not after a hell of a lot of problems.

Run, Killer, Run features an outstanding cast of characters who combine to give Rand Coleman all kinds of problems after the heist. The hot girlfriends of the thugs cause no end of trouble as they scheme for the money and tempt the guys. Needless to say, the guys are at each other's throats with jealously and betrayal, even Borgman has some unknown game going. Rand and Kitty find themselves in the middle of all this chaos, become allies, and eventually much more.

One interesting thing about the physical books themselves is that there are some significant differences between the two editions. And not just superficial.

The Rainbow digest contains catchy exploitative chapter titles, such as, "Dangerous Dame", "Good-Time Bad Girl", "Watch Those Dames!", "The Ex-Con and the Tramp" and "Floating Brothel", which are *not* in the Avon edition. You don't get that kind of creativity in the average crime novel these days! Rainbow Books was an early digest sleaze publisher mixing crime with sexy or risqué topics to sell books. The cover art helped and it was often some of the most sexy and provocative pin-up art of the era.

However, the cover art on this particular Rainbow digest is a bit different. It shows the over-sexed Pam confronting Sam, the Black first mate in an interesting scene from the story. Sam is a white-hating fellow who likes to exercise his racial hatred by getting back at white women for all that the white man has done against him. His grievances may be real or perceived, but because Sam is a hateful racist and a twisted criminal, who can tell for sure. In fact, in Sam, the author may have created one of the first overtly Black racist characters in crime fiction. The Rainbow Books cover art shows Sam's coal black face sweating bullets in a detailed close-up as he plays with a knife menacingly. He sits with a booze bottle nearby, deciding what to do with the girl placed in his room. Pam stands behind Sam swigging from a bottle of booze, a slit-skirt wicked temptress full of danger — or perhaps she is endangered herself? Pam and Sam cause considerable problems for Rand to deal with as the hoods take a boat to make their escape to Florida. The atmosphere in this tense George Gross cover is explosive, sexual and overtly racial. In the early 1950s mass-market genre paperbacks did not often show African-American images in cover art, and such images in sexy digests like Rainbow Books are not common at all. So Sam's depiction so prominently in the cover art back then might have been groundbreaking. It was certainly attention getting!

By comparison, the cover art on the Avon paperback (cover artist unknown), while more violent and showing intense physical contact, is more obscure. It shows a more explicit scene from the book, a man forcing himself upon a woman, but you can not tell if the man is Sam, nor whether or not the man is even a Black man. So while the cover image on the 1959 Avon edition shows a more explicit scene from the story, it has toned down the overt racial imagery that was much more a central theme in the cover art of the 1952 edition. It is also a more obscure cover image.

With non-white characters like Sam, as well as the Mexican punk, Manny, some readers might detect a bit of unpleasant stereotyping in this book. That would be a shame if this puts off some people from reading what is a finely wrought crime noir.

However, the most interesting difference between the two editions is the ending.

It seems White rewrote parts of the book for the 1959 Avon reprint. So what we have in the later Avon edition - is an alternate ending!

In true noir fashion, we have two editions with two very different endings. What happens to Rand and Kitty? And Borgman? What is his fate? You will just have to read this one — in either — or both — editions to find out. I know you will enjoy it. Either edition, in any condition, is a tasty noir caper novel that makes a great read and will not disappoint. It is a long-lost mini-masterpiece in either version.

Fortune:
Tough Guy Heroics as Noir Poetry

It will remind you of Mickey Spillane in a tough mode. *That* says a lot, but even more so, Ennis Willie's Tripp Fortune will remind you of Richard Stark's Parker, because of Fortune's single-minded, straight-ahead, take-no-prisoners devotion to getting his job done. In this case – Fortune's *job* is to get his memory back. You see, all he can remember of his past, is his name.

Originally published in 1963 under the sensational but misleading title of *Luscious, Teasing Body* (Merit Book #661), by a lower-than-low-end sleaze paperback outfit from Chicago called Camerarts – this book only goes to show packaging can be crucial. Camerarts didn't even try to market it as the gritty, dark crime novel it is, but rather focused on their desire to sell soft-core sex books. Their Merit and Novel lines used racy exploitative titles, while their cover photos often showed sleazy painted ladies with overdeveloped bosoms – the black & white cover photos retouched to show women with yellow, red, or even green hair and with lips blood red or even blue! – eerie and freakish. Hence the term 'sleaze'. There is nothing quite like these paperback books.

Ennis Willie is a writer whose work primarily appeared in this soft-core 'adult' ghetto of the 1960s. Like many other writers – some of whom left that ghetto and went on to greater things like Harlan Ellison, Robert Silverberg, Lawrence Block and Donald Westlake – and some who never left it like Willie – these books had a visceral, hard edge attitude and were almost always crime novels. The sex – as nominal as it was for those days, was never explicit – but in fact added to, and rounded out, the stories to make them more realistic. More realistic than much of the so-called 'quality' genre fiction of the day. These guys could write! They were pros and masters at telling a story full of action and conflict. Ennis Willie fit right in with the best of them. This is a neglected writer and novel. The man and his work have never been given the attention they deserve – until now in this book!

Now, Fortune's Back! And this hard-boiled hero as 'nobody' novel gives us a true outsider trying to make sense of himself and his world. It approaches the lofty heights of classic tough-guy poetry as written by greats like Dashiell Hammett, Raymond Chandler, and yes, even Mickey Spillane.

Tripp Fortune has no memory. As the novel opens all he (or we) know is his name and that he's looking for a girl named Joy – whom he assumes may have some answers about his past. Meanwhile, everyone else seems to know *all* about him – or about the *old* Fortune – but they ain't talking and he can't ask without giving away his vulnerability. You see, Fortune's in a jam. Not knowing his past means he doesn't know what to do, who's on his side, or who is after him, and why. It's an interesting dilemma.

We're along for one interesting ride as he discovers that the previous Fortune seems to have been some kind of mob bookkeeper who worked for a real brute named Big Jake. But what's the connection between him and Joy? Big Jake? The local mob? Fortune seeks to find out. The old Fortune seems to have been a quiet, meek sort of guy who always did as he was told. It seems he's thought of as a wimp and a looser. Why, he's even believed to be scared of Lister, a nasty little dwarf thug who for some reason hates him. But not this new Fortune. Nothing seems to fit at first. Fortune has changed his stripes, into a totally different animal – he's dangerous and he's on the prowl for his lost memories.

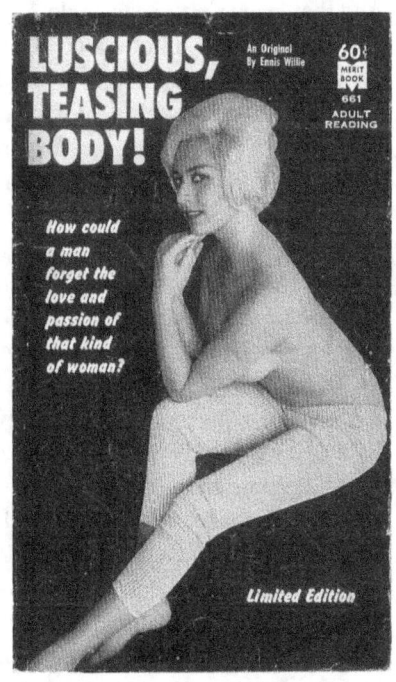

The interaction between the 'new Fortune' and his old 'friends' is excellent. One great scene takes place as he confronts two thugs in a bar. Knowing him as the old Fortune, they decide to teach him a lesson for showing his face. Fortune stands his ground, and tells them:

> "So you've dealt yourself a hand," Fortune said. "Either play it or run alone home to mama."
>
> Pretty Boy's face turned colors that proved he didn't like that kind of talk. But he wasn't quite ready. He looked into the big man's face, and what he saw there shook the notion that this was going to be the

lark it had started out to be.
He punched Arnie in the ribs as he had earlier and forced a laugh. "Look at this guy, will you, Arnie. Trying to make like he grew his self a backbone while he was gone."
He said it but he wasn't so sure anymore, and he wasn't ready.
Fortune's eyes held his. "Maybe you'd better run home. You're beginning to smell like your diaper needs changing."
Pretty Boy couldn't take that. He had to fight now. He had suffered a real enthusiasm drain, but he had passed the turning point in this road. Besides, it was just Fortune for God's sake – that wimpy piece of shit Fortune.
"Come on, Arnie," he grunted. "Let's take this bastard apart!"
It didn't occur to Fortune he had been waiting for them to move, waiting like a grenade with the pin pulled to explode all over them. It still didn't occur to him as he went into action.

Throughout this book you're wondering, who is this guy? What happened to him and why? Perhaps Joy knows the answer, but Fortune can't find her, or she doesn't want to be found by him. Only the three sexy strippers he's hiding out with now are able to fill in a few pieces of his puzzle, even as he avails himself of the other *pieces* these three luscious femme fatales offer him quite readily enough as sustenance. And that brings in the sex angle.

You see, while Camerarts novels were early 1960s sleaze, what passed for 'sex books' in those days — this novel has nothing sexually explicit in it at all. It's a straight crime novel. Nevertheless, as the action heats up, so does the sex (or what passed for it back then). This is about as hot as it gets when Willie describes blonde and brazen Greta:

Her body was satin and silk molded into erotic valleys and mountains and curves, her lips carved in flame… As she moved into the room, Fortune could see she wore no bra to confine her large breasts, protruding weapons in the war of carnal delirium.

I mean, you just gotta love it! They don't write stuff like *that* anymore! In fact, they wouldn't dare today! More's the pity too, because there is a sense of crime and poetry melded with genuine hard noir attitude and it all works to make the book live and breathe. The entire story is full of action, gritty dialog and noir attitude.

So Fortune is on a quest in this book, but not in the typical 1960s fashion so popular in the era it was written. He doesn't want to find out who he is – he knows that quite well. He wants to find out who he *was*.

He needs to discover the truth about his past and the reader can't help going along with him for the ride. You'll enjoy every page of this story, which you won't be able to put down until you reach the surprise ending. That will grab you and put everything into perspective.

UPDATE: This article was unpublished until appearing in this book and was originally written to be the introduction for the book *Fortune's Back* by Ennis Willie. I am not sure if that book ever appeared.

Introduction in *Sand's Game*: for the story "Too Late To Pray"

Ennis Willie is a writer whose work primarily appeared in the soft-core "adult" ghetto paperbacks of the 1960s. Like many other writers – some of whom left that ghetto fairly soon and went on to greater things, such as like Harlan Ellison, Robert Silverberg, Lawrence Block and Donald Westlake. There were also some who never left it like Ennis Willie. It's a real shame because the hard crime reader and fan have missed out on his fine writing, incredible stories and memorable characters only because of the sleazy book packaging and cheap formats these works appeared in.

Ennis Willie deserved better and thankfully *Sand's Game*, published by Ramble House, in 2010, will in some measure remedy those shortcomings. The book collects all of his Sand hard crime stories in one volume.

In the story "Too Late To Pray", Willie's protagonist, Sand – he uses just one name and there's no need for any more than that because everyone knows who he is – he is the quintessential outsider hero.

Sand is an ultra tough guy — the word itself is a byword for toughness. He's a gangster who wanted out of the Mob and left – but now he's back! You see, an old flame has been snuffed out and Sand has come back to find her killer — even if it kills him, which it just might. Then he's going to send that killer straight down to hell and we get to go along for the ride.

As Sand himself puts it, "For a man like me, revenge is law."

This story is brutal, fast and violent hard-boiled fiction, satisfaction guaranteed! And it is just one of eight stories and articles that make up this book — each one introduced by a well-known crime and mystery author!

What could be better than that?

Gary Lovisi Bibliography

Sherlock Holmes:
The Secret Adventures of Sherlock Holmes Series:
The Secret Adventures of Sherlock Holmes (Ramble House, 2007)
More Secret Adventures of Sherlock Holmes
  (Ramble House, 2011)
Secret Adventures of Sherlock Holmes: Book Three
  (Ramble House, 2016)
More Secret Files of Sherlock Holmes (Linford, UK, 2017)

Souvenirs of Sherlock Holmes (Gryphon Books, 2002; non-fiction)
Sherlock Holmes: The Great Detective in Paperback & Pastiche (Gryphon Books, 2008)
Sherlock Holmes: The Baron's Revenge (Airship27, 2012)
The Mystery Surrounding Watson's Lost Dispatch Box
  (MX Pub., UK, 2014)
Happy Birthday, Mr. Holmes (Gryphon Books, 2016)
The Affair of Lady Westcott's Lost Ruby & The Case of The Unseen Assassin
  (Black Gat #11, 2017; novellas)
Sherlock Holmes in Oz
  (Wildside Press, 2022)
Crime:
Extreme Measures (Gryphon Books, 1996; stories)
Ultra-Boiled: Hard Hitting Crime Fiction (Ramble House, 2010; stories)
Murder of a Bookman
  (Wildside Press, 2011)
Driving Hell's Highway
  (Wildside Press, 2011)
The Nemesis Chronicles
  (Bold Venture, 2016; stories)

Griff & Fats series
Hellbent on Homicide
  (Do Not Press, UK, 1997)
Harvest of Homicide
  (Bold Venture Press, 2017)
Hardcases & Homicide
  (Bold Venture Press, 2022)

Vic Powers series
Dirty Dogs (Gryphon Books,
  1999; stories)
Blood in Brooklyn
  (Do Not Press, UK, 1999)

Violence is the Only Solution (Wildside Press, 2012; stories)
The Last Goodbye
   (Bold Venture, 2015)

Science Fiction /
Fantasy & Horror:
Sarasha (Gryphon Books, 1997)
Gargoyle Nights
   (Wildside Press, 2011; stories)
Mars Needs Books
   (Wildside Press, 2011)
When the Dead Walk
   (Ramble House, 2014)

The Jon Kirk of Ares Series: (Wildside Press)
#1 The Winged Men (2014)
#2 The Invisible Men (2015)
#3 The Space Men (2015)
#4 The Mind Masters (2017)
#5 The Time Masters (2017)

Other Fiction:
West Texas War and Other Western Stories (Ramble House, 2007)
The Sicilian, Book 1: Augustus the Undefeated (Wildside Press, 2017)
The Sicilian, Book 2: Augustus the Conqueror (Wildside Press, 2022)
The Sicilian, Book 3: Augustus the Bold (Wildside Press, 2023)

Edited Anthologies:
The Great Detective: His Further Adventures (Wildside Press, 2012)
Battling Boxing Stories
   (Wildside Press, 2012)

Non-Fiction:
The Sexy Digests
   (Gryphon Books, 2001)
The Swedish Vintage Paperback Guide (Gryphon Books, 2003)
The Pulp Crime Digests
   (Gryphon Books, 2004)
Modern Historical Adventure Novels (Gryphon Books, 2006)
The Antique Trader Paperback Price Guide
   (Krauss Books, 2008)
Dames, Dolls & Delinquents (Krauss Books, 2009)
Bad Girls Need Love Too
   (Krauss Books, 2010)

About the Author

GARY LOVISI is an author who has done work in many genres, both fiction and non-fiction. He has been an avid reader, fan and book collector for most of his life. He is a Mystery Writers of America, Edgar Award Nominated author for his crime fiction. His twin joys of reading crime fiction and writing about crime fiction has formed a life-long joy. This has led him into editing and publishing. Through publishing his book collector magazine *Paperback Parade* (now in its 37th year!), and sponsoring his late lamented New York City book shows for 25 years, he has had the opportunity to get to know many of his literary heroes in the mystery, crime and noir genres. He has even published some of their work in his now legendary crime fiction magazine *Hardboiled*.

PHOTO BY LAURA CALI

Lovisi's main joy has been being able to get to know so many of these fine, fascinating people and fine writers—and the artists who did the cover art for their classic vintage paperbacks. Lovisi often writes on the subjects of the pulps and crime fiction. His previous books include the non-fiction survey, *The Pulp Crime Digests* (Gryphon Books, 2004); as well as the hard crime fiction books in his hard-as-nails Vic Powers series: *Dirty Dogs, Blood in Brooklyn, Violence is the Only Solution* and *The Last Goodbye*; and his tough 1960s-era coppers Griff & Fats series: *Hellbent on Homicide, Harvest of Homicide* and *Hardcases & Homicide*. He is also very active in writing fiction and non-fiction about the Great Detective, Sherlock Holmes. *A Sherlock Holmes Notebook* (Stark House, 2022) is an avidly illustrated cornucopia of all things Sherlockian. You can find out more about Lovisi and his work at his website www.gryphonbooks.com, or you can check out his Youtube videos that showcase all types of collectible books and related items.

Books on books from Stark House Press...

Paperback Confidential
by Brian Ritt $19.95
"This is a terrific book and one that is thoroughly interesting. I think it should be on the shelf of everyone who loves old paperbacks, crime fiction and just cool writing about a great time period."—Jon Jordan, *Crimespree* magazine

Hardboiled, Noir and Gold Medals
by Rick Ollerman $17.95
"This is an important book and a must-have for anybody who cares about good criticism, about the writers discussed, and about crime fiction in general."
—Bill Crider

Manhunt Companion
by Peter Enfantino & Jeff Vorzimmer $19.95
"*The Manhunt Companion* is not only a must for readers and collectors of the magazine, but for anyone interested in cutting-edge noir fiction of the 50s and early 60s."—Bill Pronzini

A Sherlock Holmes Notebook
by Gary Lovisi $15.95
"Whether you're a die-hard fanatic or a casual fan, there is plenty to delight in here... a joy to read from first page to last."—Richard Krauss, Larque Press
"...a must-have for devoted fans [and] pop culture buffs who want to know more about the vast reach of the famed resident of Baker Street."
—Pat. H. Broeske, *Mystery Scene* magazine

Stark House Press, 1315 H Street, Eureka, CA 95501
griffinskye3@sbcglobal.net / www.StarkHousePress.com
Available from your local bookstore, or order direct via our website.

www.ingramcontent.com/pod-product-compliance
Lightning Source LLC
LaVergne TN
LVHW021803060526
838201LV00058B/3217